Underestimated

ENDORSEMENTS

"In a time of rising pessimism about life, work, and our fracturing societies, Donald Thompson offers a personal, powerful reflection on believing in oneself and securing a just future in which diversity makes us stronger and more united."

– Jamie Merisotis, President and CEO, Lumina Foundation

"DT's journey and life story in *Underestimated* shows that while the pursuit of one's goals, hopes, and dreams might not be easy…the pursuit can definitely be worth it!"

– Carlester T. Crumpler, Bank of America and former NFL player Seattle Seahawks and Minnesota Vikings

"For anyone who is either starting their career or looking to make a switch to the world of business owners, then Underestimated will provide you with the crumbs to follow to ensure success. A worthwhile read!"

– John Murphy, John Murphy International and bestselling author, *10 Key Traits of Top Leaders*

"An incredible story of perseverance, resilience, instinct, and the power of relationships. What struck me most was the prevailing lesson he leaves with all of us: the health and prosperity of our country depends on the health and prosperity of all. Empower the marginalized, heal communities, and don't be afraid to disrupt the status quo."

– Eileen Park Robertson, Filmmaker and Founder, Anecdotia

DONALD THOMPSON

UNDERESTIMATED

A CEO'S UNLIKELY PATH TO SUCCESS

NEW YORK

LONDON • NASHVILLE • MELBOURNE • VANCOUVER

Underestimated

A CEO's Unlikely Path to Success

Published in New York, New York, by Morgan James Publishing. Morgan James is a trademark of Morgan James, LLC. www.MorganJamesPublishing.com

Proudly distributed by Ingram Publisher Services.

Morgan James BOGO™

A **FREE** ebook edition is available for you or a friend with the purchase of this print book.

CLEARLY SIGN YOUR NAME ABOVE

Instructions to claim your free ebook edition:
1. Visit MorganJamesBOGO.com
2. Sign your name CLEARLY in the space above
3. Complete the form and submit a photo of this entire page
4. You or your friend can download the ebook to your preferred device

ISBN 9781631958953 paperback
ISBN 9781631958960 ebook
Library of Congress Control Number: 2022931808

Cover & Interior Design by:
Christopher Kirk
www.GFSstudio.com

Morgan James is a proud partner of Habitat for Humanity Peninsula and Greater Williamsburg. Partners in building since 2006.

Get involved today! Visit MorganJamesPublishing.com/giving-back

TABLE OF CONTENTS

INTRODUCTION

Underestimate (verb): to think that something is less or lower than it really is, or that someone is less strong or less effective.

There were plenty of reasons for me not to succeed in the business world. As a Southern-born African American with no college degree and no technological background, I could have been angry or had a chip on my shoulder. The easy choice would have been to sit around wishing things were fairer or easier. Except that I come from a family of fighters.

When my parents—two teenagers from smalltown Louisiana—were raising my sister and me, I watched them work tirelessly to create a better life. Though the odds were against them, they overcame the pressures and challenges inherent to young Black families in 1970s America.

My parents blessed me with their example of being *thankful* for what you have, *responsible* for your choices, and *courageous* enough to chase success. They taught me that the world is not fair, but it is my job to win, even if the odds are stacked against me. Through them, I learned that each struggle I face and each obstacle I must overcome is building my strength to achieve greatness despite adversity. They showed me I have a responsibility to clear the path for those who will follow.

It's not that I'm unaware or overly optimistic about the social challenges we currently face around race, politics, and prejudice. I've just decided that my dreams are big enough to overcome an unfair playing field. That's why my story and this book focus not on problems and setbacks but how I rebounded and adapted to make even the most difficult situations into learning experiences.

Over the course of my career, I have grown companies, sold companies, and coached global business leaders. By most standards, I've done well, but my success was built on years of working hard, learning from poor decisions, and understanding how to dream big (and win big) even when I was underestimated based on someone else's vision of "success," usually defined by pedigree or pigmentation.

If your road to success has ever brought you to a dead end or a broken bridge, read on. If you feel your potential is underestimated and underutilized, read on. Even if things are going well, but your dreams are big, and your goals are next level, read on. This is for you.

In these pages, you'll read about the journey of my life, the challenges I faced, the support I received, the bad decisions I made, and how I recovered. I learned what works and doesn't work in business by actually *doing business*, so I'm presenting these lessons to you as I learned them: in action.

Finally, reader, it's important that you know my sharing of these stories is motivated by a deep sense of responsibility to honor those who helped me along the way. I hope what I learned along my journey will inspire you and give you courage to overcome the challenges that are keeping you from achieving your dreams. If so, I'll be paying forward what others gave to me.

Okay. Your time is precious, so let's get started.

1
QUITTING IS NOT AN OPTION

"What do you mean you're not going back?"

My mother, only a teenager, sat on the worn sofa in an off-campus apartment near my father's school. As I picture it now, she was reading a book when my father barged into the living room and announced he was dropping out of college. I can see her, turning her full attention to him, staring at him with narrowed eyes.

I can see him too, just nineteen-years-old, pacing across the threadbare carpet. "I'm burnt out, Gilda. Between football, school, and being a parent, something's got to give."

Mom shook her head. "Absolutely not."

I was only two years old, too young to understand, but I have heard this story so many times that, now, I can tell it just as well as they do.

"You have a baby to care for," she continued. "You will graduate. That is the only possibility. End of story."

You see, my parents believed that education was the only path to a happy, successful future. When my mother told my father that he *would* graduate, she was serious, and he knew it. They had been high school sweethearts in Bogalusa, a small paper mill town in Louisiana, the kind of place where people did everything they could to ensure their children would grow up to be a little

3

better off. That way of life was deeply imprinted on my mother. When she got pregnant with me at sixteen, she stayed in school. I was born in August 1971 during summer break, just before the new school year began. For her, education was mandatory, not optional. She committed to school, despite having a newborn. She had to persevere on her own because my dad had moved 1,300 miles away to attend the University of Connecticut.

Every morning of my mom's junior year of high school, my granny would drive us to the babysitter's house. From there, my mom would catch the bus to school. Then, in the afternoons, she took the bus back to the babysitter's house, put me in the hand-me-down stroller with a wobbly wheel, and walked the hot half-mile home. After a long day at school, she played with me, fed me, put me to bed, and worked on her homework long into the night. Despite the difficult schedule, she was serious about staying in school. Education was the answer she believed in.

When Mom finished her junior year, we moved to Connecticut to be with my dad. She immediately started toward earning a GED and made plans to attend college.

My parents had always talked about education as a way to get out of Bogalusa and build a better life with more opportunity. Yet, now, my dad seemed just as serious about quitting college. After two years of a tough football schedule, plus school, plus full-time classes, *and* parenting, he'd made up his mind. He couldn't keep going. As the story goes, despite my mom's protest, he just shrugged and said, "Nope. I'm not going back."

Mom pressed her lips into a tight line and gave my father a no-nonsense glare (I would later come to know that look all too well). "Well, then, I'll go to your classes for you. At least until you come to your senses."

Always the backbone of our family, my mother would do whatever was necessary to make sure we had the best life possible. So, she attended classes at the University of Connecticut in my dad's place—a Black woman from Bogalusa at UConn in the 1970s. Backpack in hand, she arrived on campus, sat in huge lecture halls with mostly White male students, took detailed notes, and listened to world-class professors talk about finance, economics, math, and history. With all her family and friends halfway across the country, she tried to blend in, a Louisiana teenager with a baby at home. In the afternoons, she'd return home to take care of me while my dad attended football practice. Afterward, they reviewed her notes from the day. Bit by bit, she taught him everything he missed.

The arrangement worked well for the first few weeks. However, when it was time for midterms, my mother put her foot down. "You have exams in econ and math next week, and I'm sorry, but I draw the line at taking tests for you," she insisted over dinner one night. "You at least have to go for those."

Dad didn't hesitate. "Yeah, of course. I'll take the tests." After paging through the composition book Mom handed him, he shook his head and smiled. "Gilda, you take more notes than anyone I've seen. Are you enjoying going to classes?"

I can picture her throwing him that same no-nonsense glare. "It's not about enjoying it," she said, matter-of-factly. "It's about doing what needs to be done."

Dad knew all about that. He'd learned it the same way Mom had: from his family, and especially his father.

My grandfather, Aaron Thompson—"Big Daddy" to his grandkids—was larger than life. As a young man, Big Daddy was a star running back at Southern University, earning the nickname "Cheetah Thompson." He later played in the NFL for the San Francisco 49ers. When he came home to Bogalusa, he worked as a football coach, school counselor, assistant principal, and minister, all while raising a large family. He lived a disciplined life and expected the same from his five sons: no drinking, no partying, home by ten o'clock, earning good grades, and holding yourself accountable for your actions.

Growing up with my grandfather's strict standards for excellence had given my dad a deep sense of responsibility, a feeling that had only intensified once he'd become a father himself. Watching my mother go to his classes every day didn't sit well with him. He was still a young man who wanted a break, but during those days spent at home with me, I know he often thought about what it meant to be a good father and provide for his family.

Making the Grade

"How'd you do?" Mom asked after his econ exam.

Dad looked down at the ground, letting his shoulders droop. Her smile quickly faded.

"Oh, well . . ." he trailed off, then flashing a grin, exclaimed, "I did well, Gilda. I might even make an A!"

Mom squealed with delight and swatted him with her dishtowel. "Donnie don't tease me! You nearly gave me a heart attack." She gave him a hug. "I knew you could do it."

Dad nodded and smiled, never one for unnecessary celebration, then put his hands on Mom's shoulders. He looked her in the eye. "I'm going to go back to taking classes. I want a good life for you and Binky. I want to take responsibility for getting us there."

That lesson in teamwork and perseverance was a turning point for my parents. Three years later, my dad graduated from UConn with a degree in business administration and began working toward a master's degree in psychology. Mom soon earned her GED and then went to college, eventually earning a bachelor's degree in child development while I was still in elementary school.

Through their example, my parents proved that hard work and determination were keys to success. They didn't believe in self-pity. If something was tough, well, that was life. You just had to get on with it and find a way to turn an obstacle into an opportunity.

Many years later, I'd be grateful for their lessons of stubborn work ethic. When something goes wrong in business, you can't just stop and close shop. You must fix it and move on.

I'd grown up seeing my mom and dad go to classes, do homework, and study for tests, so when it was my turn, I couldn't wait to begin. But I soon discovered that kindergarten was drastically different than hanging around at home. There were so many rules! Even then, I couldn't just accept a limitation without understanding the rationale behind it.

At the end of a frustrating first day of kindergarten, Mom met me at the bus stop. We'd recently moved out of student housing and into a small apartment near campus. Dad had been hired as an assistant football coach at UConn.

"How was school?" she asked as we started down the sidewalk.

I wrinkled my nose like I'd smelled a skunk. "It was okay," I said with a shrug. "Do I have to go back?"

She squeezed my hand and smiled. I'd been waiting all afternoon to tell her about the worst part of the day.

"Did you know about this nap time?" I asked, looking up at my mother suspiciously but not waiting for an answer. "When the teacher said to lie down, I said 'No, thank you.' I wanted to keep playing with the train set, but she said I had to nap. Only, I wasn't tired! Naptime is for babies. I think I should just stay at home. You can teach me school stuff, right?"

"Oh, I don't know, Binky. I'm busy with my own schoolwork." Mom unlocked the door and sat her purse on the table near the couch. "Are you hungry?"

I dropped my backpack and hurried to the kitchen. "Very hungry. Learning is hard work!" I sat in a kitchen chair—1970s avocado-colored vinyl—and watched her make a peanut butter sandwich.

"When you're finished eating, come sit with me on the couch. I want to show you something." She caressed my head before leaving the room.

As I ate the sandwich, I could hear her rummaging around in the bedroom. It sounded like she was taking things out of the closet. Finishing the last bite, I ran into the living room and dropped to my hands and knees. I shimmied across the yellow shag carpet, pretending I was G.I. Joe on a top-secret mission.

"Binky, what are you doing? You'll ruin your school clothes." She stood with her hands on her hips, shaking her head. What happened to her quiet baby—the one who sucked his pacifier so intently he'd been nicknamed Binky? She sat on the couch and patted the space beside her. She couldn't hold me in her lap because she was almost seven months pregnant with my sister, Amie. I sat as close to her as I could and rested my head on her arm.

She unfolded a newspaper clipping and pressed it on her leg to get the wrinkles out. "What do you see in this picture?"

I took the paper in my hands and studied the grainy, black-and-white image. "I see a lady walking with a little girl. They're holding hands. And there's an old car in the back."

Mom smiled and moved my finger to the woman in the photo. "That's Granny," she said. "And the little girl is Aunt Sharon—my sister."

I held the photo closer to my face. "Really? Granny was in the newspaper? Was she famous?"

"No, she wasn't famous. What you don't see in this photo is all the U.S. Marshals walking with Granny and Aunt Sharon."

I looked up at her. "What's a U.S. Marshal?"

"They're like the police."

I gasped. "Was Granny in trouble?"

Mom shook her head. "No. She wasn't. You know how your daddy and I tell you that sometimes people treat other people badly because of the color of their skin?"

I nodded.

"Well, when your daddy and I started going to school, schools were actually separated. White children went to one school, and Black children went to different schools. But the schools that Black children went to didn't get much government money. They were rundown and didn't have enough supplies for the students."

I bit the inside of my cheek and screwed up my face in anger. "But that isn't fair."

"No. It wasn't. Finally, the government decided to integrate the schools. That meant that all children, no matter their skin color, would go to the same schools."

I sighed with relief and sat back on the cushion. "Oh, that's good."

"Except many of the White people in Bogalusa didn't want Black children in their schools. They held protests, and sometimes things got violent. On the first day that Aunt Sharon went to the new school, people were protesting. They yelled hateful, nasty things at her and Granny. The U.S. Marshals had to walk with them to keep them safe."

I looked at the picture again. "Granny doesn't look scared."

Mom smiled down at her mother's resolute profile. "Yeah. She's a tough lady. A few people yelling some foolish words wouldn't stop her from doing what was right."

I leaned into Mom's body again. She wrapped her arm around me.

"It wasn't just Aunt Sharon who went to integrated schools," she went on. "Your dad and I went too, although we were a little bit older than Aunt Sharon. Sometimes, bad things happened, but we kept going because we knew that going to school was an opportunity to better ourselves. We didn't want the ignorance of others to keep us from achieving our dreams."

I pushed away, staring up at her. She looked as strong and calm as she always did. "What bad things happened?"

"Kids we knew got beaten up," she explained. "Other students said hateful things. Once, all the Black students were dismissed early because the principal found out that some White students were planning to come to school with guns. I was on a school bus that someone shot at." She paused and squeezed me closer.

"Were you scared?" I asked, my eyes wide.

"Scared and angry. I hated that I had to leave school early because people couldn't be kind. I hated that I had to choose between my education and my safety. Your dad felt the same way. He was so frustrated. We didn't think we couldn't change people's minds or make them think a different way, but we knew we *could* change our circumstances. That's why we're here in Connecticut. That's why we moved so far from our home. For a good education, for opportunity, and for a fighting chance."

It was a lot for a five-year-old to take in. I didn't know what to say, so I just laid my head on Mom's arm and stared at the photograph.

"So. When you ask me if you have to go back to school tomorrow, do you know what I'm going to say?"

I looked down and pulled the Velcro straps of my shoes open and closed a few times. "Yes."

"And now you know why school is so important to your dad and me?"

I nodded slowly. "Yes."

As my mother stood to put the photo back in her bedroom, she asked, "Do you have any questions?"

"Yes," I said.

She turned to face me and raised an eyebrow.

"Do I have to sleep at naptime? Because maybe I could just be quiet and close my eyes. I don't actually have to *sleep*, right?"

Mom looked up at the ceiling, probably wondering if anything she'd told me had sunk in. In that moment, it might not have seemed like I'd learned much from her story, but I had.

In later years, I faced my own struggles that reinforced the lesson from that day, obstacles that helped me understand that my parents and grandparents had worked hard and faced danger so I could be here in this city, in this apartment, going to a good school. They had struggled to build something better for me than they'd had for themselves. That knowledge stayed with me for the rest of my life.

"So…do I?" I asked again when my mom's silence stretched on too long.

"No," she said finally, shaking her head. "You don't have to actually sleep during naptime."

Pushing Boundaries

People hear the words "football coach" and think of glamour and money. That may be true in today's NFL, but it sure wasn't the case in the lower rungs of the college football world in the 1970s and 1980s. My dad was gone a lot. During the regular season, he was on the road with the team. When he wasn't on the field coaching, he traveled to scout and recruit. Yet, the absences only made his time at home more special to me. My dad was my hero. I looked up to him the same way he looked up to Big Daddy.

On my dad's side of the family there was a line of intense, powerful men of passion and conviction. As you can imagine though, their passions flew directly in the face of many everyday realities for Black people living in the South. Black men were expected to accept a lower social station and fall in line. Their decisions to stand up to overwhelming discrimination and racism cost my family dearly.

In the late 1930s, Samuel Thompson (my great-grandfather and Big Daddy's father), sold newspapers advocating for better treatment of Blacks. Area members of the Ku Klux Klan confronted Samuel, making threats when he refused to stop selling the papers.

Like most of the men in Bogalusa, Samuel worked at the local paper mill. One afternoon, two employees pushed him into the paper-chopping machine, and he died. The mill called his death a "tragic accident," but the Black community in Bogalusa knew it was murder. Many years later, no one was surprised, least of all my family members, when a local man made a deathbed confession, admitting his involvement in the murder. Like too many Black families, ours had experienced the egregious and personal nature of racism.

Trying to make amends, the company offered Big Daddy a job at the mill, since his father's death meant he had to start helping support his family. Every summer when school ended, Big Daddy went to work in the mill. He continued there for a long time, but refused to let his own sons follow in his footsteps. As a father, he was strict, but the core of his philosophy was focused on keeping his sons alive and safe. Later, he applied the same philosophy to me, his first grandchild.

At least once a year, my family went back to Bogalusa to visit Big Daddy, Granny, and all our relatives. The trip was a big deal, a twenty-hour summer drive when my dad could take several weeks off.

Although long, the trip was also fun. It could have been a scene from a Chevy Chase movie. Dad drove while Mom sat next to him. Amie and I filled the long stretches of I-81 with games, bickering, and multiple rounds of "are we there yet?"

We'd spend a week or so with Big Daddy and Granny then another week with my mom's parents Granny and Pop Fred. The whole family loved having us home. We were like celebrities. I played with my cousins, worked in the garden with Granny, and helped Big Daddy set up for his six a.m. Bible study classes. My memories of those trips are filled with love, but also the rotten egg smell of the paper mill, always heavy in the humid air.

The stories my parents had told me about Bogalusa came to life on these summer visits. There were stark differences between this small, Deep South mill town and our larger, scenic Northern college town. Bogalusa had fewer trees and no sidewalks. The houses were smaller. Some homes had bars on the windows. There were rusty, broken-down cars sitting on blocks in at least half of the front yards. This was my family's home though, and I enjoyed exploring our roots.

One warm summer afternoon when I was seven, I decided to do what I did best—test the boundaries of how far was too far to explore. Just like in kindergarten, I needed to understand the context for rules that didn't make sense to me.

Whenever we drove past a certain part of town, Big Daddy slowed the car to a crawl and made deliberate eye contact with people on the street. These were young men with hard faces. Many held paper bags wrapped around bottles of beer or malt liquor. Some of them would meet Big Daddy's eyes in defiance. Others dropped their gaze to the sidewalk. Shouts of "Hey, Reverend!" were common, but others didn't even look up from the ground, except maybe to make sure we weren't the police.

Once we'd passed them, Big Daddy would look at me in the rearview mirror as he sped up the car. "I don't ever want to see you on this side of town. Do you hear me?"

I nodded, but couldn't keep my curiosity from bubbling over. "But why?"

"Because it's dangerous. Nothing good happens over here. These people lead tough lives, and that has made them tough people. There's drinking, drug dealing, and all kinds of stuff that my grandson doesn't need to get caught up in. Understand?"

"Yes, sir."

I looked out the window and watched the rest of the town roll by. Big Daddy didn't live in a mansion, but his little house and yard were always well tended. He took pride in what he owned and accomplished. He was also proud of Bogalusa. Big Daddy often preached about how people could overcome their circumstances.

Earlier that day, his sermon had retold the David and Goliath story. I'd sat in the hard, wooden pew and listened in awe as Big Daddy explained that no matter what your circumstances were, if God was for you, then nobody could be against you. If you had faith and courage, like David did, you could slay a giant.

It's strange to think that a story from so long ago can stay with a person their whole life. Yet I have been inspired by Big Daddy's sermon at many different points in my journey toward success. That day, his words inspired me. They made me want to prove myself as a giant-slayer. When we got home, I changed out of my church clothes and raced outside to the garage, where my bike leaned waiting against the wall, a second-hand ten-speed Big Daddy had fixed up for me.

I hopped on and pedaled furiously down the sidewalk, closer and closer to the forbidden neighborhood. I rode past one house, then the next, then the next, glancing repeatedly over my shoulder toward Big Daddy's house. Then, I turned around and rode back, repeating the circle for what felt like hours.

Finally, I decided to go for it. I passed all the houses on the street until I got to the stop sign. This time I didn't stop. I steered toward the part of town where I wasn't supposed to go. I had to see it up close. *Just once*, I told myself.

I heard my grandfather's warning in my head, but I needed to see what I was missing. I wanted to know if I was brave enough to take the risk, brave enough to stand up to my fears. Brave, I thought, like David.

I pedaled faster as I approached the street. Gripping the handlebars tightly, I turned and could hear my grandfather's voice, whispering in my head that what I was doing was dangerous. But I wasn't afraid.

The street didn't seem much different than the ones before it. The houses were rundown. I saw furniture scattered in yards. Guys sprawled on porch couches wearing nothing but sweatpants or shorts. People were drinking and playing cards or dominoes. Even up close, it seemed just like it had from the safety of Big Daddy's car.

About halfway down the street, the thrill of the adventure wore off. In the back of my mind, I realized I was breaking the rules—Big Daddy's rules. I'd never done that before. Sure, I'd gotten in trouble for questioning rules, but I'd never intentionally disobeyed my grandfather.

My palms started to sweat, making the grips on my bike slippery. I noticed that people were looking at me, giving me sideways glances like they were trying to figure out what I was doing there. Maybe they recognized me? Everyone in town knew Big Daddy. Certainly, they wouldn't hesitate to tell him they'd seen his grandson riding down their street. The realization hit me with a sickening crash. There was no way I'd get away with this.

I raced home, hoping I'd at least beat my uncles home before lunch. As I turned the corner and Big Daddy's house came into view, I saw him standing in the driveway with his arms crossed. Although it had been years since he'd left the NFL, he still hadn't lost his running back physique. He was a very big man. I gulped a little and slowed my pace. *No need to hurry toward a whooping*, I thought.

As I rode up the driveway, his eyes narrowed. I stopped and got off.

"Where have you been?" he asked me.

I looked at my feet and kicked some pebbles. "Nowhere."

He stepped forward and took the bike from my grip. He lifted it with one hand and held my wrist with the other. "Don't lie."

Big Daddy knew exactly where I'd been. Big Daddy knew everything. I bit my lip and shrugged. I couldn't find the words to explain why I'd done it, so I said nothing.

"I came out here to see if you wanted something to eat before the family gets here, but I couldn't find you. I'm assuming you were somewhere you weren't supposed to be?"

He walked, bike and wrist still in hand, toward the garage. He put my bike back and turned to me, then picked me up and tossed me over his shoulder. He marched into the house and brought me into the little sitting room off the hallway.

Then, without another word, he spanked me, wearing me out until my backside was sore enough that I'd think twice about getting on my bike even just to go down the driveway, never mind across town. When he finished, he didn't let me go. Instead, he tucked me tightly between his knees and stared directly into my eyes.

"Do you understand why I'm disappointed?"

I gulped through heavy sobs and nodded. "Yes, sir."

"Tell me."

"Because I wasn't supposed to go over there, and I did."

"No." he paused. "That's not why."

I looked up, confused.

Big Daddy grabbed my arms and held them tightly. "Your mama and daddy got out of this environment to make a better life for you. You can't get caught up in the stuff that goes on in those neighborhoods. You can't put yourself in situations where you'll get hurt and derailed."

My eyes widened. I could tell that what he was saying was important, even though it would be years before I understood the full weight of his words.

I wiped my nose with my t-shirt and squeaked out, "Okay."

Then, he leaned forward. "I mean it, Binky. God has a plan for your life and it's not in those streets. You're on a special path. You're going to be the first millionaire in our family."

2

A WINNING STANDARD

M uch to my mother's relief, I stayed in school past kindergarten, although my independent spirit only grew stronger. I wasn't a bad student. In fact, I liked academics. That part made sense to me. To get what I wanted, I needed to study and work hard. My parents followed that advice themselves. They'd firmly instilled the same lesson in me. Sometimes though, when they saw me going after what I wanted, I'm sure they wondered if I really understood anything they were trying to teach me.

The Christmas season was a tricky time. It meant celebrations and visits with relatives, but it was also when we'd find out whether my dad would have a job the next spring. If the football team failed to rank or earn a trip to a bowl game, it was likely that we'd soon be packing—another year, another college town. Those early holidays were pretty great though, since my dad coached the defensive line at UConn for five years. Our Christmases weren't full of expensive gifts and toys, but we had stability, and we were happy.

One of those holiday mornings, after I'd finished opening my presents and helped my parents clean up, I sat on my bed and admired my new Hot Wheels fire truck. The red paint was perfectly shiny, with no chips or scratches like my other cars. It was cool, for sure, but how did it compare to the cars I already had? I opened my toy box and looked over my collection. The blue Trans Am, my favorite car, caught my eye. It was dirty and had some dents from that time I dropped it down the stairs. Yet, when I placed the Trans Am next to the fire truck, there was really no contest. I still liked the Trans Am more. I studied both toys and an idea came to mind. I pocketed the fire truck and tossed the Trans Am back in my toy box.

Looking around the room, my gaze landed on the eight-track tape my parents had given me earlier that morning: Carl Douglas. Boy, did I love that song "Kung Fu Fighting." I'd run around dancing and throwing kicks and punches while I sang along. Though it was a great song to play at home, I figured that since I heard it on the radio all the time, I didn't really *need* the tape. I started humming to myself as I grabbed the eight-track and a stuffed lion toy I'd gotten from a relative. I put on my coat and crammed the toys into my pockets before I ran into the living room.

"Dad, can I go ride my bike outside?"

My dad craned his neck around me to see the TV. "Move out of the way, son. This is an important game." He waved me aside. I took that as a yes.

I reached for the door handle as Mom called from the kitchen, "Don't forget your hat and gloves. It snowed last night!"

I pulled on my boots, hat, and gloves, and bundled up. I hopped on the banana seat and started pedaling around the parking lot. It didn't take long before my friend, Joey, joined me. Eventually, we ditched our bikes and went over to the playground where a few other kids were playing on the swing set. As we trudged through the snow, I pulled the fire truck, eight-track, and stuffed lion out of my pockets.

"Hey," I announced. "I just got these presents for Christmas."

The kids gathered around to look.

"Man, I love that song," a second-grader named Gary said as he reached out to touch the tape.

I raised an eyebrow. "Well, today's your lucky day. You can have this eight-track for only five dollars."

"Five dollars? I don't have five dollars!" Gary said, givng me a wild-eyed look.

I had no idea how much a tape cost, so I didn't know where to start the bidding. "Well," I said. "How much *do* you have?"

Gary emptied his pockets and inspected the contents. "Two quarters."

"Sold!"

I quickly unloaded the fire truck and the lion on other neighborhood kids. When my hands were full of coins instead of toys, I said goodbye and went home. I dumped the change on my nightstand, next to a pile of books I'd gotten that morning. I curled up in bed and read until my dad called me.

"Binky! Come here!"

He didn't sound angry, but my eyes still darted to the pile of change. I closed my book and raced down the hallway.

My dad nodded at the TV. "It's halftime. Let's throw in your new eight-track and give it a listen."

I clasped my hands behind my back and dug my feet into the carpet. "I don't want to."

"What are you talking about, boy? You love that song. Go get it."

He waved toward my bedroom, so I turned and walked down the hall, but I didn't get far before I remembered that, with my dad, honesty truly was the best policy. Telling the truth wouldn't save me from a spanking, but it might save me from a spanking *and* a lecture.

I dragged my feet and walked slowly back down the hall to the living room. "I can't get my tape because I don't have it."

Mom had joined Dad on the couch. They both stared at me. "What do you mean you don't have it?"

I pointed to the door. "I just sold it to Gary."

My dad bolted upright. He looked even bigger than usual. "You did what?"

"I sold some of my new presents when I went outside to play." I kept my eyes on my feet.

"What were you thinking?" Mom asked. "Why'd you do that?" She stepped between my dad and me. "Donnie, sit down. Let's hear what happened."

"Well, I already know the song, so I don't need the tape," I told them. "And I like the fire truck, but I *love* my Trans Am. And I just thought maybe someone else would like the lion more than I did."

Mom looked over at my dad. He was staring at me with a mixture of anger, disbelief, and… something else. I couldn't tell what it was, but it reminded me of the way he'd looked at me the first time I hit a baseball without using a tee.

"Okay," Mom said, quickly summing up the situation. "The first thing we need to do is go get your toys back and return your friends' money. Your father will go with you." She patted him on the shoulder and gave him an encouraging smile.

I thought about protesting, but the look on my dad's face was enough to make me back down. I ran to my room and grabbed the change, handing it to him. He looked at it in his gloved palm and asked, "You made all this, huh?"

I nodded and tried not to smile.

Yes, I got a spanking that afternoon, but I also knew there had been just a little pride in my father's eyes when he saw the money. Of course, there was some anger too. Because of my scheme, my dad had been taken away from his football game and forced to trudge around the apartment complex in frigid temperatures. Under all that annoyance, I still knew there was a part of him that couldn't help but be impressed.

Learning About Learning and Hard Work

Since Dad's career was going well, and my mother now had both a degree and a job, the Thompsons started gaining some financial stability, enough that my parents could buy a home in Manchester, Connecticut. It was a small, yellow, Cape Cod-style house with a huge, wooded backyard. There was a small, open, grassy area, too—just big enough for my dad and me to play catch. Most importantly, it was ours, and we were all—Mom, Dad, me, maybe even baby Amie—very, very proud of it.

There was one part of the house, however, that I didn't like: the basement. It was musty, smelled funky, and had cobwebs everywhere. My dad saw potential.

One day, he stood in the doorway leading down and declared: "We are going to finish the basement this summer. Make a playroom, maybe a TV area for adults. What do you say, Binky? You going to help?"

Like he had to even ask. Even musty and funky, the basement suddenly became my favorite room in the house.

My father was handy. He could fix almost anything and owned lots of lovingly tended tools. Even when we lived in rented apartments, he kept them well maintained. Of course, he'd never done a project as complex as finishing a whole basement, but somehow that didn't seem to worry him at all.

A few weeks later, in August, right before football training started for my dad and school began for me, we were down in the basement finishing up. Dad called out, "Wrench!" so I grabbed it and scurried over. He secured the TV stand to the wall so it wouldn't tip over, then stepped back and surveyed his work. The room had come along just as he planned. He'd started at the library by checking out a couple of books on home remodeling. Then, he went to the hardware store and got advice about buying the best supplies.

Dad grinned as he examined his work. "Tell your mom to come down here and see this. Amie too!" he yelled as I raced up the steps.

When Mom got to the bottom of the stairs, her face settled into a slow expression of delight. She put Amie down to let her toddle across the carpet, and then she walked around, brushing her fingers along the paneling.

"Wow," she said finally. "You boys outdid yourselves!"

"Haha!" My dad turned to me. "And just in time for football season. We'll be able to watch all the games down here!"

My father's face radiated pride. He'd never done anything like this before, but he didn't let that stop him. He knew he could learn anything he needed to know by reading the right books, talking to the right people, and believing there was really no reason he couldn't do it perfectly.

That summer in the basement, my father taught me that there are no limits to what I can accomplish if I'm willing to learn and put in the time. He never sat me down and spelled out the lessons he was teaching because he didn't need to. Watching him live his values and commitment was more powerful than any lecture.

Paintings, Cheerleaders, and Injustice

My parents were my teachers and protectors, but that didn't mean they weren't tough—especially Dad. When it came to my entrepreneurial spirit, he may have been willing to let me test the boundaries, but when it came to being disrespectful, disobeying, or not doing my schoolwork, he didn't give an inch. It was crystal clear that if I pushed the limits too far, I'd spend the next day being careful when I sat down.

As much as I wished I could get away with rule bending, I still believed my dad was fair. His rules were designed to make sure that Amie and I stayed safe and lived by the values our parents embodied. I grew up understanding that good rules have good reasons and all my actions have consequences.

My dad, however, knew all too well that the world at large didn't operate like the Thompson household. Some rules were senseless and unjust, while others were nothing more than a way for bullies, big and small, to get what they wanted. When I talked about standing up to bullies or acting out in response to things I thought were unfair, my dad was always in my corner. He taught me to stick up for myself and for others who didn't have a voice. He knew that running to a grown-up or teacher wasn't always going to be an option, so he supported me as I learned to speak up and fight back.

My dad learned that philosophy from his father, who was even tougher on my dad and his brothers than Dad was on me. Big Daddy raised his sons to understand that the world was not built for their success. He wanted them to know—as young Black men coming from the South—they were starting life with the deck stacked against them. But, this unfortunate fact just meant they had to try harder. People and institutions wouldn't offer them support. Instead, they would have to fight every single day to find success. My dad had been waging that battle his entire life. He passed those ideas to Amie and me: *Learn to fight for what you want and what you think is right.*

Although my battles back then were small compared to what I would face in the business world, I took my father's message to heart. I was never shy about anything, but I was especially outspoken when I felt that I or anyone else had been mistreated. And I wouldn't hesitate to fix the injustice. While I'd cheer for a fairly matched schoolyard fight, there was almost nothing I hated more than seeing someone big or strong pick on those who couldn't defend themselves. It was as if I had an allergic reaction to bullying.

For example, one day in third-grade art class, the teacher asked us to paint of a landscape scene. I'd chosen to paint a football field because it was something that I could easily picture. I wandered over to the paint center and held the stained plastic dish under the bottle of green paint. I squeezed out a big blob of paint and headed back to my desk. The art teacher, Mrs. Pearce, was circling the room, looking at everyone's paintings. She stopped next to one student's desk, slid her glasses down her nose, and frowned.

"Hmm…that's not very good, is it?" she said with a pinched expression. "Look at those trees." She pointed at the student's work. "They're on top of the mountains in the background, but they're as big as the ones in the foreground. We're supposed to be working on *perspective*, Jocelyn. Weren't you listening?"

Jocelyn's lower lip began to tremble. "I'm sorry…" she started, but when the tears came, she couldn't finish her thoughts.

As Mrs. Pearce moved away, I put down the paint dish and walked over to Jocelyn's desk. She'd painted a picture of rolling hills and some trees with lots of different colored leaves.

"I like it," I told her, and I meant it. "It's bright and cheerful. It makes me think of a sunny day."

Jocelyn just sniffled in response.

I tried again. "But I wouldn't like to rake up all those leaves when they fall!" I gave her a big grin to let her know I was joking, but she didn't laugh at all.

"Hey," I said softly. "Don't listen to Mrs. Pearce. Your painting is really nice." I turned to Barry, who was sitting next to Jocelyn. "Don't you think her painting is nice?"

Barry craned his neck and glanced over at the painting. After a few seconds' consideration, he nodded and went back to his own painting—a space scene, complete with asteroids and UFOs. His response wasn't as enthusiastic as I'd hoped. Jocelyn didn't seem to feel any better, so I grabbed her painting and climbed up on a stool. I steadied myself and then stood tall, holding her painting for the whole class to see.

"Hey! Who thinks this painting is good?"

I watched all eyes turn toward me. My classmates didn't seem fazed. They knew me well enough not to be surprised by this behavior. There were a few murmurs of appreciation, and then everyone's hand went up.

"Mrs. Pearce, I think you're wrong about Jocelyn's painting," I said and hopped down.

"Young man, you are disturbing this class," said Mrs. Pearce, walking over to me.

"You made Jocelyn cry. That's not right." I crossed my arms and waited for punishment.

She pointed to the door. "Go to the office this minute."

I shrugged and went willingly. I hadn't done anything wrong, except stick up for a classmate. Mom had to come pick me up from school, but she wasn't mad. By this time, not only she was used to getting calls from school, but she was also used to me being in trouble for trying to right injustices. Though I'm sure she wished I were in class and not the office, I knew she was proud of my conviction.

After all, my mother was a big part of the reason I always questioned things, not because she was outwardly rebellious, but because she was always questioning me herself. She never accepted a statement at face value. Instead, she always pushed my thinking and helped me develop the ability to express my opinions and make strong arguments.

For instance, when I was in fourth grade, I had a poster of the Dallas Cowboys cheerleaders hanging in my room. My dad had been on a recruiting trip to Texas and brought it back for me as a surprise. I'd hung it up without a moment's hesitation. The women on the poster were posing in their short shorts and crop tops with blue and silver pompoms in their hands. I thought it was great.

"What is *that*?" Mom said. She's come to check my homework and was standing near the door, pointing at the poster.

"Oh, Dad got it for me…" I trailed off as she marched over to the wall, yanked the poster down, and ripped it to shreds.

When she finished, she glared at me, the remains of the poster hanging in her hands. "Is this what you think of women? They're just objects for you to look at?"

"I never said—"

"You didn't have to say anything. Just having this poster tells me enough about what you think."

I balled my hands into tight fists. This was some serious injustice right here.

"I'm going to tell Dad!"

Mom just laughed. "Good. Tell him. That's not going to change the fact that this poster is in shreds, and nothing like it will ever be allowed on these walls again."

She turned and left the room. All I could do was watch her walk out. She was right. Regardless of what my dad might say later—and something told me he'd side with my mom on this one—the poster was gone for good.

Later that evening, when I finally dared to come out of my room, Mom was sitting on the couch, reading. She smiled when she saw me hanging around the hallway.

"Come sit with me," she said, putting down her book. "Tell me why you liked that poster."

"Because the Cowboys are my favorite team," I explained, which was true, although it wasn't the *only* reason.

"And why is that?"

"Well," I thought for a minute. "I like how Coach Landry never gets mad. He just gives directions for a new play and moves on. As if he knows they can fix the mistakes. And I like how they win a lot of games. And they have good players."

Mom nodded thoughtfully. "And who is your favorite player?"

"Roger Staubach!"

"What do you like about him?"

"He's the quarterback. So, he directs the game. He knows what he's doing out there. The other players respect him. And, he's a good person," I explained.

"Oh? How do you know?" she pressed.

"He was in the Navy and served in Vietnam. He's a hero."

"Well, sounds like you know a lot about this Roger Staubach. I'm glad you've thought about this."

I smiled a little, thinking maybe Mom was coming around. Maybe she was starting to see what a good idea that poster had been. Maybe she'd get me a new one!

"Now tell me," she continued, "Were any of those excellent qualities about the Cowboys and their quarterback demonstrated on that poster?"

Checkmate. Another victory for Mom.

No "I" in Team

While I wasn't winning any debates with Mom in my elementary school years, there was something I was winning: baseball games.

"How's that arm, Ace?" Big Daddy asked when I swung open his car door. About once a year, he and my grandmother drove up from Bogalusa to spend a few weeks with us. Though he'd just been in the car for hours, my grandfather would always get right to business. "Once we get your grandmother settled," he'd say, handing me a suitcase to carry inside, "you and I are going to go work on that curveball."

Even though I was still young, he treated me like one of the high school athletes he coached. We spent hours on curveballs, knuckleballs, and sliders, and I was probably the only kid in the Connecticut Little Leagues who could throw so many different pitches. Big Daddy showed me how moving my fingers a fraction of an inch or gripping the ball in a slightly different way could totally change my game.

It might seem odd to someone who doesn't come from a sports family to invest so much time in teaching a kid the intricacies of a game. But not for the Thompsons. My dad's motto: *if you're going to do it, be good at it. Otherwise, don't bother doing it.* Just like Big Daddy, my dad spent hours at the park or in our backyard making sure I was the best baseball player I could be. And the best I could be was really good.

But in sports, as in anything, you can get overconfident. Although my dad wanted me to have a strong self-image based on my capabilities and work ethic, he was also a coach. Coaches work with *teams*, and the goal of team sports is to win. That was sometimes easy to forget in baseball, where so many of the plays were made by single players.

One evening, I barreled into the house, excited to tell my dad about my game. He was in the kitchen, making himself a snack after a long drive back from a recruiting trip.

"Dad!" I exclaimed, collapsing into a chair at the kitchen table. "You missed a great game!"

"How'd the team do?" he asked before taking a big bite of his sandwich.

"Well, first, coach put me in at shortstop. I tagged out a couple of guys and had a bunch of assists on outs at second base. This weekend can we work on my throw to first? I want to get better at throwing on the run. And I hit two home runs! Two homers in one game! And then, later, I got to pitch two innings, and I struck out four people and hit two, but that was on purpose. Man, it was so much fun."

I took a deep breath. Praise from my dad was a rare gem, but I was expecting at least a little smile or a nod of pride. Instead, he finished chewing. Then he looked at me and asked again, "How did the *team* do?"

"Oh," I shrugged. "We lost 9-7."

"Well, what difference does it make how well *you* did if your *team* lost?"

His words stung, but not because he was wrong. Instead, by that age, I was beginning to understand what he meant when he said things like that. Looking good and playing well didn't mean anything if I couldn't also lead my team to victory. Developing a winning standard meant working hard and leading my teammates, not just coasting through a game as a solo player.

It's often hard to pinpoint the exact moments that have changed your life, but that night at the kitchen table with my father, I knew this was an important one.

3

SCHOOLYARD LESSONS

My father's hard work and winning standard paid off in 1981 when he got a job as the defensive line coach at the University of Pittsburgh. The Pitt football program was always one of the highest ranked in the country and had a particularly strong team at the time: an 11-1 season record; seven first-round draft picks; and twenty-three players who'd go on to start in the NFL, including legendary quarterback Dan Marino. Talk about a step up.

The job also meant we had to move to Pennsylvania. Connecticut had been my home since I was a baby, and that house in Manchester held great family memories, but this was my father's big shot. At the end of fourth grade, I said goodbye to all my friends and the only home I could remember.

We moved into a large house in Bethel Park, Pennsylvania, a comfortably middle-class, suburban town about ten miles from Pittsburgh. Working for an elite football program meant more money. With Amie starting kindergarten, Mom enrolled in graduate school. My parents' dreams of building success for themselves and smoothing the path for us started to come true.

I didn't realize it at the time, but the move to Bethel Park marked an uptick in our family's fortunes—and my own.

"Time for lunch," my fifth-grade teacher, Mrs. Kimble, announced.

My classmates and I rushed to put away our books. We ran to the door, trying to be first in line. As I waited, I shoved my hand in my pocket to get the piece of candy I'd stashed there before school. The wrapper crinkled a little. As I started to open it, I felt a finger jam into my shoulder blade.

"Hey, Don, give me one of those," Michael whispered.

I didn't even turn around. "No way, man. Get your own."

He paused and then jingled the change in his pocket. "I'll give you fifty cents."

A quick consideration. On one hand, I liked Jolly Ranchers. On the other, I could do a lot more with fifty cents than one piece of candy. I thought back to when I'd sold my Christmas presents but decided, this time, there was no way I could get in trouble. I'd bought the Jolly Ranchers with my own money, so they were definitely mine to sell.

"Okay," I agreed, handing him the candy. "And hit me up again tomorrow. I'll have way more flavors."

Michael dropped the quarters in my outstretched palm, then unwrapped the candy and popped it in his mouth before Mrs. Kimble came over to lead us to lunch. He didn't care about the future of the Jolly Rancher market, only about his momentary satisfaction. I, on the other hand, spent the lunch period calculating potential profits from selling candy to my classmates. An entrepreneur was born.

Thank goodness for Woolworth's, America's most famous five-and-dime. I bought Jolly Ranchers in bags of twenty-five for $2.50. I figured if I could sell each candy for a quarter, I'd bank a cool 150 percent profit. Not bad for a day's work. In my fifth-grade mind, I saw a budding empire about to unfold.

The next day, I brought the rest of my Jolly Ranchers to school, stashing them in my locker. I used old-school word-of-mouth marketing to spread the good news that I'd be selling candy for a quarter apiece, before school, at lunch, at recess, and after school.

"Grape, please," Christine said, sliding her quarter across the lunch table.

I smiled at her and pulled a purple Jolly Rancher from my backpack. Christine had long eyelashes and a bright smile. I was *almost* tempted to give her a discount, but I thought better of it. I wanted to be seen as a respectable businessman. No room for matters of the heart in the candy business.

A few weeks into my side hustle, business was booming. I'd even hired another kid, Daryl, to help me hand out the candies and keep a lookout for teachers so that I could keep my mind free. I had to figure out new ways to make an extra buck or two. Adding Daryl to my team paid off one day during social studies when I had a brilliant idea.

As soon as I got home from school, I raced into the kitchen. Mom sat at the table going through her checkbook. I gave her a hug—first because I loved her, and second because I wanted to get her in a good mood—and then walked to the refrigerator.

"Mom, can I ask you something?"

"Yes, Binky?"

I paused. "Don't you think it's time to stop calling me 'Binky'?" I asked, forgetting momentarily what I wanted to talk to her about.

"Well, let me think about that." She tapped her pen against her chin and made an exaggerated expression of concentration. "No, now what do you need?"

I reached into the fridge, found a piece of American cheese, unwrapped it, and folded it in half. I was about to shove it in my mouth when she cleared her throat.

"Are you trying to cool the whole house? Close that refrigerator."

I did and sat down at the table. "Mom, I'd like to go grocery shopping with you."

She leaned toward me and wrapped one hand behind her ear. "Excuse me? Did I hear that right?"

"Yep," I laughed.

"Why do you want to go? You've always complained when I've asked you before."

I'd already figured out a response. "Dad said I ought to help you out more now that you're back in school. I thought maybe I could, you know, help carry things for you or something."

Technically, I wasn't lying. My father *had* asked me to pitch in, although I was pretty sure he hadn't anticipated I'd be able to get a little something for myself out of the deal.

"Aren't you a gentleman? I certainly can't say no to that. I'm going tomorrow to get fish for dinner. How does that sound?"

"Perfect!"

I hopped up, gave Mom a quick kiss—just to generate some extra goodwill—and went to my room to do my homework.

Here's the deal with my sudden interest in grocery shopping. I'd been buying my Jolly Ranchers at Woolworth's because I walked right by the store on the way home from the bus stop. But the A&P grocery store, which was much farther away, sold candy *by the pound*. That meant I could get Jolly Ranchers for about five cents each and keep selling them for a quarter. I did the math and realized—that's 400 percent profit.

I didn't exactly *need* the money, but I thought I could use it to buy some of the things my parents had decided weren't worth the expense. Like sneakers, for example. My parents always bought me PRO-Keds—comfortable, practical, perfectly fine—but lately, like my classmates, I wanted the cool things I saw on television, like high-top Converse All Stars.

Convincing my mother to let me come to the store was only half the battle though. There was no way she was going to let me buy Jolly Ranchers in the quantity I envisioned, especially since we weren't allowed to have candy at school in the first place. On the car ride to A&P, I worked out a plan. Once we got there, I put my scheme into action.

I followed my mother through the produce section, holding the grocery list and crossing off items. At the meat counter, however, there was a long line—just as I had hoped. I went up to the counter, took a ticket from the dispenser, and handed it to my mother at the back of the line. Time to enact my plan!

"Looks like this is going to be a while," she said with a sigh. In hopes of getting the shopping done quickly, she turned to me for help. "Binky, run over and get eggs and milk while I wait here. Don't forget to check the expiration date."

I grinned as I made my way through the aisles. I didn't have much time, but if I hurried, it might be just enough. At the bulk bins in the front of the store, I grabbed a bag and poured in huge scoops of Jolly Ranchers. I paid for the candy and ran as fast as I could to stash the contraband in our car. In those days, it wasn't uncommon for people to leave their cars unlocked, so I got in easily and was able to hide the candy under our back seat. Then, I dashed back inside, grabbed a carton of eggs and a gallon of milk and made it back to the meat counter before my mother reached the front of the line.

"What took you so long?" she asked as I put the groceries in our cart.

"I had to check all the egg boxes," I said, giving her my sweetest smile. "I wanted to make sure I got you the perfect one."

My mother narrowed her eyes. "So this has nothing to do with all the candy you just took to the car? I hope you plan on sharing that with friends."

How did she know? Somehow, she always knew. I began making up a story, but just then, the butcher called out our number. She didn't bring it up again, even as we unloaded the groceries. I pulled the bag out of the back, figuring I was home free.

The candy-by-the-pound conversion turned out to be an excellent business decision. In my best week, I cleared fifty bucks, but as I have since learned to expect, when a business is thriving, competition is typically close behind.

"Don!" Daryl shouted, running up to me as I walked into school.

"Where's the fire, Daryl?" I asked like the slick businessman I was becoming. This was the Monday after my $50 week, and I was riding high.

"Trevor Dixon is selling candy, too. He's telling everyone you're ripping them off!"

I looked around the schoolyard for Trevor and saw him standing by the water fountain, surrounded by a small crowd.

"Don't worry, I got this."

I causally strolled over to Trevor with a friendly but curious expression on my face.

"Ah, there he is now." Trevor smirked at me over the heads of the kids he was trying to convert. "Don is selling Jolly Ranchers for a quarter. That's a rip-off! I'll sell them for twenty cents—five pieces for a dollar. Don's only giving you four."

I smiled at Trevor. Another big business decision: I said loudly, so everyone heard, "We're changing our prices. Everything is ten cents."

Suddenly swarmed by savvy shoppers, Daryl whispered to me, "We won't make any money."

I waved away his concern. I'd already done the math. The lower cost of the bulk candy from the grocery store meant I could slash prices and still make a good profit—my first lesson in retail margins.

I was on my way to being the head of a candy empire when someone ratted me out to the principal.

"You need to stop selling candy at school," Principal Bowman said after the secretary led me to his office.

I crossed my arms. "Why?"

He raised an eyebrow at my backtalk, but decided he'd let it slide for now. "Well for starters, it's against school rules."

I shrugged. "Who made those rules? You could change them."

Mr. Bowman sat back in his chair, interlocked his fingers, and rested his hands on his chest. "Well, it's not just my rules. Part of our job is to think of our students' health. Candy isn't healthy. You're not even allowed to *have* candy at school, let alone sell it!"

I looked at him with a you've-got-to-be-kidding-me expression.

"What about the soda in the vending machine? Those drinks are just as bad for you, and the school has no problem selling them."

It didn't matter to me that I was talking to the guy in charge. If I saw unfairness or hypocrisy anywhere, I wasn't afraid to point it out.

The principal pressed his lips together for a moment. Whatever they were paying him, the look on his face suggested it wasn't nearly enough to be dealing with me. He abandoned logic and tried a new approach.

"It's just not an acceptable practice at school."

"But you also sell cookies and ice cream in the cafeteria! What's the difference between that and Jolly Ranchers?" He opened his mouth to interject, but I was on a roll. "I'm not *making* kids buy the candy. They *want* it."

I smiled to myself as I concluded. It was true; I had a great business model, fair and square. My argument was so convincing that I wouldn't have been surprised if the principal had handed me a dime and asked for watermelon Jolly Rancher. Instead, he reached across his desk ad grabbed the phone.

"You're being extremely disrespectful. I'm calling your mom and dad to pick you up. You're on the verge of suspension, young man."

I knew I'd pushed too far. Now there was nothing to do but accept the consequences.

I sat in the office for almost an hour, just waiting. When Mom arrived, she promised the principal I would no longer be a candy entrepreneur. Her sincerity saved me from being suspended, but her message was difficult for me to accept. I was good at the candy business. I loved the rush it gave me as much as I loved the cash. I didn't want to give it up.

I held it together in the office, but as we walked toward the car, I started to cry. My dad sat in the driver's seat waiting for us. Mom was so late in coming to get me because she'd picked him up at the airport on her way. He'd been on a recruiting trip.

I crawled into the back seat, still crying.

As Dad pulled the car onto the road, he looked at me in the rearview mirror. "What's all this crying about?"

"My…candy…business," I sobbed. "Mom…shut it…down."

Mom shook her head like she couldn't believe she was getting blamed. She explained what I'd been up to.

My dad gave me another glance in the mirror. "How much were you making?"

I wiped an arm across my running rose and sniffled, "Like $30 a week."

He laughed and looked over at her. "Well, now you're going to make *me* cry! That's good money!"

His support and pride made me feel a little better. Though my dreams of becoming a pre-teen tycoon ended for now, I kept an underground Jolly Rancher business going on a much smaller scale for a little while longer. The wheeling and dealing of running a business had given me a glimpse of what it felt like to use my smarts and competitive drive to my advantage. That was a good feeling. Perhaps an addictive one. Plus, I couldn't just go cold turkey on all that cash.

What Did You Call Me?

Since my dad was on my side, and my mom couldn't figure out anything I'd actually done wrong, the Jolly Rancher business didn't result in any punishments, other than Mom watching my candy purchases more carefully.

Overall, I got along well with the other kids in Bethel Park. After just a few months at my new school, I already knew everyone in my grade, and even though I had my close group of friends, I wasn't cliquey. I was friendly with everyone I talked to, happy to play with anyone at recess, and kind to whomever I sat beside at lunch. I was also okay with being alone. My parents and grandparents had taught me to be confident. I felt good about myself and knew I was doing the right thing, so there was no reason to worry about what other people thought.

Of course, being a nice guy didn't mean that *everybody* liked me. In Bethel Park, at just age ten, I had my first real experience with hateful ignorance.

One afternoon, we were playing kickball in the gym. The red rubber ball came bouncing at me while I played my beloved shortstop position. I grabbed it and tagged the runner in front of me, causing the third out.

As I jogged over to where the other kids on my team were lining up to kick the ball, Ronald, the pitcher on the other team, called, "Hey, give me the ball, blackie."

At first, I was sure I misheard him. Admittedly, I was one of maybe three or four Black students in a school of close to 1,000 kids, but I hadn't yet felt discriminated against or singled out because of my skin color. So, I gave Ronald the benefit of the doubt as I walked toward him.

"What did you say?"

He cocked his head to one side and smirked. "I said, 'Give me the ball, blackie.'"

Without giving it another thought, I punched Ronald square in the face. He fell to the ground, stunned, while I rubbed my throbbing fist.

I was sent to the office, and Mom had to make another trip to get me. The principal considered suspending me, but other kids had heard what Ronald said. Instead, he let me off with a warning and a suggestion to my mother that I learn to control my temper.

She looked at him, her lips in a perfectly straight line, and said, "We'll have a long talk when his father gets home."

After my parents' experiences in Bogalusa, it was no wonder that my father's reaction to the incident was far different from his usual response to my rule breaking.

"Good," he said at dinner that night when Mom told him the story. "That boy deserved it. You don't let anyone treat you that way."

Mom, on the other hand, was frustrated by my violent reaction. She glared at him across the table, then turned to me.

"Yes, what that boy said was wrong," she acknowledged. "But so was your reaction. *You're* the one who ended up in the principal's office. *You're* the one who was nearly suspended. *You're* the one who has a mark on his record."

"But Mom, listen—"

"No, Binky, you listen. When you react with violence, you brand yourself as the bad kid. Nobody will take the time to get to know you, to see how smart and talented you are."

"But what he said was wrong," I insisted. "He shouldn't be talking to people like that."

She nodded. "I agree. It's not right. But you can't go around physically stomping out hatred every time you see it. It's one thing to defend yourself when you're in physical danger. It's another to use your fists to fight name-calling. When you do that, people see you as a kid who can't control his temper. You'll have an even bigger target on your back if that's the path you choose."

I wasn't totally convinced. I guess I sort of saw her point. I didn't want to be limited because people thought I was mean or violent. Then again, punching Ronald in the face had felt like the exact right response to a kid who didn't care who I was or what I thought.

But for the moment, I swallowed back the arguments that were bubbling up and nodded. "Fine. What do I do instead?"

"You save the fight for another day. You own your response. You don't let bullies and people filled with hatred and ignorance determine how you act. You be the better person, and don't let anyone else dictate your path."

Mom's words sunk deep into my core. Until that point, I'd thought power was solely physical. That's what I'd seen on the football field. The most powerful players were strong, fast, tough, and never shied away from a block. But that evening, she showed me power was also mental. I'd given up my power to Ronald when I reacted to his words without thinking. It would take some time to learn how to control my reactions, but once I mastered that skill, I'd find that it gave me more power than I'd ever be able to put behind a punch.

Moving Again

In the summer before my sixth-grade year, when the lease was up on our house in Bethel Park, my family moved to Shadyside, an area much closer to Pitt's campus. It turned out to be an eye-opening experience. A few weeks after we got settled into our new townhome, I started at Reizenstein Middle School. It was a magnet school—a public school that offered special programs in math, science, and the arts—and drew its student population from across the city. For the first time, I experienced other students who looked like me and got to know kids I wouldn't have met in the more insulated neighborhoods where we'd lived before.

We stayed in Shadyside for nearly two years, but when I was in eighth grade, the Pitt Panthers had a rough season, which resulted in a staff shake-up. Most of the coaching staff lost their jobs, including my father. This was the life of a coach, challenging, but not unexpected. Dad had broken through the college football ranks, so we knew he would find a job soon.

A new job meant we also faced another move. Breaking the lease on our townhouse, paying first and last month's rent on new place, and all the logistics of moving would be expensive. Not to mention, my dad would be traveling frequently during the holidays for interviews at colleges all over the country.

"What do you think?" Mom asked as she put the star on top of the Christmas tree.

I hung the last ornament in the box and stepped back to survey the tree.

"I mean, it's nice, but why are we bothering?" I shrugged. "We'll just have to take it down when we move."

"I like it," Amie said.

She gave Mom a sweet smile and shoved an elbow into my side, reminding me to be less grumpy. Even as an eight-year-old, my sister always kept me in line.

Mom plugged in the lights, then brought in a plate of Christmas cookies. We sat on the couch to eat and admire our handiwork. After a few quiet minutes, she swallowed her last bite and turned to us. She was suddenly serious.

"You both know what your dad's job situation is right now," she said, looking from me to Amie and back. "I think you know that Christmas will be light this year."

We both nodded. It was true that for the last few weeks I'd been eyeing a new boombox I'd seen at Sears, the kind with the microphone, detachable speakers, and dual cassette players that let you record from one tape to another. Like kids my age across the country, I'd already started planning a mixtape I wanted to make for a girl I liked. When I found out that my dad had been let go though, I dropped any hope of receiving that expensive, unnecessary boombox. I knew there were more important ways my parents needed to spend their money.

On Christmas morning though, I woke up to find a boombox under the tree. To this day, I consider that stereo among the most meaningful gifts I've ever received. My parents were willing to make sacrifices to ensure that I would have a wonderful Christmas. The $150 price tag was a lot of money in the mid 1980s and an even bigger deal to a family with limited income.

Holing up in my room and listening to one of my casettes on my new boombox was my favorite way to escape the real world. Sooner than I could have imagined I needed that distraction. In January, we moved again when Dad got a coaching job at Western Kentucky University. I had to finish the second half of eighth grade in a new school and the transition wasn't easy. If moving to Pittsburgh taught me that kids could be bullies, then my early experiences in Bowling Green taught me that adults could be just as bad.

Academic Prejudice

When Dad went from UConn to Pitt, the move had been a step up; he had a more prestigious position at one of the nation's elite football programs. The move to Western Kentucky University, on the other hand—well, it wasn't a bad job, but my dad was moving from a big, urban school to a smaller, rural school with a less successful program. Then, like now, there were a limited number of coaching positions, especially for African Americans, which forced him to accept the best one he could find. His goal for us never wavered though. He would continue to do whatever necessary to ensure that Amie and I had a smoother path.

For me, however, "smooth" is not the word I would use to define that spring. I attended the county school for grades K-8 because my parents had enrolled Amie there. They liked that we could be in the same place, available to support each other if need be, and it was supposed to be a good school.

For the first few weeks, I tried to make my way in a new environment nearly five hundred miles away from where I'd been just weeks before. I went to the classes on my schedule without questioning whether they were right for me. Quickly though, I realized that most of what the eighth graders were studying here in Kentucky was material I'd already learned in Pennsylvania. I never thought what I'd learned at Reizenstein as "advanced material," but some of this schoolwork was stuff I'd learned a couple of years earlier. I cared about school, but I wasn't interested in repeating lessons I'd already mastered. I made an appointment to see my new counselor.

"Come in, Donald. What can I do for you?" Mr. Hopkins asked when I stood in his doorway.

"Well, sir, I'd like to switch to more advanced classes. The ones I'm in now aren't challenging."

Mr. Hopkins pulled a manila folder from his filing cabinet. I assumed it was my school records from Reizenstein. "The school I just came from was a magnet school. I was in a lot of advanced classes, and I'd like to keep up with that type of work."

"Hmm…" the counselor scanned the folder and then leaned back in his chair. "And what types of advanced classes would you like to be in here?"

"Definitely math and English," I said eagerly. Those two classes were the worst parts of my day at the county school. I finished worksheets in pre-algebra so quickly that the teacher had started to make extras just for me. And I hadn't liked Ernest Hemingway's *The Old Man and the Sea* the first time; no way was I reading it again.

Mr. Hopkins opened his desk drawer and chose a pen. He clicked it repeatedly before writing a few notes in the folder. "To get into algebra, you needed to have completed the district math placement last year."

"But I wasn't here last year," I said leaning forward in my chair. "I took algebra at my old school though. You can see I was getting good grades in that class."

Mr. Hopkins frowned. "Donald, I'm sure you're *very* bright."

Funny, I thought, *he's making his words sound like they mean the exact opposite of what they're saying.*

"But at this school," he continued, "you're going to have to *prove* to us that you can handle advanced math. These transcripts," he waved the folder in his hand, "don't mean anything to us. We don't know what your other school taught, so we can't be sure you've had a rigorous enough preparation for honors classes. Just keep doing your work, and we'll let you know if we think you should be moved up."

My volume rose slightly. "But sir—"

The counselor tapped a finger on the folder. "That's quite a behavioral record you've got there."

It was clear he'd looked right past my stellar grades.

I sat back in my chair. "So, you're not going to let me switch classes."

"You'll need to earn it. We don't give handouts here," he said. "Come see me in a few weeks, and we'll reevaluate your situation."

I burst out of his office fuming. Handouts? I wasn't asking for a favor. Let me know in a few weeks? By the time they'd "reevaluated my situation," the school year would be nearly over.

The counselor didn't have any intention of moving me to advanced classes. He already knew everything he wanted to know about me. He'd made his estimate about who I was and what I could become. To him, I was a Black kid who talked too much and questioned authority. He'd decided to show me my place rather than give me the placement I had earned through hard work at my school in Pittsburgh.

I also made a decision then and there. I knew, as long as I passed eighth grade, my middle school record wouldn't play a role in my long-term success. I could test into honors courses when I went into high school. If they were going to make me miserable, then I'd at least provide them with some ongoing classroom entertainment.

Passive Resistance, Backfired

"Okay, class, turn in your verb phrases worksheet," Mr. Burrell said. "Then I want you to get out your books and read chapter nine while I grade these."

I grabbed the papers that the guy behind me was passing forward, added mine to the top, and then handed the pile forward. Instead of reading, I wrapped a rubber band around my finger and thumb, aimed toward the open window, and let it rip. Then, I tapped the rhythm to Tina Turner's "What's Love Got to Do With It" on my desk.

"Someone didn't put their name on their paper," Mr. Burrell called out.

I held my hand up. "Yep. That would be me."

Mr. Burrell cleared his throat. "You also didn't answer any of the questions."

All eyes in the class were now focused on me. They'd seen a version of this exchange a million times at this point. Don doesn't do his work. Mr. Burrell yells at him. Don makes a snarky comment. Mr. Burrell ignores it and pretends Don isn't there for the rest of class.

"Nope. I sure didn't."

"Do I even want to know why?" Mr. Burrell asked, pinching the bridge of his nose like he was getting a headache.

I shrugged. "Because I already know how to use verb phrases. I've known since elementary school. In fact, I'm pretty sure my little sister did that same worksheet for homework last night, and she's in third grade."

A few eyebrows rose among the students. They waited for Mr. Burrell's response. As usual, he didn't bother.

I kept up this pattern for weeks. I knew there would be consequences, but I was prepared to deal with them. In my mind, I fought the good fight. Unsurprisingly though, my parents didn't see it the same way, and they found out about it in the worst way possible.

School administrators may not have thought much of my academic capabilities, but that didn't mean they were just going to ignore my rebellion. To make my parents aware of the situation, the school sent letters home that outlined my behaviors. These notes had to be returned with a parental signature.

The letters did go back. They had my dad's name at the bottom—but he never saw a single one of those notes. I forged my father's signature.

A voice in the back of my mind told me that this was a bad idea…a really awful idea. I pushed down those internal objections, however, by telling myself that, although my methods weren't ideal, they were justified by my goal—fighting against an unfair system. In the context of that struggle, I thought, what was a forged signature or two? Yet, the voice got a little louder with each additional forgery, warning me that this couldn't end well.

The voice was right.

That spring, when the school sent home flyers with each student advertising a student-parent-teacher social, I tossed mine on the kitchen counter without thinking. Mom would most likely need to stay home with Amie and Dad's long hours and frequent travel meant he rarely came to school events.

That evening, however, the neon yellow paper caught his eye as we cleared the dishes from dinner.

"What's this?"

My pulse quickened. "Oh, some social event for parents and teachers," I answered, trying to sound casual. "Nothing special. It's probably just to make a big deal out of eighth-grade graduation or something. You definitely don't have to go."

"I know I don't *have* to go," he said as he skimmed the flyer. "But I'm in town that night, and recruiting has been pretty smooth, so I don't have to be there every night. I know it's been tough for you at this school, so…" He looked up at me, smiling. "I think I'll go!"

Despite the queasiness in my gut, I managed to smile in return. "That's great!" I choked out. "Can't wait."

I started sweating the moment we entered the school on the night of the social. I knew this wasn't going to end well. We walked over to the refreshment table, but my palms were so clammy I didn't trust myself to hold a cup of punch. I shoved my hands deep into my pockets. Each time Dad met another teacher or administrator, my heart raced faster. Would this be the conversation where the truth came out? I knew it wasn't a matter of *if* but *when*.

"Mr. Thompson? I'm Howard Burrell, Don's English teacher."

"Good to meet you. Don's a big reader, so I expect he's pulling his weight in your class. I hope he's not getting into any trouble—not talking back about paintings or selling candy or anything." He winked at me.

Mr. Burrell had a confused expression, then seemed to determine that my dad was making a joke. He chuckled. "Well, the teenage years can be difficult. Students do sometimes act out. But it seems like you have the issue in hand, the way you always return the notes from us so promptly."

I honestly thought my heart was going to explode.

Dad's cheerful expression froze.

"Excuse me?"

"Yes, well, um…" Mr. Burrell stammered.

With my father's stare trained on him, Mr. Burrell looked almost as uncomfortable as I felt. Almost but not quite. "You know, the notes about Don's behavior. You always sign and return them right away. It's very helpful."

He didn't respond for a few seconds. I started hoping that a meteor would choose that exact moment to crash down on me.

"Yes, of course," Dad finally replied. "Happy to do it."

Mr. Burrell wandered away to talk to another parent, looking relieved to be somewhere else. When he'd gone, my father turned to me.

"We'll talk about this when we get home."

That night, I got the whooping of my life. First, I'd embarrassed my father. Second, I'd been acting up at school. Third, I'd been lying to his face for weeks.

Long after my father had finished his lecture and shut the door to my room, I was still awake. Looking back, it seemed so obvious. Yes, my anger at the school's treatment of me was justified. But the way I'd handled it put me in the same position I'd been in back in elementary school, when I'd hit that kid in gym class. By choosing this form of rebellion, I was just reinforcing people's wrongheaded and ignorant judgments. My teachers in Kentucky thought I wasn't a good person or a serious student. Instead, they viewed me as a behavior problem that needed to be managed. Rather than prove them wrong, my choices had actually confirmed their beliefs.

Even worse, I'd disrespected my parents. I knew their rules weren't arbitrary. They set boundaries and goals for me to help me achieve larger dreams. How could I have thought an action that flew in the face of everything they'd taught me could be a good choice? All their lives they had sacrificed and worked extremely hard, yet I was taking shortcuts. They saw a future for me that I couldn't even comprehend.

This wasn't the way to win, and I knew it. The school year was nearly over. I couldn't undo the many bad decisions, but in the fall, I'd be in high school and would have a fresh start. I promised myself that the next year would be different.

4

MY TURN TO PLAY

Another blazing August day in Bowling Green. Not even nine in the morning and already the temperature pushed ninety degrees. Any sane person would have been in an air-conditioned building, in cool summer clothes, and maybe even sipping a tall glass of lemonade.

But we weren't sane people. We were football players deep into pre-season training.

Dad insisted that I wait until high school to start playing football. He saw the injuries firsthand and determined that I should give my body a chance to develop before such intense training. It felt as if I had been waiting forever just to get on the field.

Every summer I could remember, I'd been at his side during pre-season training. Nothing was too insignificant. I loved it all, from carrying equipment and refilling water jugs to cleaning up the field after practice. I'd gotten to know the players, shouting their names along with my dad if he thought they weren't pushing hard enough. When I was little, the players would let me tackle them, so I thought I was strong enough to lay them out flat. Once I got older, they gave me pointers about throwing the perfect tight spiral.

When I started ninth grade at Bowling Green High School, it was finally my turn to play. After all that time by Dad's side, I thought I knew what football camp was like. But on the second day of preseason work-outs, as I wiped away the sweat from my face and neck, I realized that the view from the sidelines hadn't prepared me for the experience on the field. Actually training with a team—and a good one like the Bowling Green Purples—was more intense, exhausting, and aggressive than anything I'd ever done before.

But football was in my blood. I loved every minute.

An assistant coach blew his whistle: "Okay, short break! I want you back on the field in ten for shuttle runs."

As I walked to the benches, I pulled off my helmet and shook my head.

"Whoa, watch it! You're like a sweat sprinkler system over here!"

I snapped my head around, ready to defend myself, but the guy who'd said it grinned as he shielded his paper cup. I knew he was a ninth grader like me, but I didn't know his name. There had been lots of new people to meet the day before, and besides, by the time my mom had come to pick me up, I'd been so tired that I could barely remember my *own* name.

I laughed. "Sorry, man. Didn't see you there." I took a cup, put it under the spigot, and gulped some water. "I'm Don. What's your name again?"

"Chris. That's John and Trey," he said, pointing at two guys on the bleach-ers. They waved back. "Come on, let's go sit down while we still have a few minutes. My legs feel like Jell-O."

We made our way over to the bleachers. I introduced myself to Chris's friends. Soon, we were talking and laughing like we'd known each other for years. That's one of the reasons football training works: when you suffer through suicide drills together, you tend to bond quickly.

Chris was giving me the inside story on the ninth-grade teachers when another group of players walked by. "Ooh, look at da widdle babies," one of them jeered, scrunching up his sunburned face. "The widdle babies is so cuuuuuuute in their teensy weensy unifowms!"

They all laughed as if they'd never heard anything more hilarious. As they walked by, one of them shoved Trey's shoulder, nearly knocking him off the bench. Another took Chris's helmet, lying on the ground, and threw it onto the fifty-yard line. They continued laughing and gave each other congratulatory arm punches.

The whole thing ended before I even had a chance to get upset. Mostly, I was just confused. Weren't we teammates? What about all that unity and team spirit stuff the coaches had been talking about?

I turned to Chris. "What the heck, man? What's with them?"

Chris rolled his eyes. "The junior and seniors on varsity love to torment the younger players. It's tradition." He hopped up and went to retrieve his helmet.

"Sounds stupid," I said as he jogged back. I glanced over at the group, who'd joined the other upperclassmen around the water cooler. They high fived, joked around, and laughed loudly. Every move seemed intended to communicate to the rest of us that they were in charge.

"Yeah, it's pretty dumb," John chimed in. "We're all on the same team, but my older brother says that hazing is normal."

I'd seen the results of hazing plenty of times when I hung out with my dad's teams. On the field, the teams played as a unit, but off the field, the new players were put through some rough stuff. Inevitably, they'd come to practice limping or babying certain body parts. When my dad asked them what was wrong, they'd look at their feet and cough, "Duct tape." Dad would laugh, but then quickly put on a straight face and make the player run extra laps for being late.

Back then, I'd thought it was funny too, but now that I was facing the prospect of being on the receiving end, the pranks suddenly didn't seem so entertaining anymore.

"Well, it might have been normal before, but…" I leaned in toward my new little group of friends, lowering my voice to a whisper, and asked: "What if we changed that?"

They stared back at me for a second, dumbfounded. Trey frowned, but the others looked intrigued.

"Change it how?" Chris asked, his eyes darting over toward the varsity players. "They're like twice our size. We can't fight them."

I tilted my head to one side. "That's not true. We can fight them."

My new friends exchanged looks. They didn't say a word, but their opinion was clear: *This guy is nuts.*

"I mean, you're right that none of us could fight them *alone*," I conceded. "But, well, think about it. How many freshmen are there on the team? Four? Five?"

Chris shrugged. "Something like that."

"Exactly! And yeah, we're younger, but it's not like we're weak or anything. Look at you, Chris! You're six-three at least. I bet you could bench two of those upperclassmen at the same time."

Everyone laughed. "Okay, sure, they could pick on us individually, just because they're older and think they're better than we are. But if we stick together all the time—and I mean *all* the time, in the hallways, in the locker room, after practice—they're not going to be able to touch us. We could do some serious damage to them. Because no matter how tough they think they are, I guarantee you that all of us together…" I grinned at the group, all listening intently, their eyes trained on me: "We're tougher."

And that was how our football crew got started. Chris and I convinced the other freshman to follow our lead. For the first month or so of the school year, we traveled in a pack. If one of the older players tried to mess with one of us, four of us were immediately there ready to protect our friend. With this strategy, it didn't take long for the upperclassmen to get tired of harassing us. We were the first freshman class to stick up for ourselves. Our victory reinforced what my father had always taught me about sports: win or lose, you do it as a team.

Our bond gave us confidence in what we could do on the field. We promised each other that when we got to be juniors and seniors, we'd be state champs.

The experience also gave me confidence in myself—not that I lacked confidence before. Far from it. Although my mom had often told me that I was a "born leader," as a child I hadn't understood how that could possibly be true. Leaders were teachers, coaches, or presidents—people in charge, people who had power. How could a kid be in charge?

Now, I began to understand. You don't have to be in a position of authority to lead people. You need big ideas. You must be willing to take risks and inspire people to follow you. All those traits came to me naturally. While I still didn't know where those skills might lead me in the future, I did know where I wanted them to take me in the short term: straight to first-string quarterback. For me, that's what football was all about. I wanted to be the team leader, the guy who rallied the troops, and the one who controlled every play on the field.

I knew I'd eventually win the position I dreamed of playing, but I was also realistic. I was in ninth grade and just starting out, so I didn't expect anyone to just hand me what I wanted. I'd have to put in some time and plenty of work before I was ready to earn the starting QB spot.

In the meantime, I'd spend the off-season focusing on the sport I was already good at. Once football ended and spring semester rolled around, I was the first kid signed up for baseball tryouts. Being new to the school, I didn't realize the quarterback coach from the football team was also the head coach of the baseball team. I wasn't thrilled about it when I found out—Coach Morgan and I didn't exactly see eye-to-eye. But baseball was my sport. I felt confident I'd make the team, no sweat.

After a week of tryouts with players auditioning for different positions, Coach Morgan posted the official lineup on the locker room bulletin board. I almost didn't bother checking it. I'd spent most of the practices and tryouts playing shortstop, the position I'd always played. Simply put: I'd crushed it. There were a couple other guys who'd played shortstop too, but neither of them had the speed or the range I had. All arrogance aside, I didn't think there was really any competition for the spot. But just to make sure, I shouldered my gear bag and walked over to the wall where the list was posted.

"What the—"

I squinted hard at the list. Maybe I'd misread it the first time, matched my name with the wrong position. I ran my index finger across from my name to the column on the right side of the paper. But there it was, in black and white: "Don Thompson: Right Field"

Right field? It was bad enough not to get shortstop, but I wasn't even an infielder! This made no sense. Couldn't be right, I decided.

Then again, a lot of things hadn't seemed right during the football season. Sessions with Coach Morgan were full of subtle indications that I was not his favorite player by a long shot. I always got the ball that was in the worst condition—new and slippery, or ancient and deflated. I had to take a knee when he needed a QB to demonstrate a new play. No matter how well I did, he always found something to criticize.

Despite those moments, he never really held me back in football. I was clearly the best QB on the JV team. I thought that if I talked to him, I might be able to convince him that I was the best shortstop too. Whatever the outcome, I couldn't accept this outfield position when I knew I'd earned an infield spot. I knocked on his open office door, and Coach looked up from his desk.

"What is it, Thompson?"

"Coach, I think there's some sort of mistake. I'm listed in right field," I said, motioning toward the bulletin board.

He put down his pen and stared right at me. "Nope," he said with a short shake of his head. "No mistake."

I frowned. "Did you see the double play I turned in the scrimmage yesterday? Or how I got Kessler out in that rundown on Tuesday?"

"I did."

I waited for the coach to say something else, but he just kept staring at me.

"Coach, I'm telling you, I'm an all-star shortstop," I went on, trying to keep from sounding desperate. "No joke. I was actually on the Pittsburgh All-Star team a few years ago—as a *shortstop.*"

Coach Morgan crossed his arms over his burly chest. "Well, here, you're an outfielder."

I bit my lip and thought for a second before trying another angle. "But I've never played outfield. I can't give my team my best if I'm playing a position I don't know anything about."

"I guess you'll have to learn," he shrugged. "Is that all?"

"Actually, I do have one more question."

He barked a short laugh. "Of course you do."

The two guys he selected for shortstop were fine players, but no way were they better than me. One had bobbled and dropped several groundballs. The other shied away from line drives, like he was scared of getting hit.

"Do you really think Bennett and Green are better shortstops than me?"

He wasn't expecting that question. He blinked and broke eye contact for a moment, then cleared his throat. "That's none of your business. It's my decision, and it's final. I'll see you at practice tomorrow."

I could have argued, believe me; I had plenty of fight left. But the thin line he'd drawn his lips into told me that he wasn't going to listen to anything else I had to say. Without another word, I turned on my heel and marched to my locker.

I played outfield in the scrimmage that week. I made it through a couple of actual games too; but my heart wasn't in it anymore. I didn't want to play for a man who had some unspoken resentment against me. I was good at baseball—really good—but not long into the season, I quit the team and the sport altogether. Dad didn't exactly approve, but he didn't disapprove either. Baseball had never been his thing. Mom, on the other hand, was disappointed.

"Well, I can see why you wouldn't want to play for him," she said. "But I don't see why you have to stop playing baseball altogether. There are plenty of club teams around town that I know would be glad to have you. Why don't you try out for one of them?"

I sighed. "Mom, I'm burnt out on it, okay? I just want to focus on football now."

I wasn't entirely sure that was true. Deep inside, I still loved baseball, but I was definitely discouraged by what had happened. I wasn't interested in another fight. I still had football. I'd put my energy into that.

"Well, you're not a kid anymore, Don. You need to make your own decisions." She gave me a small smile. "But I want you to consider that, by quitting the team, you're letting this man make decisions about your life."

I opened my mouth to protest, but she held up her hand, stopping me in my tracks. "I'm not saying you need to play. I'm just saying that it's important to think about who we give power to."

"Sure," I grumbled. "I'll think about it."

It didn't take much thought for me to decide I wasn't playing for Coach Morgan. But as usual, Mom was far wiser than I understood at the time. Despite my stubbornness, her advice stayed with me. For years, that life lesson guided the way I thought and acted even when I didn't realize it.

Giving up baseball is one of the biggest regrets of my life. Once I understood the ramifications, I vowed that it would be the last time I let someone else limit what I did or who I became.

Success is the Best Revenge

As school wound down that summer, I had to admit that, outside of the baseball situation, my freshman year had been pretty good. I'd made friends and, much to my parents' relief, I got back on track academically. I'd taken advanced classes and made honor roll each semester. I did so well, in fact, that in early June, my parents received notification that I had qualified for the National Honor Society.

At the induction ceremony, while the principal welcomed parents and community members out on the stage, my fellow inductees and I stood in the wings. I wore a new suit, complete with a square-bottomed knit tie, and I felt pretty good about myself. So, when I saw a couple of girls I hadn't met during the year, I went over to introduce myself.

"Hi, there," I said, flashing a smile. "I'm Don Thompson. Football player, good student, nice guy."

The girls giggled and looked at each other. "I'm Echo Moore," said one of them who had long brown hair. She pointed to the girl beside her. "This is Jana Burrell."

I raised an eyebrow. Burrell, eh? Related to the teacher I'd forged my dad's signature for?

"Are you lovely ladies ready to hit the stage? I think they're calling for us."

We lined up on the side of the stage. I made sure to stand next to Jana.

The crowd gave us a standing ovation as we walked out. I saw my little sister waving wildly at me and mouthing my name. I gave her a wink, turning my attention back to scanning the auditorium, searching for salt and pepper hair and big ears.

Sure enough, there was Mr. Burrell, my eighth-grade English teacher. He was crouching in the aisle with a camera pointed right at Jana. Once we'd taken our places on the stage, he lowered the camera and waved at his daughter. Then his eyes flicked to her right, where I stood. For a moment, he seemed to be unable to do anything but stare at me, his mouth slightly open. I could almost see the thoughts churning through his mind: *An honor student? That kid?*

I grinned a smile so big it nearly split my face in two. I gave my old nemesis a cheery wave. It was true what my mother had told me back in elementary school. The best way to defeat low expectations is to succeed.

5

CHALLENGE ACCEPTED

During my sophomore year, our freshman crew all made the varsity football team. Though I didn't step into the role of starting quarterback, I learned a lot as the backup and still got plenty of time on the field. We were tough: one of the toughest high school teams the city had seen. Our squad stuck together, played hard, and supported each other on and off the field. I understood more clearly why my father worked so hard to get his college players to unite. Football was physically demanding. If a player didn't put in his best effort, his teammates could get seriously hurt. To be a great football player, you had to be on a great team.

The Bowling Green Purples were a great team. As freshmen, the new players and I had vowed we'd go to the state championships, and three years later, that prediction came true. The Purples did go to state my senior year. But there was a catch.

I didn't go with them.

Instead, in the last semester of my tenth-grade year, my father got a job offer too good to turn down: defensive coordinator for East Carolina University. I finished out the school year in Bowling Green. Then, the summer before eleventh grade, we moved to Greenville, North Carolina. Although all our moves were difficult, this one was the hardest. I had made good friends and promised the team that I would be the quarterback to lead them to the championship. Now, I'd have to wish them luck and start over somewhere new.

Years later, I learned that my leaving was hard not just on me, but the whole football community. Some of the football players' families had even offered to let me live with them so that I could stay on the team. I also found out that Mom considered letting me stay in Bowling Green, knowing it would make me happy to fulfill the goal I'd set for myself. My father had said he couldn't leave me behind; he'd miss me too much.

After struggling to find my place on the Purples during my freshman and sophomore years, I knew how hard I'd have to work to earn the quarterback spot at my new school. Luckily, football is all about finding the best man for the job. I had no doubt that I was meant to be a starter.

When Dad got the job at ECU, he and I did some research about the local schools. We decided that I'd attend Junius H. Rose High School. Chip Williams, the football coach, had a reputation for being tough, but his programs worked. Players thrived under Williams' direction, developing into one of the top football programs in North Carolina. It would have been easy for me to go to a different high school in Greenville and be the starting quarterback. At J.H. Rose though, I'd have to prove myself—a challenge I was ready to face if it meant playing for a strong team.

As usual, there was summer football camp before the school year began, so at seven a.m. on another hot August morning, I hauled myself to the first practice at my new school. I was eager to meet my new teammates. I missed Chris and my friends back in Bowling Green, but I knew I'd find a new crew, especially once they saw me on the field.

The first thing I had to do, though, was get in good with the coach.

I got to school early, before most of the other players had arrived, and wandered around the locker room until I found the coaches' offices. One door was open, so I poked my head in.

"Coach Williams?"

A man with wire-rimmed glasses and buzzed, graying hair looked up at me.

"I'm Donald Thompson. I'm new to the team this year—just moved here from Kentucky. I wanted to introduce myself."

Coach Williams pushed his chair back and stood, waving me into his office.

"Don. Great to meet you," he said, shaking my hand. "I've seen your tapes. You've got a real command of the ball." Coach Williams clapped me on the back. "Have you had a look around, yet?"

"No, sir. I came right here to your office."

He smiled. "Smart man. Well," he said, gesturing toward the door. "Let me give you a quick tour."

We walked out into the locker room, then through a door next to a huge green and blue Rampants logo. "So...locker room. Weight room. Offices. And...through those doors is the field. That's pretty much it."

I scanned the weight room. I'd spent my fair share of time lifting and spotting, so the equipment and charts were nothing new. There was, however, something different about this space: one wall was covered with framed photos.

"Who are those guys?" I asked.

"My 300 Club—people who can bench more than 300 pounds." Coach looked me up and down. "What do you bench? 215?"

I cleared my throat. "More like 250." *On a good day.*

Coach patted my shoulder. "Don't worry about it. You just do the best that you can, okay? You don't *have* to get your picture up there."

Was this guy talking smack already? Coach had just laid down a clear challenge, whether he'd meant to or not. Suddenly, I was all about the 300 Club.

"So *when* I bench 300, I get my picture up there?"

"Yes. And a special t-shirt," he said, pointing to a green shirt hanging in a frame. "And first dibs at whatever machine you want. Basically, you get special privileges because who's going to mess with a guy who benches 300?"

From that day forward, I worked so hard to get my picture on that wall of fame. Every so often, Coach would remind me that it wasn't about the 300 Club. He just wanted me to do my best. I'd thank him, say I agreed, then up my weight, increase my reps, and put in extra time before and after school. I wanted to perform to the best of my ability, really push it to achieve my goals. If I'd known that benching 300 pounds was totally out of the question for me, I would have accepted maxing out at a lower weight. But, if my best could be *the* best, then there was no reason not to do everything I could to make it happen.

Finally, a few months into the season, I did it. My arms shook, and my face was drenched in sweat, but I did it.

The other players cheered as the bar clanged back onto the stand and yelled for the coach to come see what I'd done. They were almost as happy as I was, partly because they were good teammates who wanted to see their peers succeed, and partly so I'd shut up about the 300 Club, which had been my obsession.

Coach Williams brought out my t-shirt and tossed it to me with a wink. "I always knew you'd do it. But I saw from the get-go that you're motivated by people telling you 'no.' I just wanted to push you to do your best."

I pulled that shirt on over my sweaty workout clothes and didn't wipe the grin off my face for at least a week.

The academics at J.H. Rose were just as strong as the football program. I did well in classes, except maybe the few times when I let practice—or time with girlfriends—get in the way.

"Hey, Mom?" I asked tentatively, shoving my hand in my back pocket to fish out the folded-up paper.

She didn't look up from the book she was reading. "Hmm?"

I held out the sheet. "My Algebra 2 teacher said you needed to sign this test."

"Why?" Mom asked, putting her book to the side and reaching out her hand. Her eyebrows rose slowly as she glanced over the test. "You got a C?"

"A C isn't a bad grade," I reasoned as I joined her on the couch.

"No, for most people, it's not. But I know this doesn't show your best work. You can do better."

I rested my elbows on my knees and sighed. "I was just a little busy. I forgot to study."

"Busy with what?" She frowned.

I suspected she already knew the answer.

"Well, I'd gone out with Cheryl and—"

Mom's frown deepened. "Mmmhmm."

"I'll do better on the next one. I'll get my grades up for you," I said, trying to smooth-talk her.

She shook her head. "Don't do it for me. I've got my college degree. My career is fine. This grade isn't going to impact me. It's going to impact you."

"Mom, one C isn't going to stop me from getting into the NFL and making tons of money."

"And what's your backup plan in case that doesn't work out?" she asked, getting up from the couch.

I followed her into the kitchen. "Plan B? I won't need a Plan B when I'm rolling in dough."

"And that will make you happy? Being a millionaire?"

I laughed. "Um, yeah. Definitely."

She began chopping tomatoes for a salad. "Well, I don't think it's that simple. You can have money and not be happy. You can have money and not be rich. You can have money and not be respected. *How* you achieve is just as important, probably more so, than *if* and *what* you achieve." She tossed the tomatoes into a bowl and gave me a level stare. "Does that make sense?"

I nodded. Mom wasn't saying that I couldn't or wouldn't join the NFL and be a huge star. She was just making sure that I respected the process as much as the outcome.

A few minutes later, I heard the front door open.

"Gilda?"

"In the kitchen, Donnie." Seeing my nervous expression, she shook her head, and then turned to get the roast in the oven. I knew what that meant— she wasn't going to help me weasel out of a punishment. I'd made my own lazy, careless bed, now I had to lie in it.

Dad strode into the kitchen, grabbed a soda from the fridge, and then turned to me. I realized the test sat on the table in front of me, the C looking bigger and redder than ever. My dad's eyes went right to it.

"What's this?"

He picked up the paper and stared at it for a few minutes, reading the teacher's note at the bottom. My stomach sank. That note used phrases like "disappointed" and "not putting forth his best effort," the kind of words most likely upset my dad.

"My algebra test." I cleared my throat. "Yeah, umm, I didn't do so great, but see, I talked to Mom about it, and she was going to sign it for me, and I've already got a new study plan…"

I trailed off. Better not to dig myself in any deeper.

Dad folded the paper into a small square and put it in his back pocket. He walked out of the room, and I heard him walking down the stairs into the basement. When he came back, he was holding his toolbox.

"Let's go," he said, grabbing his keys.

I followed him to the car.

"Where are we going?" I asked.

My dad kept his eyes on the road. "You'll see."

We pulled into the local hardware store, and he handed me the empty toolbox. I took it and jogged after him, trying to keep up.

"Dad? What are we doing here?"

"Getting you some tools." He started in the first aisle and pointed at a wall of small tools. "See anything you like?"

I stared at him. "Anything I like? They're *wrenches*."

"Well, a wrench is a useful tool. Or a screwdriver's always handy." He pulled a couple off the hooks and held them up to me.

"What are you talking about? You are about the weirdest dude on the planet right now."

"If you're not going to do the work in school," he said with a shrug, "then you're going to need to learn a trade so that you can get a job when you're eighteen. I'm not going to force you to go to college, but I will force you out of my house. So, what are you thinking? Plumber? Mechanic? You can make great money fixing cars."

"Dad." I shifted my weight from one foot to the other. How serious was he right now? "You know I hate doing that kind of stuff."

He carefully hung the tools back on their pegs and turned to me. There wasn't the trace of a joke in his expression.

"If you don't care about school, fine. I can't make you. But then it's time for you to start learning something that will help you make a living. You won't need advanced math and history classes as a mechanic, but you will need to learn cars. If you bring home another C just because you were being lazy, then you will spend every afternoon learning to fix engines and unclog drains." He folded his arms. "Do you get me?"

I looked down at the empty toolbox in my hand. "Yeah, Dad. I get you."

He wasn't saying that plumbing or auto repair were bad jobs. He was saying that learning a trade would be my only option if I didn't stay focused. I wasn't anywhere near dumb enough to tell him that I didn't need multivariable equations to be in the NFL. He knew better than anyone what a long shot that was, and the players who succeeded there were anything but dumb or careless.

So, I got myself back on track in Algebra 2 and never brought home a C on a test again.

Thompson for President

In the spring of my junior year, I was in homeroom, putting the finishing touches on my essay for English class. The vice-principal had been droning through a list of afterschool activities. I tuned him out so I could focus on writing the perfect concluding sentence. My train of thought was interrupted when a cheery voice crackled over the PA system.

"All right, Rampants," she said, filled with enthusiasm. "Get ready to flex your patriotic muscles! In three weeks, you'll vote for your Student Government Association representatives for the coming school year. Candidates, tomorrow is the last day to sign up to run for election. May the best Rampant win!"

One of my football buddies looked over at me.

"So you gonna run for president, Thompson?"

I grinned. My friends liked to tease me about my enthusiasm for participation. When Coach Williams asked for volunteers or leadership, I'd have my hand in the air before I even knew what he was asking us to do. I didn't care.

I knew that I was doing what I needed to do to get ahead. Plus, when it came to trash talk, I gave just as good as I got.

"Maybe I will," I said. "It would look good on a transcript—really round me out as the total package."

"Don't be ridiculous, Don," came a voice from over my shoulder.

I turned to my right and saw Ken glaring at me. I didn't know him well, but he was a star on the tennis team, the spring sport I'd taken up after baseball. He moved in different social circles than I did. What I did know was that he was the kind of person who just had to contradict others.

"Ridiculous. Huh. Interesting." I slowly stroked my chin. "And what makes you say that, Ken?"

He rolled his eyes. "Edward Almeida is going to win. He's been class president since we were all in diapers. No one even knows who you are."

I detected a challenge. I'd just been joking around before, but hearing Ken say I couldn't do it made me want to give it a serious shot.

"Oh, really, Ken? You don't think I could win?"

He shook his head. "No. I'd bet *anything* you can't win."

"How much?"

Ken eyed me for a moment, trying to tell if I was serious. "Fifty bucks."

"Ha!" I clapped my hands together. "You're on. You'd better have my money ready in three weeks."

Then I stood and asked my homeroom teacher for permission to go to the office and submit my official request for candidacy.

After dismissal that day, I went to the office supply store and bought five pieces of poster board. At home, I dug out the thick Sharpie and, in big, block letters, I wrote the same message on every sheet: *I Will NOT Be an Administrative Puppet! Vote for Donald Thompson!*

I didn't have a clue yet what I'd do as student body president—besides impress college admissions counselors and get out of class a few times a month—but I liked the way the motto sounded. More importantly, I knew the other students would feel the same way. I rolled up the posters and sat them by my backpack. I had officially joined the campaign trail.

Over the next few weeks, I chatted up everyone I could. The process took a lot of time, but it wasn't hard to get people to listen. Although new to J. H. Rose, I had friends from just about every clique. I played football with the jocks and tennis with the preps, had honors classes with the smart kids, and was even cool with the guys who were usually up to no good, since most of them liked sports, and through my dad's job, I could hook them up with tickets to ECU games. I was the *perfect* high school politician, all my constituencies neatly lined up.

It hadn't been some big strategy, though. I hadn't made friends because I hoped their friendship would one day come in handy. I genuinely liked connecting with all types of people. It didn't matter what sport someone played, how well they did in school, or what they looked like, if I thought a kid was cool, that was good enough for me. And I thought lots of different kinds of kids were cool.

That's not an easy mindset for teenagers—or adults—to get their heads around. In the past, my classmates hadn't always appreciated my viewpoint. For example, back in Kentucky, I dated Echo Moore, my fellow National Honor Society inductee and member of the tennis team. She was scary smart, and we hit it off. Since she was White, I got a lot of flak about the relationship from my peers. But I couldn't have cared less. I moved at my pace with my plan. I felt that if people didn't like it, then they could pound sand.

Of course, my general popularity didn't mean I could get everyone at school on my side. Still, it didn't stop me from trying.

"Hey, Devon," I said as I filled my water cup from the cooler after tennis practice.

Devon nodded back without saying anything. He wasn't on the team, but since he worked with the coach privately, I often saw him around the court waiting for a lesson. We weren't friends, and though we shared a similar interest, our personalities were different. But that was exactly why I wanted to talk to him.

"Can I ask you something?"

For a second, Devon didn't respond, just took a long drink from his water bottle. I waited. During our few interactions, I'd gotten the suspicion that Devon didn't like me all that much. Rather than let it bother me, I viewed it as an opportunity. I'd been pitching myself to people who already knew me. I'd ask them how they were doing, what activities they were in, and what improvements they felt needed to be made at J.H. Rose. Then, after listening carefully, I'd thank them for their time and encourage them to vote for me. For a few of my more-deserving future constituents, I may have even slipped them some Jolly Ranchers.

With Devon, it was different. This conversation offered several advantages for an SGA presidential candidate. First, getting Devon on my side might earn me some votes with his friends. Second, talking to him would allow me to practice campaigning on someone not impressed by my smooth-talking football star persona. I'd have to work harder to bring Devon around to my point of view, but that was just fine with me. There was nothing that got me more fired up than a challenge.

After a long silence, Devon finally put down his water bottle.

"Sure, I guess. What do you want to know?"

I wanted to play it cool, not like I was trying to get his vote. "I was just wondering if you're going to go out for the team next season."

Devon shrugged. "I don't know. I like tennis, but I'm not really into the whole school spirit thing."

"I get you, I get you," I said, nodding. "But I saw your backhand the other day—the team could use you, man. And you know, if I get elected SGA president, I bet I could hook you up with a nice parking spot so you don't have to carry your gear all the way from the back of the lot."

Devon burst out laughing. I chuckled too, although I wasn't sure what was funny.

"Nice try," he said after a few moments, shaking his head. "But I don't even vote in those stupid elections, so you can save your little speeches for someone else." He lifted his gear bag onto his shoulder and walked to the benches on the side of the court.

I started to call after him, but decided against it. Why waste my time on a vote I'd most likely never get? It was always good to try a new tactic, but you also had to know when to cut your losses. I picked up my own bag and started walking toward the parking lot. On the way, I noticed a group of girls from the varsity cheerleading squad. One of them spotted me.

"Hi, Don!" she called, waving with a big smile.

I grinned and jogged over.

"Nicole! How's it going? Have we talked about what a great SGA president I'd make?"

If Devon didn't want to talk, I'd just have to find other voters with more interest.

The day after the elections, the current SGA president got on the morning announcements to declare the winners.

"And finally," she read out once she'd gone through all the class officers, "the student body president for the 1988-1989 school year is . . . Don Thompson!"

Around me, my homeroom broke out in loud cheers! They chanted my name. I didn't say a thing. I just turned to my right where Ken was hunched down in his seat, stuck out my hand, and waited for my money.

A Car, No Butts About It

Senior year as SGA president—not a bad deal. I played my new status up to its full advantage. First, I got myself assigned to all three lunch periods (my rationale was that I needed to be "accessible to my constituents"). Next, I did an independent study that mostly consisted of hanging out in the office and running errands for the secretaries. And then, I took over the duty of selling parking stickers to the students so that I could get the best parking spots for girls I liked.

It wasn't just cute girls who got good spots though. I sold myself a prime location with my own metal sign declaring that the spot was only for the SGA president. Every morning, I rolled up into that spot in my light blue 1985 Dodge Lancer. I felt like a king.

Dad bought the Lancer for me the previous summer. In fact, I hadn't even asked for it. A few months before, he'd quietly told me that it was time to start looking for a car. He said because he'd raised me, he trusted that I was responsible, so he'd rather have me behind the wheel than some reckless kid he'd never met. I certainly didn't argue.

"This is your car. You'll decide when to drive it. You'll decide where you go. You're responsible for it," he said, reaching out his hand to give me the keys.

I held out my palm, almost buzzing with excitement.

"But—" He paused with the keys dangling over my hand. "If I even *suspect* that someone has been drinking alcohol or smoking cigarettes in this car, it's mine again."

I nodded. "Yes, sir."

He wasn't joking around. If I broke the rules, he would take that car away so fast I wouldn't even know what happened.

Not long after Dad gave me the Lancer, I was cruising down Memorial Drive with a bunch of friends, rapping along with Run-D.M.C.'s new version of "Walk This Way." We were all dancing in our seats and trying to see who could screech as high as Steven Tyler, when suddenly I smelled cigarette smoke. I frowned. The windows were down, but the smell was so strong—it couldn't be coming all the way from the sidewalk.

I looked in the rearview mirror and saw one of the guys in the back about to take a second drag on the cigarette he'd just lit.

"Are you kidding me?" I yelled. "You *cannot* smoke in my car! My dad will take this car away. Put that thing out!"

"Oh, come on," he said through a puff of smoke. "It's just one. I'll keep the window open. Your dad won't even know."

"Fine."

I glanced around at the cars in front of me just long enough to make sure I wouldn't cause a wreck, then swung the steering wheel hard to the right. I pulled up to the curb, wrenched the car into park, and turned around.

"Get out."

"What's up, man? Aren't we going to the mall?"

"We are. You're not." I pointed to the cigarette. "My dad could be any-where and he always finds out somehow. I'm sorry, but I'm not taking the risk just so you can smoke a stupid cigarette."

He got out, and I drove away, leaving him standing on the corner. Every action has consequences and with Dad it was simple—good choices have good consequences and bad choices have bad ones. To keep my car, I erred on the side of good.

Meeting the Doctor

As I got closer to graduation, my career path was as undecided as ever. All my classmates were making big college plans, deciding where to apply based on the future jobs they wanted. I felt confident that I'd make it to the NFL, although perhaps playing a different position than I'd originally imagined.

During senior year, I switched from quarterback to safety. There was a new potential quarterback on the Rampants, Jamie, and even I had to admit that the kid had skills. We were evenly matched, so it was an intense battle in early training. I never knew for certain, but I told myself the deciding factor ended up being that I was more aggressive. I wasn't afraid to hit or get hit, which made me a better candidate for a defensive position. Jamie became quarter-back, and I moved to free safety.

That was a tough pill to swallow. I'd always thought of myself as a quar-terback. Initially, moving to a new position felt like a consolation prize. Like so many times in the past though, my dad helped me see the truth of the sit-uation. He preached about the value in the team when I was still not mature enough to do more than worry about my personal feelings. I could mope around, feel like I'd been cheated, and whine about something I couldn't change, or I could pull my weight, be a starting player, and help my team get to the state championship. When I looked at it that way, there wasn't a ques-tion about what I should do. I was free safety now, and I was going to be the best free safety the Rampants had ever seen.

Dad wasn't the only adult who helped me through this transition. Dr. Larry Hines, a psychology professor at East Carolina and the sports psychologist for the Pirates, had become a good friend of the family. I met Larry one afternoon while helping out at practice. Before the coach ran video of the previous weekend's game, Larry stood in front of the team and explained what it meant to be "mentally tough." He demonstrated a few relaxation techniques to help the players keep their heads in the game and stay calm.

Larry's work intrigued me. Unlike my dad and other football coaches, who talked about strength and focus, Larry approached the game from a different angle, saying things like "clear your mind" or "focus on your breathing." After Larry had finished talking to the players, I introduced myself. I asked him to tell me more about what he'd taught the team. Then, we had a long conversation about the power of the mind. The talk that day led to a lifelong friendship.

What a funny pair—the seventeen-year-old football player and the psychology professor. Despite our outward differences, Larry and I clicked. I looked up to him based on what he had achieved, earning a doctorate in psychology in the early 1980s, a time when there weren't many African Americans with those qualifications in North Carolina (or anywhere really). Larry, like my parents, had worked through other people's ignorance, fought back when presented with limited opportunities, and came out stronger. He used his confidence to move to the top of his field.

Our friendship had a profound effect on me as a teenager. Larry's example and life lessons fueled my belief that I too could climb to the top of my field—whatever that profession might be.

Even though I was so much younger than Larry, he still respected my opinions. He recognized me as a fellow dreamer. We shared a common bond.

In addition to his work in psychology, Larry was also an inventor. He always tinkered with things and came up with big ideas. For example, he created a hair-care product in his bathtub, figured out how to package it, and started selling it from his house. To this day, people love the stuff and buy it by the caseload.

In high school, I especially liked talking to Larry because, when I explained that my career goals were uncertain, he didn't try to steer me down one path or another. He just listened. My parents were concerned about my lack of clear direction. Larry, on the other hand, understood what I meant when I said that I didn't care if my ideas were all over the map; I just wanted to figure out how to be financially independent. His philosophy centered on coaching people where they were, but with a strong belief in what they could be.

"Hey, Larry!" I said, sliding the screen door open to the back porch.

I'd just gotten home from my job at Monk's restaurant, and the family cookout was in full swing. Dad was at the grill. ECU players and coaches crowded the porch. My mom served as hostess, drifting from guest to guest, making sure everyone had enough sweet tea.

"How's school going?" Larry asked as I joined him at the wooden picnic table.

"Pretty good, actually."

"How are your grades? Keeping up with your classes?"

"Oh, yeah," I laughed. "I won't be having any trouble with grades. Dad promised he'd buy me a brand-new car if I got straight As this year."

Larry laughed. "Well, I know you're not going to disappoint him or yourself."

"No, sir." I smiled and took a big swig of iced tea. "What about you. Working on anything special?"

Larry tapped the side of his head. "You know me. Always something happening up here. But nothing I'm quite ready to start work on yet."

"Well, you'll let me know when you've got something, right? I could use a new project."

We talked some more about school, football, and books we'd both been reading until I had to excuse myself to finish my weekend homework.

"Will I see you at ECU next year?" Larry asked before I left.

I shrugged. "We'll see. Or maybe on TV during Sunday night football."

Larry chuckled. "Well, either way, I'll be rooting for you."

As it turns out, I'd be seeing plenty of Dr. Hines the following year. I was recruited to play college football for the East Carolina Pirates. I had no doubts about attending ECU. During the recruiting process, I'd worked only with the other coaches to keep things fair, but I couldn't wait to play for my dad. On signing day, the ECU reps came to J.H. Rose and set up a table in the auditorium. I sat there with the two other athletes who'd be playing collegiate sports for ECU and signed my letter of intent while my parents and school officials looked on proudly. Dad took the opportunity to make sure my teachers hadn't made any mistakes with my grades though, because not only did I get the scholarship, I also got straight As. Here came a new car and my dream of playing college football, all at once!

After I said goodbye to my parents and walked down the hall to my next class, the assistant principal, Mrs. Jackson, stopped me for what I thought would be a congratulatory speech.

Instead, she crossed her arms in front of her. "Just so we're clear, I'm not excited about your scholarship to play football. In fact, I'm disappointed."

My jaw dropped. I struggled for a second to find a cool, calm, and collected response, but all that came out of my mouth was "What?"

"Your talent and skill are supposed to take you to more important places than a football field." She narrowed her gaze. "I'm not happy with what happened here today."

I didn't understand her reaction. Everybody was excited about my scholarship! ECU was a good school. I'd be getting a free education and chance to play football. What was the problem?

"I still don't—"

She shook her head. "Nothing wrong with playing football. But you? You're supposed to be a leader and that's *not* going to happen on the football field."

Without another word, she turned on her heel, leaving me dumbfounded. All I could hear was Mrs. Jackson's shoes clicking as she walked down the long hallway.

At first, what she said seemed ridiculous. Who did she think she was to put a gray cloud over my big day? But later, after I let Mrs. Jackson's words sink in, I started to understand. She meant that I hadn't really considered what to do with all my talents. I pursued college football because it seemed like the next logical step, not because I had thought carefully about all the avenues available to me.

I've remembered that brief exchange with her ever since. In many ways, she was right.

Recruited, but...

Remarkably, my college football career at East Carolina almost ended before it even began. Although the experience was tough on me personally, it gave me insight that would help me much later as I tackled the business world.

Throughout the recruiting process, my dad didn't openly advocate for ECU. He didn't try to persuade me one way or another. Instead, he encouraged me to choose a school that made the most sense for me. But, given that football had always been such a strong bond between us, how could I *not* want to play for him now that I had the chance?

Soon after I signed, I came home from school. He waited for me in his study and called me in for a chat.

"So you're all set at ECU," he said, the question sounding more like a statement.

"I sure am!" High school hadn't even ended yet, but in a month, I would begin summer training with my new college teammates. "Don't work me too hard in the heat," I joked.

"Well, that's what I want to talk with you about." He got up from his desk and flopped down beside me on the old couch.

There was an awkward pause—and my dad's not really an awkward pause kind of guy. *Uh-oh*, I thought. *What's going on?*

Dad looked down at his hands. "I think you know that I'd hoped for more than I've gotten at ECU."

I did know. From the start, the job had been a series of disappointments, many of them well beyond my dad's work or success as a coach.

For example, each ECU coach received a free membership at the local athletic club or country club, whichever they preferred. Dad had been excited about that perk. He didn't have much free time, but he enjoyed blowing off steam on the golf course. Yet, when it came time to choose between his options, he learned that the option for a country club membership had been revoked—only for him—because of his skin.

This was 1989. Many people at that time might have thought that this level of blatant racism no longer existed. Yet here it was in plain view. A decade into his coaching career, my father still had to battle against open prejudice.

There were also challenges within the system. Dad had been hired to coach ECU's defensive line, but he hoped to be promoted to defensive coordinator. After a year, the position became available. Finally, he would get his chance—an opportunity that could potentially be a steppingstone to a head coaching position.

I looked at him incredulously. "Coach Lewis *did* offer you the defensive coordinator job…Right?"

"He didn't," Dad said simply. "So, I went looking elsewhere. And Mack Brown has offered me a defensive line coach job at UNC."

Wow. The University of North Carolina was a more prestigious program, and Coach Brown was a rising star, known nationwide.

"Dad—" I began.

He interrupted me. "I know. We have been looking forward to working together at ECU. And you're only just starting out. He cleared his throat again, more forcefully: "If you'd like me to stay, I will."

For nearly as long as I could remember, I'd been waiting for my chance to play for Dad—to learn from him, excel with him, and experience something that few players ever get to do at this elite level.

I looked him right in the eye. "No. Don't make me a consideration. I'll just be here a couple of years. You have your whole career to consider. Do what you think is best."

For a minute, we just sat there, kind of frowning at each other. Then he smiled, I think in a mix of pride and relief.

"Good…Good man. Now, I'd like you to do one more thing. Wait in the hall while I call Coach Lewis and break the news."

I nodded and stepped outside the office. Though I heard little of the conversation, I knew exactly what was happening. My new head coach was losing one of North Carolina's best recruiters to his biggest in-state rival. I imagine he had answered the phone in his typical, gruff tone, but as soon as he realized what my dad was saying, Coach Lewis must have been confused, then anxious.

The snippets I could make out were clear. My dad repeated, "I'm afraid it's too late" and "my answer is still no."

Coach Lewis must be panicking now, I thought. I could almost see the surprised expression on his face as he realized, soon, all the top young high school players in the state would be picked off, one by one, headed to UNC.

After hanging up the phone, my father came to the study door and motioned for me. "Don, I asked you to stay for two reasons," he said, settling back into his chair. "First, after the fact, people may say different things—some might say I quit or was fired or was pushed out. I think you heard enough of what I said so that you are certain of the truth."

I nodded.

Coach Lewis made offers, hoping to keep him. The more my father said no, the more he offered. In the end, Dad had everything he'd wanted on the table—the promotion, a raise, and the country club membership. He explained this all to me, because he wanted me to learn from this experience.

"The second reason I wanted you here," he explained, "is that I want you to understand that college football is a *business*, and in business, loyalty is situational. Trust is situational."

While lots of people get business lessons from textbooks or case studies delivered in a lecture hall, my dad gave me a gift that day. This was a potentially career-defining moment for him. On the spot, Dad had to decide: do I stick to my convictions or do I take what is being offered? What I later saw unfold in my own career is that, in business, people don't do things because they're right; they do things because it serves their interest. When it was in the head coach's self-interest, he offered Dad everything he had previously denied him, but by then, it was too late.

At that time, the situation made me angrier than my father. Yet, the lesson didn't make me hate people or judge them. Instead, I gained insight—a new understanding of how people ticked. I couldn't have known back then, still a senior in high school, but one day it would make me a much stronger salesperson. I realized I could thrive by addressing the potential customer's needs and self-interest. I learned that you must talk to people as they are in reality, not as they hope to be.

An additional lesson here also helped me when I became a leader and employer: if you want to keep a valued employee, manage their happiness. Find what motivates people and give it to them before they go somewhere else. If you don't understand what they care about, then you can't lead them to their highest performance. Whether it's money, title, perks, flextime, or praise, figure out what tells your employees "I value you, and I'll prove it on your terms."

I wonder what might have happened if Dad had been at ECU when I played. Would my experience have been better? Perhaps, but that wasn't the way things unfolded. Looking back is important, but I've never found it useful to speculate on things that couldn't have been changed. Instead, I look forward to what I can do in the future.

Although it wouldn't be under Dad's supervision and guidance, I still got to play football with an unbelievably hardworking and talented group. The experience left me with lessons that would guide me for the rest of my life, particularly after I stepped off the field.

While I appreciate the lessons now, they didn't come cheap. College football operated at a level of competition far beyond anything I had experienced in high school. Competition permeates every aspect of the game, from interschool rivalries to interactions with teammates. We were a close-knit team, but another truth sat just behind the cohesion—each ECU Pirate competed against one another for prestige, visibility, and playing time.

Think about it this way. An exceptional school athlete is a big fish in a small pond. When you're good enough to get a scholarship, that means you're one of the top two or three people on your team. If you're one of the top two or three people on your team, then you're one of the top ten percent of players in your league. That, in turn, makes you likely to be one of the top hundred players in the entire state and in the top ten percent of young athletes in the country.

That's a lot of numbers, but here's the gist: a kid like me gets used to running with the first team and getting lots of playing time.

Then, I went to college.

6

BLAZING A NEW TRAIL

When I started at East Carolina University in the fall of 1990, I thought I had the whole college thing down. In the wake of an impressive high school football career, student government, National Honor Society, and my general popularity, I could see the next four years clearly: I was going to be a big deal. The path seemed lit up, just waiting for me to fulfill my destiny.

My self-assurance wasn't *pure* swagger though. I had good reasons to be sure of myself. First, I received a full athletic scholarship to one of the most competitive football programs in the Southeast. Given that only two percent of high school athletes go on to play Division I sports, that recognition of my dedication and talent meant a lot. I knew, too, that I'd be able to handle whatever academic challenges came my way. I'd learned that I could do just about anything if I wanted it enough. After all, getting straight As had been easy when there was a brand-new car on the line.

Also, the transition culture shock that hits many first-year students wasn't a problem for me. Because of my dad's career, I'd been hanging out on college campuses and with college students for almost as long as I could remember. ECU had a reputation as a party school, but by the time I started, the social scene—parties, clubs, hooking up—felt like old news to me.

Football came first, so the effort became my focus. I wanted to make a name for myself and play at the next level, so the social aspects of college were not on my radar. Plus, I knew that if I got out of line, my dad would have something to say about it. It didn't matter that I wasn't living under his roof anymore or that he was down the road in Chapel Hill. He'd know.

I began college as I'd begun every new challenge: with focus, determination, and a big dose of confidence. But I was also realistic. I knew that being a college-level student-athlete was no joke. Since I'd be working harder than I ever had before, I took a few classes that summer to complete some required courses. I figured that the extra work would lighten my academic load.

Even after watching my dad coach for my whole life, I never anticipated how difficult life would be as a college football player. On the weekdays, we were normal college kids, at least during the early part of the day. But at two p.m. every day, our lives changed, dominated by dedication to football. First, we met with coaches, learning plays and reviewing tapes. Then, we were on the field, running drills and practicing. Next came dinner, mandatory study hall, and an early bedtime so we could get up and do it all over again the next day. The weekends were even busier as we prepared for games or traveled to other colleges for away games.

Today, many people assume that a Division I football player's life is all hundred-dollar handshakes and big, off-campus parties. Actually, that's rarely the case. The people I hung out with were far from spoiled superstars. We were working too hard. The most lavish perks: a priority parking pass and a free meal or two around town. A few of the best players might have benefited from some extra incentives, but I simply wasn't that good.

For most of my ECU Pirates teammates and I, football wasn't glamorous at all. It was about hard work. Those long hours on the field, in the weight room, and watching tapes made us into a close-knit group. The coaches designed our training programs to not only strengthen our bodies but also create camaraderie. If you're going to play a sport that feels like getting into a series of car wrecks every Saturday afternoon, you've got to be able to trust your teammates on the field with your life. That commitment to the team is one of the reasons that former athletes are often attractive to employers, as I'd discover later.

At ECU, every single player was *that guy* on his high school team. I showed up having spent the last four years being better than most—I'd been that big fish—but now the pond included every other exceptional athlete from schools ranked even higher than J.H. Rose. Suddenly, the other fish weren't minnows. They were sharks, each and every one.

Overnight, my football life literally became a fight, not just during game time but all the time. I fought to get noticed, battled for playing time, searched for an opportunity.

From an athletic standpoint and, equally importantly, from an ego standpoint, the competition was tough. We all ran drills and practiced plays, but there were always players who were bigger, stronger, and faster. Every day, I noticed a teammate who could do the same things I could but a whole lot smoother. The game sped by so fast it felt like we were going double time. It was fun, but it wasn't easy.

Every second on the field was under surveillance, whether game time or practice. When a coach told me that I did something wrong on the field, he wasn't commenting on a singular moment; he was describing an action he'd watched and analyzed during late nights in the video room.

I was still getting used to this new part of training when, one day during practice, the defensive back coach, Chuck Pagano, asked to see me.

"Thompson," he said as I sat down. "I watched last week's practice tapes, and I noticed that you false-stepped."

I was more than a little annoyed at the accusation. False stepping is when a player takes a step backward during a play rather than exploding forward to make a tackle. It's a move of hesitation, uncertainty, or possibly even fear. I would never use any of those words to describe myself, especially not on the gridiron.

I shook my head. I wanted to be respectful, but I didn't want my new coach to think I'd given less than total commitment. "No, I didn't, Coach. I didn't false-step."

Coach Pagano stared at me.

"You sure? I think you did. So…either I'm a liar, or you're incorrect and wasting my time. Which one is it?" He folded his forearms and narrowed his eyes.

If my life were a movie, this is the scene when the audience would be yelling at the screen. *Don't be an idiot! It's obvious he's seen the tape! Just shut your mouth!*

But there are times in life when you just need to learn the hard way.

"I don't know what to say," I shrugged, too proud to back down, "but I didn't false-step."

Coach Pagano picked up a VHS and popped it into the deck. "Well, there's only one way to settle this then. We'll watch the play and figure out what really happened. And let's just make it clear right now. If I was wrong, I'm happy to admit it."

He turned to me, pointing his finger at my chest: "But if you false-stepped, the two of us are going to talk about it after practice while you run stadium steps."

Maybe I should have been nervous…felt hints of uncertainty. *Had I erred? Did I get it wrong?* Instead, I just sat down, totally confident and ready to watch myself perform, if not perfectly then at least with conviction. He pressed play.

Sure enough, Coach Pagano was correct. I had false-stepped, which slowed my pursuit of the ball carrier.

The bottom of my stomach suddenly dropped out. I searched for a good response but came up empty.

"Yeah," I said, watching the play for the third time. "That is not great."

And, for the record, neither was running those stadium steps.

What I learned from the exchange with Coach Pagano stayed with me long after the pain of running steps. As a matter of fact, the lesson I learned continues to influence my interactions with executives and leaders today.

In that moment, I couldn't see my own mistakes. I made the situation worse because I wasn't really interested in learning from a person who not only had a better view of the situation than I did, but also had years of experience playing and coaching. I limited myself by not being open to receiving Coach's help or realizing that his criticism wasn't personal. He was criticizing me as a person, rather pointing to my performance on the field. His job was to prepare me and the team to win.

From Scrimmage Line to Downline

Despite my lack of playing time at ECU, I still felt convinced that my destiny was in the NFL. My parents supported my pro football dream, but they insisted that I receive a strong education as well. They had worked so hard and sacrificed so much to earn their degrees. They wanted college to be as pivotal for me as it had been for them.

I expected a much different experience though. I learned interesting facts, but my professors seemed to think that I was there to train for a specific career. It felt like there were pre-defined tracks that you were supposed to slot yourself into. Do you want to major in biology and become a doctor? In economics and become an accountant? In philosophy and become a…well, it was unclear to me where some of the tracks led.

After my career in the NFL, I thought I might become a stockbroker or launch my own firm, so I chose to major in finance. Really though, I just wanted to be like Gordon Gekko, the late 1980s "greed is good" antihero from the movie *Wall Street*. Although I took my classes seriously and learned a great deal, the requirement of specializing in just one field felt like a limitation. I felt forced into a narrow, restrictive category. The field I would work in didn't really matter very much to me. I had just one overarching goal: to make money and be successful. None of my classes seemed to be teaching me how to do that.

I tried to put this feeling aside, but my discontent grew stronger as time passed. I was learning what other people thought I needed to know to follow a prescribed trajectory through my life. Instead, I hoped to chart my own course. My classes focused on how to get a job and then work for someone else. Yet, the wealthiest people I knew of were professional athletes and business owners—people who worked for themselves.

In the spring semester of my sophomore year, a perfect storm brewed. One part of spring practices it that the coaches develop what's called "the depth chart." Essentially, it's a graphical representation of where each player ranks in position to the rest of their teammates. They listed me as the second team free safety, which meant that even though I wasn't the starter, I was going to get a lot of playing time and be part of special teams. My hard work had paid off and would get me on the field constantly to help ECU win football games.

Suddenly though, I was reminded of Dad's life lesson about self-interest. Another week of spring practice ended. A a new depth chart went up. I'd been demoted to third string. No one from the coaching staff explained the move to me, but I realized immediately what happened. The previous third-string player—the one from the original depth chart—went to the same high school as several players ECU was recruiting. He was moved up so those potential recruits—and their coaches—could see how well the Pirates treated students from their school.

The politics behind the scenes were nothing new to me. I'd watched Dad suffer through far worse. Still, it hurt—a lot. I had put in too much work and gone through too much pain to lose my chance now. The worst part was losing out due to something I couldn't control. After I saw the new depth chart, I just sat on the bench in the locker room. I stared into the distance and thought:

There is a path where I can be great and football isn't it.

That day, I skipped practice. As I was packing my gear to leave the locker room, one of the other players came jogging in. His cleats clacked on the tile. It reminded me of high school when Mrs. Jackson had expressed her displeasure with me for choosing football over something more important.

"Thompson, you've got to get on the field. Coach sent me to come see what's taking you so long."

"Just go back out there," I shook my head. "I'm done." And just like that, I turned a page I never imagined I would turn.

I left Greenville and drove two hours to my mom and dad's new house in Durham. On the drive, I alternated between being so upset that I couldn't even think straight and worrying about how the news of me walking out on a football practice would go over at home. I considered the possibility of transferring and trying to walk on at UNC. Then, at least I could fulfill my dream of playing for my dad.

Instead of making me feel revved up, as a new plan of attack usually did, the idea made me feel even more frustrated. Transferring—to UNC or even one of the smaller schools that had recruited me—and making a name for myself on a new team would require a huge amount of work. There was no guarantee I'd get any more playing time (or treated more fairly) as a Tar Heel than I had as a Pirate.

As I neared my parents' house, I realized that maybe it didn't matter where I played football. I just didn't want to do it anymore. I also realized that, without commitment and passion, the risky game of football could become dangerous. Players whose hearts aren't in it, whose minds are somewhere else, whose senses aren't tuned to every little movement and nuance—they are the ones who get hurt. I wasn't going to be another football statistic.

By the time I arrived, my decision was clear. I was leaving the team. It wasn't about giving up or being angry. It was about accepting that, regardless of whether I was good enough to play in the NFL player, I didn't want it badly enough to get there. There were other ways to achieve the success I'd always imagined. For the first time in my life, I realized football wasn't my future.

That decision felt good, but I still had to break the news to my parents. I sat in their driveway trying to figure out what I was going to say, but after a few minutes, I gave up and got out of the car. Whatever words I used, the truth was that I was quitting. There was nothing to do but go in there and tell them exactly what I'd decided.

When I opened the door, I could hear Dad's voice coming from the kitchen. To put it mildly, he didn't sound pleased. Amazingly, he'd already heard through the coaching grapevine about my move to third string.

I sat at the kitchen table and waited for my dad to hang up the phone. Once he did, I took a deep breath.

There was an explosion, but I was ready for it. I stayed quiet while he got his initial surprise and anger out. Although the conversation that followed wasn't easy, I kept calm and stuck to my position. I didn't have to play football to achieve my goals. Mom got in on the discussion too. She didn't love the idea of me just quitting, but truthfully, he wasn't too heartbroken about me moving away from a career in sports. After a couple tense hours of back-and-forth, my dad finally sighed. He placed his hands on the table.

"Well, seems like you've got your mind made up. You're not a kid, so I can't tell you what to do. But, I hope you'll think long and hard about what this decision means for you."

I nodded. "I will, Dad."

I followed his advice. Even after sleeping on the issue for a few nights, my thinking didn't change. I met with Coach Lewis to discuss my decision to leave the program. He tried to talk me out of it, but not too hard. We shook hands and parted ways. My college football career was over. Little did I know that it wouldn't be my only life change on the horizon.

Now that I wasn't spending all my time on football, I began to seriously question what I was doing at school. I'd been dissatisfied with the academic parts of college almost since my first day of classes. To top it off, my scholarship would end after spring semester, which meant I'd have to foot the bill.

I was still determined to make money—big money. Now that a multimillion-dollar NFL contract was off the table, there was more pressure to figure out the path to earning that fortune. Facing my future with optimism and determination instilled in me by my parents and mentors, I didn't get discouraged. I was going to work until I found the idea that sparked the journey I knew I was meant for.

As it turned out, the idea found me.

My life changed in what seemed like the blink of an eye. I moved out of the football dorm and into student housing. My schedule was completely different. And I got to know Todd Humble, a walk-on quarterback who'd also left the team. Todd was kind enough to listen to my late-night speeches and dreams of getting rich. One afternoon, toward the middle of spring semester, the phone in my dorm room rang.

"Hi, Don. This is Allen Bass. Todd Humble gave me your name. Do you have a second to chat?"

Allen was Todd's brother-in-law. He was a few years older than we were and had already graduated. Todd had mentioned to me that Allen was involved in some kind of networking venture that might interest me. There was almost nothing I wasn't willing to try.

"Hey, Todd told me you might call. What's the deal?"

"It's called Amway. Basically, it's merchandising for all kinds of things, including products from Fortune 500 companies. But it's also about networking: making connections, talking to people, getting them interested. Todd said you're good at that."

"Yeah," I grinned and thought about the traits that set me apart from most people I knew. "I'd say it's one of my strengths. What exactly would I need to do?"

"Well, I'd be happy to meet up and share some information. The pitch will only take ten or fifteen minutes. At that point, if we feel like you qualify and you're interested, I'll explain the next steps."

I knew without a doubt that I'd qualify. The question was whether I wanted to do this thing or not. I agreed to meet with him. Allen visited the dorm a few days later. He showed me Amway's qualifying interview brochure and explained how the organization worked. He showed me some of the products we would sell and told me that people were making thousands, even millions, of dollars with this business.

"If this is something you're interested in," Allen explained, "we can get you a seat at the next open meeting."

The next week, I went to the Ramada Inn in Greenville and sat in the conference room with about fifty other people. Jake Baker, an ex-Marine and engineer, stood in front of the room and sold me on the dream. He earned a six-figure salary working for himself. In the presentation, Jake featured the story of Larry Winters, a former car wash manager turned millionaire through Amway.

If this thing costs less than $100 to start, I thought to myself, *I'm in.*

Later that week, I sat in Todd's living room looking through my Amway starter kit. Todd became my sponsor. We flipped through paperwork and checked out the sample cleaning products. Todd explained the basics of how to recruit others into our network. A business that depended on how good you were at connecting with people? I knew I could do this.

I threw myself into the Amway business full throttle. The more I suc-ceeded, the harder it was to convince myself to care about school. The future my professors offered me seemed increasingly distant from my personal vision. With Amway, I was selling the dream—wealth, self-sufficiency, and influence. This was my definition of achieving the American dream. My goals felt closer than they ever had before, but to reach them, I realized I'd have to leave the traditional trail behind.

7

MORE THAN ONE WAY TO AN EDUCATION

On a Sunday evening in the spring of my junior year, I had one of the toughest conversations of my life. After this, future business negotiations would seem like tea parties. I was at my parents' house for dinner. I didn't visit every weekend like they wanted, but occasionally I'd come for a meal or a driveway game of father-son basketball. These short trips gave me a bit of a break and let my parents know that I was happy and on the right track.

Our conversation started off smoothly enough. Dad was in the middle of recruiting for UNC. Amie excelled at school—as usual—and was staying at a friend's house to work on a fancy science fair project about bacteria. We spent a good half-hour discussing the upcoming NFL draft, analyzing every player, and constructing our personal dream teams until it was time for dinner.

"All right, all right, enough with the football talk," Mom said as she passed me a bowl of broccoli. "I get more than my share of that as it is even without you encouraging him," she raised an eyebrow at me. "Let's talk about something else, shall we?"

Dad nodded. "Of course. We can talk about whatever you want." Then he winked at me. I knew we'd pick up the conversation right where we'd stopped after dinner and dishes.

Mom beamed.

"Don, have you decided which classes you're taking in the fall?"

She didn't look up as she asked me the question, just tossed it out while she cut up her pork chop, like it was no big deal, like she wasn't at all concerned about the answer.

And why *would* she be worried? In her mind, I felt the same way she and my father did: a college education was the foundation for the future and the primary path to wealth, security, and happiness. Didn't their lives prove the point? College got Dad out of Bogalusa and set him on the path to coaching. College enabled Mom to be more than a wife and mother—not just a supporter of my father's career—but also a successful businessperson in her own right. Education meant everything to them. In turn, they expected it to be my focal point. I couldn't remember a time in my life when my parents hadn't been discussing which college I would attend, wondering about my major, or stashing away money to make sure they'd be able to support my college career. It had been the endgame for nearly every choice they'd made for me from day one. To them, leaving school would be a rejection of the opportunities they'd so carefully prepared for me.

I knew what I was about to say wasn't going to go over well.

It was time to face my new reality. As a matter of fact, if I were honest with myself, I should have admitted this to all of us long before. For months, I'd been drifting further away from school, checking out little by little.

When I stopped playing football, the change had been immediate. One day, I was on the team, all in and ready to fight. The next day, I was done. This realization about college, on the other hand, had been a more gradual process. At first, I didn't want to admit my new life to myself, realizing it would be rough on my parents. Initially, I just slacked off a little, not finishing assignments or studying extra for quizzes. Later, I began skipping classes. First, one or two a month, then several every week. When I finally broke the news to Mom and Dad, I was skipping more classes than I attended.

That wasn't the way I wanted to do school; that wasn't the way I wanted to do anything. If I couldn't fully commit, there didn't seem to be any point. Plus, it was weighing on me that the tuition bill for next semester would soon show up in my parents' mailbox, leaving them financially responsible when my heart wasn't in it. Facing those facts, it just didn't make sense to register for fall. I had to be honest with my parents. The conversation might be difficult, but I was sure that it wouldn't be long before they'd see I'd made the right choice.

I placed my fork on the table, taking a breath.

"Actually, I have something I've been meaning to tell you." I turned, looking each of my parents in the eye. "I'm not registering for classes in the fall."

They looked at each other and then at me.

"What do you mean 'not registering'?" Mom said. "You have to register for your senior year."

"Well, that's the thing," I went on, keeping my voice light. I wanted them to hear the optimism that I felt about this decision. "I'm not doing my senior year. I'm leaving school." Although the silence that followed couldn't have lasted more than a minute, it felt like an hour or more.

"Don, I'd ask if you're joking, but I know you wouldn't joke about this," Mom finally said.

I shook my head. "Not joking. I mean, I should have done this months ago, maybe last year, but it took me a minute to get clear about the right path."

"The right path?" Mom's tone echoed her disbelief. Her voice trembled. "Don, how can you say that quitting college is the right path? Putting aside your career, your future, it doesn't even make sense! You're already three-quarters of the way to graduation. You're almost done! Why on earth would you quit when you're so close?"

Before saying another word, I reminded myself about the difficulty of this conversation, especially for Mom. When I'd stopped playing football, she was quietly excited. She figured I'd focus on my studies and start on the road to becoming a brain surgeon, astronaut, or the President of the United States—no dream was too big for her vision of my future. What she didn't see was that my dream was big too. The only difference between our visions was the path to get there. I wanted them to see my future the way I did, but even more importantly, I wanted them to understand that this move away from formal education wasn't meant as disrespect. In fact, it was the ultimate compliment: my dreaming, my goals, my choices, even the fact that I *had* choices—it was all a direct result of how hard they'd worked and how far they'd come.

"I get that this decision seems weird to you, but to me, it makes perfect sense. And it doesn't matter how close I am to being done. Why would I keep doing something that isn't getting me where I want to go?"

"But education is *always* the way to get to where you want to go," she said. "It gave your dad and me a chance to be what we wanted to be, to do what we were meant to do."

"I get that," I said. "You both have great careers. I know you've always expected that I'd follow in your footsteps and get a college degree. Until now, I expected the same thing. But that's changed. I've had a chance to see that that there are other ways to chase my dreams."

I could feel Mom's pain. Finally, she spoke in a voice that, although soft, contained deep anger and fear. "I want to be understanding, but Don, I don't know if *you* understand the impact of what you're saying—for you, for your father, and for me. It feels like you're rejecting every opportunity we prepared for you. Our plan since day one has been to provide you with the chance to get an education. An opportunity, I might add, that wasn't just handed to us. We fought to get it for ourselves. We fought to give it to you. To make things easier for you."

Under the table, I gripped my knees and one leg bounced nervously. Everything she said was true. I could never fully understand what their sacrifice had entailed because they'd made sure I didn't have to. As a result, my life had been easier than theirs. I could imagine how much this decision hurt Mom and probably Dad too, even if he wasn't showing it as much. I didn't know what else to say to explain that I wasn't trying to blaze my own path to spite them. If anything, I made this decision *because* of them, because of what they'd set up for me.

Clearly too angry for tears, she turned to my father. "Donnie…"

I braced myself. When Mom appealed to Dad, things tended to get real in a hurry.

He sat up a little straighter in his chair and fixed me with one of his *I'm-not-playing* stares.

"Don, is this about that Amway stuff? Is that why you're quitting school?"

My parents had been hearing about Amway from me pretty much non-stop since the moment I'd walked out of that Ramada. I talked about my plans to anyone who'd stand still long enough to listen. My folks knew that I'd been devoting much of my time during the past school year to advancing my position. However, they weren't sold on the business. Like many people, they didn't see it as a legitimate way to earn a living. It certainly didn't epitomize what they considered success.

"Well, it's not *why* I'm quitting school," I replied. "But, it has shown me that there are other ways to get ahead. I'm not saying I'll be doing it for the rest of my life, but right now? Yeah. It's way more useful than school has been."

My mother pressed her lips together. She shook her head. But I continued. "I mean, I'm learning stuff they don't even teach in school." I then ticked off points on my fingers: "I'm meeting new people. I'm getting sales experience. I'm earning money. And most importantly, I'm growing something for myself."

My parents couldn't deny that I had a knack for this kind of work. They had seen me use my sales skills firsthand my whole life. They could see it now too. My business had been growing fast, adding more than one hundred independent business owners to my business network in the first eight months.

Mom jumped back into the conversation. "Don, do you know what the job prospects are like for people without college degrees? For Black people without college degrees? I'll tell you what they are: they're terrible! Do you want to work some minimum-wage job for the rest—"

I cut her off. This seemed like a turning point, and I had to speak my mind. "I don't mean to disrespect you and Dad, but you're not talking me out of this. I know what I want, and I know that this is the way to get it. I don't want to discuss how I might not make it." I glanced between my parents' faces so they could see the determination on mine. "That's not a question. I'm going to make it."

The silence seemed to last for hours. I could see my dad work the muscles in his jaw. He looked directly at me, clearly angry, but he did his best to control his temper.

"Well, it seems like you've made up your mind," he said. "I don't suppose there's much your mother or I could say that would change anything."

"Nope, probably not," I responded trying to be firm but also fully respectful of their stance.

He shook his head. "You've always been stubborn."

"How about 'determined'?"

My dad's face remained fixed. "You can call it whatever you want. But what you're doing is quitting. You're running away from school."

"Am I running away from school, or am I running toward something better? The players on your teams leave school to join the NFL. People leave their jobs for better ones all the time. I don't see it as quitting. I'm chasing my dreams."

Dad sighed. "I see why you've been doing so well. You could sell water to a drowning man." His expression became serious again. "But Don, even though your mom and I may not agree with the choice you've made, we're still here to support you."

He glanced at my mother. She didn't respond, just closed her eyes for a moment and took a deep breath. After a minute, she opened her eyes. When she finally spoke, her voice was gentle but sad.

"Don, I know you know that this is hard for me. You're leaving school. That's the last thing I thought I'd ever hear from either of my children." She managed a small smile. "But your father's right. We'll always be here for you."

I reached around the salt and pepper shakers and put my hand over my mother's.

"Thanks, Mom. Don't worry. I'll ask for help when I need it."

Climbing a Mountain While Digging a Hole

At that point in my life, it's hard to tell if I meant what I said about asking for help. The issue wasn't even on my radar. I recognized that yes, I was capable of asking, but I never thought I would. I made a decision that was the exact opposite of what they wanted for me. I was one hundred percent certain I was never going to need their financial help. I'd dig in until I could achieve on my own.

And, just as my certainty in an NFL career was based around my talent and recognition on the field, this new vision of financial success was grounded in reality too. It wasn't just an idle dream or a fantasy about making it big. This was real.

Looking back, my initial belief in Amway as the be-all, end-all path to success seems a little foolish. As I see the organization now, it's a business model that works for only a small percentage of people. But when it works, it works well. For me, success equated to grit, sales personality, and the ability to handle rejection as a step on the route to success. My strengths back then boiled down to focus, quick learning, an outrageous work ethic, and the ability to run my mouth about anything to anyone for any length of time—ideal qualities for an Amway salesperson.

At the time, I saw the company as much more than one precisely suited to my particular skillset. I wasn't just selling laundry detergent or face scrubs. I was selling the American dream and my own dream at the same time—the promise of wealth, influence, and self-sufficiency.

Preparing for life after college, Amway seemed like *it*—a straight route to the success I'd been imagining since I was a child and sold my Christmas presents to my neighbors.

My parents' skepticism didn't worry me. I understood their concern for an organization that didn't look like a *real* company to them. They were used to tradition and had traditional views of what *work* meant: an office, filling out a timesheet, and meeting colleagues at the water cooler. Even though my dad hardly had a nine to five job, they distrusted what I was doing. They also didn't like the fact that they didn't see any successful Black people in the program. Concerned about my new future, they felt like I risked being exploited for someone else's financial gain.

Ironically, their apprehensions did ring true, but I understood the opportunity. In almost every situation, whether it is companies, political parties, or football teams, people recruit others that will help the organization and its members achieve their goals. Managers don't hire employees who don't perform. Coaches don't recruit players who just sit on the sidelines. I knew my skills were being utilized to make money for those up the leadership chain, but I was fine with that because I also believed that soon I'd be the one on top.

Talking to people and being sincerely interested in what they had to say had been a gift of mine since childhood. Sales seemed to be a natural extension of my natural communication skills. Whatever I was pitching, I'd always been able to get people to listen.

I honed these sales skills not only to convince others to join my network, but also to encourage them to grow their own. For me, it wasn't only about selling products. I wanted to be helpful and pay it forward. One of my primary aims was to recruit others who also dreamed of running their own businesses.

In Greenville, I made lists of people I knew who might be interested—cousins, high school friends, football buddies—then called them up. By the fourth or fifth call, I had my pitch down to a science. First, I'd shoot the breeze on some topic I knew we shared in common.

"Aunt Theresa! It's Binky! How are the kids? I can't believe Jason is already starting high school."

Or "Hey, Brandon, it's Don Thompson. Good to talk to you. Did you see ECU lost to Florida last weekend? Coach didn't know how good he had it when we were on the team." Once we'd chatted for a bit, I'd start scoping their situation, trying to get a feel for whether they were interested in branching out. "I guess now that the kids are getting older, you have more time to yourself. Are you thinking about going back to nursing?" Or "So...I heard you've been working at that Ford dealership over on Tenth Street. How's that going?" Then, I'd give them a little teaser about my work, making sure they knew how well things were going.

"Well, you know, it's funny you should mention being your own boss. I'm working with a company that you might find interesting. Doing well with it, too. I just spent the weekend in Myrtle Beach so I could meet with all these millionaires from our leadership."

By that point, most folks were at least interested enough to want to know more. I'd give them just enough information to intrigue them but not enough that they thought they knew the whole deal. That way, they'd be eager for me to come over and give them the full pitch sooner. Then, just like Alan Bass had done with me, I'd meet them at their house or a coffee shop, bring along some literature, and try to get them to go to one of the weekly regional meetings. There, they'd have the opportunity to join the company as part of my network. It was a simple numbers game: the more people who went to the meeting, the more chances that someone I brought—hopefully, a few someones—would sign up to take part.

Larry Hines, my favorite sports psychologist, dreaming buddy, and mentor was quick to sign on, as were several others I'd known in Greenville. But one of my favorite (and at the time most surprising network additions) was Devon Wilkins, the kid from the Junius H. Rose High School tennis team that I couldn't talk into voting for me as student government president.

I remember my pitch to him like it just happened yesterday. My booth at McDonald's was filled with leaflets as I sat there reviewing some sales paperwork. With my empty tray pushed to one side, I focused on the numbers and thought about which of my contacts I was going to call next. I heard some snickering from a nearby table. When I looked up, I saw Devon sitting at a table nearby with a small group of people. I immediately thought back to my time running for SGA president. Just like they used to do from the bleachers of the high school gym, Devon and his pals were now sneaking looks at me and talking in hushed voices.

We made eye contact. I nodded then went back to my sales figures. A few seconds later, Devon surprised me when he slid into the booth across from me.

"Don Thompson! It's been a while. What are you doing sitting in a McDonald's by yourself on a Friday night?" He eyed my paperwork.

I could tell he looked forward to giving me a hard time. Answering him with a grin, I explained, "Getting a few things in order before I head home. I've been on the road all day."

"Yeah?" Devon asked, sipping his soda. "I heard you've been selling vitamins or something. That's a long way from senior class president, isn't it?"

He looked over at his friends, grinning. Back at his table, they were all laughing.

By this time, I had been with Amway long enough to be laughed at, rejected, and ridiculed. Whatever Devon could bring just rolled right off me. I folded my hands, cleared my throat, and looked Devon right in the eyes.

"It was *student government* president actually, and you're partly right. See, I work with a multibillion-dollar company, and yes, one of their product lines happens to be vitamins. But there are many other products too—basically anything you could want from just about any company you can think of. I get to run my own business—travel around, meet new people, and set my own hours. I can basically make as much money as I'm willing to work for. So yeah," I finished, my smile widening. "I'd say it's going well."

Devon's mouth hung open slightly. I'd disarmed him by not being embarrassed, and his friends had stopped laughing. He kept his eyes glued to the floor. "Oh. Well. That's great," he murmured, looking desperate to get back to his table.

"What about you?" I asked. "What have you been up to?"

"I'm in sales too."

My internal recruitment radar went off. This conversation had just gone from a chance to look good to an opportunity to create a new independent business owner. "What kind of sales work are you doing?"

"Door-to-door vacuum sales."

"How's that going for you?"

"Actually," Devon said, leaning forward and lowering his voice: "Not great. Could you, um, maybe—" He looked around. "Well, could you maybe give me a call sometime about your gig?"

I called him the next day. After that, Devon joined my network and began to put as much work as I did into growing his business.

Once I'd exhausted my Greenville connections, I cast a wider net. I spent a lot of time on the road in my Pontiac Grand Am listening to motivational audiobooks on cassette, which I thought of as a new form of personal education. I'd drive up to Richmond, Virginia, or down to Charlotte, North

Carolina, to recruit more salespeople from my network. Most of the people I recruited were connected to me—relatives or friends of friends—but every now and then, I would strike up a conversation with someone I met in line at the grocery store or waiting for an oil change. I was extra proud of those additions to my network. It takes a skilled salesperson to successfully pitch to a stranger.

My first six months in Amway were a whirlwind. The company had a program called Quicksilver, which used incentives to encourage new team members to grow their networks. To join, you had to have sponsored six people, done 1,000-points in business, and gotten at least 15 people to join your network in your first 90 days.

I was so eager to succeed and build my sales skills that I achieved the requirements for Quicksilver in just thirty days.

In that first month, I sponsored Larry Hines, and he went Quicksilver. Then I sponsored Devon, and he did too. Within a year, we were at the 7,500-point level, which made us direct distributors. Before long, we advanced to the Platinum level, which let us access merchandise directly from the manufacturer, eliminating the middleman and giving a larger share of profits to my immediate team. From a skills perspective, I threw myself into the work and studied to get better. Things were looking up.

Because I was making money, I thought I was doing well, but it soon became clear that my payouts were being quickly consumed as I rolled all my profits back into the business. The expenses added up: gas, brochures, marketing materials, phone bills, and dozens of other expenses were necessary to promote the business. The little profit I had left over got eaten up quickly by rent, utilities, and food. Far from living in luxury, I was making only enough to pay for the necessities. Even that was a tight squeeze.

The long-term solution to my financial struggles seemed clear—just make more money. Although my eagerness fueled me, I understood that financial stability would take time. Sweat equity accumulates and, eventually, pays off. I knew there would be lean times before I reached my goal, so I found some "help" to tide me over.

Unfortunately, that "help" was a wallet full of credit cards.

Dad had warned me about credit card companies before I started at ECU. They love college students. He said I'd probably get lots of offers in my campus mailbox or from representatives handing out flyers in the student center. He knew the offers would be tempting, but he made the choice simple.

"Don't do it," he told me during one of our afternoon hoops sessions in the driveway. "Your room, board, tuition, it's all paid for. Between your scholarship and all that money you saved up working during high school, you don't need a credit card. Don't get yourself caught up in that mess."

"Sure, Dad," I nodded. I dribbled the ball a few times and started lining up my shot. "I hear you. I won't." The ball swished through the net, "Aw, yeah! Nothing but net!"

I heard him, but I wasn't really listening. When I got to college, I didn't get *one* credit card—I got *five*.

I remembered what he told me, but I also remember thinking that credit cards were not a big deal. I thought, *Everybody has them, so why shouldn't I?* Besides, it wasn't like I was going to go wild or anything. I wasn't going to buy a motorcycle or spend Spring Break in the Bahamas, but still, small purchases add up. I didn't spend significant money in any one place or on any one thing. I just spent $30 here and $50 there, over and over. I used the cards for stuff that wasn't extravagant, but also wasn't exactly a necessity, from movie dates and meals at restaurants to buying new clothes. Looking back, I must have spent at least $500 at Ryan's Buffet. I just could not say *no* to those butter rolls! I also became a regular at the local Adidas outlet...tracksuits in every color of the rainbow.

After a month or two, I'd already maxed out one of the cards. I shrugged it off with the classic teenager's defense, thinking, *Credit card debt can get other people in trouble, but that won't happen to me.* All I knew was that in a few short years, I was going to be rich, so paying off the debt wouldn't be an issue. When I hit the limit on one card, I moved to the next. It seemed like a solution that could work indefinitely—at least until I made that big money I was so certain sat just around the corner.

By the time I left school, it became clear that this rotating card system wasn't really a solution but had created its own massive problem. Every month I scraped by, making minimum payments and eating up more than a quarter of my monthly income. I couldn't possibly repay it all, but I'd manage to scrape together a few hundred dollars every so often to keep them from calling the collection agencies. I mistakenly believed I was making bank with Amway until I saw that my actual bank account came up nearly empty at the end of each month.

Over the next few years, I realized how many stupid things I'd spent money on. The price for those butter rolls and teal, tear-away track pants ended up so much higher than the price on the check or tag. My financial decisions cost me late fees, denied loan requests, sky-high interest rates—all told, some ten years of struggling to get out from under the crushing effects of credit card debt.

As a result, like so many people my age, I've learned an incredibly important lesson: delayed gratification, or how to trade immediate comfort for long-term gain. In my late teens and early twenties, I was doing that sort of distance thinking about my career, but I was blowing it when it came to money. I was focused on my immediate wants without the foresight to realize the ramifications. I wanted a steak dinner way more than another peanut butter sandwich.

My father and I developed a close relationship as I grew into adulthood, but sometimes his advice hit me at a time when I wasn't ready to hear it. Instead of accepting Dad's principle about living within my means, I rebelled. I couldn't see that he was teaching me an enduring life lesson. Instead, I had to make mistakes on my own.

8

DREAM BIG TO WIN BIG

t took my parents a while to get over me dropping out of school. Their anger and hurt faded, but they still had a hard time seeing how this plan would work. Yet, they always were true to their word: they didn't agree with my choice, but they were there for me and continued to support my dreams.

In the first year after I left college—and frankly, long after that too—they would drop subtle hints about helping me out financially. I knew that they would do anything they could to support me, but I always rejected their offers for money. If I'd still been a student, it would have been a different story, but I'd already decided I was ready for the "real world." The responsibility for making it was all mine.

It's obvious to me now that my parents helping me out with rent or utilities in months when business was light wouldn't have changed who I was fundamentally—someone who works hard and strives to do better. But that wasn't obvious back then. I made things much more complicated based on misguided pride. I figured if I couldn't take their advice to stay in school and finish my degree, then I couldn't take their money either.

Today, I make it a point to teach the executives and employees I mentor how to ask for and receive support. As a young adult, I didn't understand the difference myself. I thought accepting help made me seem weak, and I mistakenly believed my responsibilities—my growth as a man—hinged on developing the toughness it took to get through the hard times without asking for a thing from anyone else.

I closed myself off to any help my parents offered. Even when I suffered, I turned them down.

Mom didn't hold back when she became concerned. She'd just confront me head-on.

"Honey, I know you're going to be a big-shot millionaire and all, but I just worry about you right now," she'd say when we had dinner together. "People don't become millionaires overnight. What are you going to do until then?" She'd frown and shake her head, then start piling food on my plate.

Dad was more subtle. He'd call in the evening, acting casual and relaxed, like he just wanted to chat about the Cowboys game. Then, after twenty or thirty minutes, he'd ask about business and whether I needed help.

"It's getting close to the first of the month," he'd say. "You selling enough soap to cover rent?"

He wasn't as subtle as he thought.

Whenever my parents pushed the conversation this way, I steered it in the opposite direction.

"I'm fine," I'd tell Mom. "I'm going to make it big, no question. And when I do, I'm going to buy you something seriously nice. Like a house in Hilton Head."

"Can I get that in writing?" she'd laugh.

"Never mind a contract," I said. I tipped my chair back and placed my hand over my heart. "You have my personal guarantee."

Although financial support didn't feel right, I constantly asked people to share their knowledge. I'd try to learn from anyone who'd give me thirty seconds of their time: friends, relatives, neighbors, and even complete strangers. To me, striking up a conversation was no different than reading a book. Some people go to the library to learn. I did that too. I continued reading to get ahead. But why stop there, I thought? Anyone could be a resource. I just had to ask.

The sales system gave me many opportunities. Most people who sold for Amway also had full-time day jobs. So, at our conferences, I'd meet dentists, politicians, software engineers, and people from a multitude of careers. They each had unique wisdom to share. When I met successful people, I'd simply ask them to give me ten minutes of their time. I took notes on how they achieved success, what they were reading, and who helped them along the way. I never passed up an opportunity to turn a casual chat into an opportunity to better myself.

In other words, I knew that anything I needed to learn could be found in books and by associating with people who had the success that I was working toward.

Most people were happy to share information. In my experience, people like to tell their stories. They love sharing how they made it. I used that quality to my advantage, but my interest wasn't insincere. I genuinely wanted to know their path to achieving their dreams. These discussions were inspirational, providing me with ideas to help me reach my goals.

I didn't limit my quest for knowledge to just the really big questions either. Instead, I focused on uncovering their strategies. For example, if I saw a guy in the parking lot getting into a gorgeous Lexus, the situation was a no-brainer: I needed to figure out how he'd been able to afford such a nice ride. Then, maybe I could do what he'd done.

"Hey, man, that's an awesome car."

It might sound a little strange, but it worked. People who buy nice cars usually love to talk about them. Inevitably, the person's face would light up. With a big grin, they would tell me every detail about the machine. I'd nod and sound impressed at every new spec, but it wasn't the car itself I cared about. When the person paused for breath, I'd ease into the questions I really wanted to ask.

"I'm obviously not doing as well as you." I'd turn and shove my thumb over my shoulder at my Grand Am. "What kind of work do you do?"

I started noticing a pattern in the answers: software, technology, and computers. I dug deeper, asking how they chose that field. Then I'd hand them my card and ask them to give me a call, explaining I'd like to buy them a cup of coffee and pick their brain some more, preferably not standing in the steakhouse parking lot. Not everyone agreed, but when someone did and offered me their card in return, I'd leave feeling pretty good.

In general, the knowledge I gained this way was a product of bits and pieces gathered over time and from many different folks. I do remember, however, a few encounters that taught me specific lessons. In one of these cases, I was waiting in a long line at the DMV when I heard a sharp beep. I saw the guy sitting next to me checking his pager, the fancy kind with a keyboard that allowed you to type messages. I waited until he put the pager back in his pocket and then spoke up.

"That's a nice pager. Are you a doctor?"

The guy could have reacted negatively, but instead, he smiled politely and nodded. "Yep—pediatrics."

"Cool. It can't be easy dealing with sick kids—at least if they're anything like I was," I responded. "Where do you practice?"

"Well, I used to work over at Vidant, but I opened up my own practice a couple years ago."

"Good for you! Must be nice to work for yourself."

"Well," he said sighing. "There are definitely advantages, but these days I'm on call pretty much 24/7. It can be exhausting."

"Makes sense," I nodded. "Do you wish you'd stayed at the hospital then?"

The guy shook his head. "Not at all. My practice is a lot of work, but I wouldn't trade it for anything. What I do for the kids and parents is worth every second of sleep I've lost."

"That's an impressive level of commitment."

"True," the doctor replied. "But in my experience, that's what it takes—not only in medicine, but in any job. You can't achieve anything that matters unless you're willing to sacrifice. Sometimes I think of my friends who finish work at noon on Fridays, take golfing trips every other month, and I wonder what I'm doing."

He smiled again and shrugged. "But then I remind myself that I want more than that. When you're building something important, you have to remember that you're putting in the time now for a major win down the road."

A few moments later, his number was called.

As he stood, I put out my hand. "Thanks for talking to me. I learned something today. I appreciate it."

I never spoke to that doctor again—didn't even catch his name—but to this day, his words stay with me. *You're putting in your time now for a major win down the road.* That idea resonated deeply. I didn't shy away from hard work. Although I would have loved quick success, I also understood that I wasn't just working for today. I was building toward the future.

And you know, in all the conversations I had, guess what *nobody ever* told me? No one ever said that I had to go to school or have a degree from a prestigious university to be successful. Not one person admitted that their degree or pedigree was the primary determinant for success. That's not to say that education didn't help or that people weren't proud of their college degrees, but college didn't seem to be the only path to success. Instead, the key seemed to exist in small habits that kept driving you forward, as well as sheer perseverance.

Working the Night Shift

In those early years while I was dedicated to building my network, I realized I needed to take on additional work, particularly after the initial explosion of growth slowed and then leveled out. I'd talked to what felt like every single person in Greenville, so I had to start casting my net wider, meaning I spent more on gas and more time on the road than I did identifying recruits. I deposited my checks but, almost immediately, watched them disappear as I attempted to get to the next level. I was running a nonprofit but not by choice.

I decided to search for steady third-shift work to pad my monthly income and make a dent in the credit card debt. I'd still have the daytime hours to meet with my team, study business books and magazines, and organize phone teams, conversations in which a few big distributors would get together and call prospects. I used the early evening hours to network with people after they'd finished their usual nine-to-fives. Also, third shift paid more because many people didn't want to work overnight. I didn't care about a late shift, as long as the job didn't impact my daytime progress.

I applied at a shipping warehouse and a convenience store. When it came down to it though, the warehouse work was too tiring. Doing manual labor all night would have left me flat-out exhausted during the day, so I wound up at The Pantry instead, a 24-hour convenience store in Greenville.

At The Pantry, I sat behind a clear plastic barrier from midnight to six a.m., three nights a week. I did all the stuff you would expect: made change, stocked shelves, and cleaned up the chili station for the rotisserie hot dogs, which was by *far* the worst part of the job. Because of the hours, I interacted with all sorts of interesting characters—the kind who frequent convenience stores at two in the morning. I generally found them entertaining, but they made the managers a little jumpy. They were so concerned with robberies that I had to lock the front doors when I went into storage. The whole store would close for fifteen minutes while I restocked corn nuts.

Fortunately, the police often checked up on the neighborhood, so I never felt too unsafe at The Pantry, and I never got robbed. I mostly dealt with harmless drunks, who were always hustling to get free stuff. Sometimes, people I knew from my network would stop in. We'd talk business late into the night to pass time. The desire to succeed was never far from my mind, even when the smell of rotating hot dogs and chili threatened to overpower the building.

When I left school, I realized that Greenville wasn't a big enough market. I needed a new audience, so I decided to move to Raleigh, part of North Carolina's "Research Triangle" that also includes the cities of Chapel Hill and Durham and three major universities. There I could reach a new network, and it was closer to my parents, who still lived in Durham.

Goodbye, convenience store job! I applied at a security firm instead. After I passed all the tests, they gave me a flashlight, and I officially became a guard. Because I seemed like one of the stronger people on the team, and I was willing to take on the tasks that no one else wanted, they gave me a job as the late-shift guard at a group of warehouses in downtown Durham.

The complex was eerie, filled with mysterious warehouses. I still have no idea what they contained—didn't ask, didn't want to know. Part of the job consisted of walking around and putting a key into lockboxes all around the building. The boxes recorded each time the key had been inserted so the managers would know how many times during the night I made my rounds. Every night I walked that scary building and turned those keys—alone.

I consider myself a tough guy, but that job felt like I was living in a horror movie. I jumped at the slightest sound, creak, and rustle that seemed to come from nowhere. My mind ran wild. Everywhere I looked, I saw lurking figures in the shadows, even when the logical part of my brain knew there was only asphalt and emptiness. I wondered how I would react to a real confrontation, which sent a shudder up my spine. I was totally alone! Even if I called someone on the walkie-talkie, they were miles away. What would I do if I encountered someone? I wasn't armed.

"Hands up! I've got a flashlight!" Somehow, I didn't think that was going to be much of a deterrent.

As I walked around for eight hours a night, I reflected on my life. When I flinched at a strange sound or envisioned villains hiding in the bushes, I couldn't find an upside in my situation. In my head, I'd give myself lectures. *Don, face it. This is awful. Right now dude, you are really not doing well. You're guarding shady warehouses and you're behind on every bill. You have got to fix this.* These real-talk sessions worked though. Soon, I was fired up to move forward, if only so I didn't have to walk that dark, scary lot ever again. Sometimes a crappy job is the best motivator.

After a few weeks, the awful job got even worse when I discovered that I was just there for insurance purposes. Security wasn't supposed to deter thieving and vandalism, although if it did, that was a bonus. We were there in case of a fire or some other catastrophic event. I was a human fail-safe alarm, there to call the police or fire department if something did happen. When that became clear, I started spending a little more time in the office. I even began to enjoy the downtime, using it to read business and motivational books I'd checked out from the library. I had no padding in my monthly revenue that accounted for buying them.

After a couple months of paying my dues in the warehouse, the security firm recognized I was trustworthy and moved me to a cluster of office buildings. The new job was a huge upgrade: nicer part of town, well lit, and another guard also on duty. No more spooking myself at three a.m.

The new location also provided a new motivation. Back at the warehouses, I'd experienced a life I definitely didn't want and that realization pushed me even harder. On the other hand, at the office complex I caught a glimpse of the life I aspired to achieve. Late at night, I'd let myself into the executive offices and walk around, careful not to disturb anything, noticing every detail. The offices always had shelves with rows of business books and magazines. I'd write down the titles and add them to my growing reading list. Just knowing I was reading the same material as people who were so successful made me feel like I was on the right path. I figured, if they learned something from these books, I could too. Sometimes, I'd even sit at the massive mahogany desks. I folded my hands in front of me and imagined I was a CEO waiting for a meeting with a big client. It might have been a fantasy then, but I knew that if I played my cards right, someday I could make the dream a reality.

9

TRYING A DIFFERENT PLAY

Those years, the most I could afford was a dumpy, one-bedroom apartment. The mattress was laid on the bedroom floor. When people came over, they had to walk around it to get to the only bathroom. In the tiny kitchen sat a wobbly, glass-top table with aluminum legs. No matter how many pieces of folded paper I shoved under that leg, it still tilted to the side.

I scrambled to pay the $275 rent each month. Would I make it this time, or would I get yet another mid-month reminder call from the landlord? To stretch my budget, I scrimped where I could. No more cool tracksuits and steak dinners. Any clothes I bought now were button-downs and slacks that made me look professional when I gave business presentations. At $2.50 for a ten-pound bag, potatoes were a staple, and there were always boxes of three-for-a-dollar pound cakes stacked in the pantry. I pioneered the all-carb diet.

Despite the unsteady financial picture, my college girlfriend and I got married in a small ceremony that my parents hosted at their house. With little money or savings, we honeymooned at a local hotel. Reflecting back, I see that the stress of those early years foreshadowed some of the challenges my new wife and I would face much later. Although the marriage didn't last, we share three wonderful children and many cherished memories. Back then though, I didn't have a moment to consider how the future might unfold. I had to focus on making money and trying to get ahead.

I was moving up in the Amway world. The same year that I had moved from warehouse to executive suite security, Larry, Devon, and I got invited to an Amway-sponsored dinner party at the Pinehurst Country Club. It was an honor to be at this annual event. Only the most successful business owners, those at the Silver Level and above, were invited. The three of us wore rented tuxedos and grinned ear to ear when we saw the decorated ballroom and its huge chandelier. It didn't escape our notice that, except for one couple, we were the only Black people in a crowd of over one hundred people. At the time, however, it wasn't the color of people's skin that struck me. It was the realization that I was doing exactly what my parents had worked so hard to make possible for me. I was getting through doors that had previously been closed, and it felt amazing. The food wasn't too bad either.

In some ways, things were looking up. I'd hit some major milestones and gotten recognition. I had a strong network, a great record, and the willingness to hustle harder than just about anyone. But there was one important thing I still didn't have: profit.

Even though it was technically possible to get rich through Amway, most people didn't. It was the same as in any other professional field. There are a few super wealthy musicians, sports coaches, and tech entrepreneurs, but there are a lot more people in those same jobs who are just earning a living. Every month, distributors had to purchase products and recruiting materials from their "upline," or recruiter. Each distributor received a percentage of their own sales and the sales of those people in their network. But, unless you were at the top, those percentages were tiny. Back in those days, distributors were also responsible for their recruits' bonuses, which could take a big slice out of a small pie. I learned from those making serious money, realizing that they were earning it from selling motivational literature and from leading seminars.

I knew that I would soon be among the elite business owners. I kept going, despite barely keeping my head above water. My fire was fueled by the company's motivational strategies and incentives—a bonus here, a new level there. The first bonus check I received was such a rush. I actually paid off one of the credit cards (a towering relief to start getting out from under my debt), then plowed the rest of the money right back into the business. Later, there were additional bonuses and trips.

I was intensely focused on building my business, but at the same time, I took away multiple leadership lessons that turned out to be invaluable in my life and career. Looking back, I view the experience as a learning journey that created the foundation for what I would later achieve. Perhaps most importantly, I developed a strong communication style by selling the opportunity to join to new contacts from all walks of life. The many, many times I heard "no" were important too. Because of those experiences, I can handle rejection better than most people and not let it stop me. Instead, I keep striving to be even better. The second important part of my learning journey was that the company's emphasis on self-improvement reignited my love for reading. Taking on the challenge to improve myself, I read everything I could find that would help me hone and broaden my knowledge.

Although I had learned so much about sales and networking, it also began to dawn on me that I was doing this thing backwards. The other successful people in my network all had day jobs. Most people didn't depend on Amway to pay their bills and support their families. Always willing to learn from the accomplishments of people in my network, I began following their playbook.

I sent out my resume, eventually getting a call for an interview with Dollar General. I put on my sharpest outfit and went to meet with David Grooms, the company's district manager. We met in an office in the back of the recently opened store in Carrboro, North Carolina. The room was nothing like the lavish offices I explored while working as a security guard. I sat in a metal folding chair at a card table that served as David's desk. Still, David was polite and professional as we began the interview.

"I'm impressed by your Amway record," David said as he scanned my resume. "But Amway's a pretty different animal than standard retail. It doesn't seem like you have any experience in this area."

"That's true," I answered, "but I'm a hard worker, and I'm a quick learner. Anything I need for the job, just point me in the right direction, and I'll learn everything there is to know about it."

It sounded like a line, but I knew if he just gave me half a chance, he'd see the truth in that statement.

David nodded. "From your record, it seems that way. It's obvious that you're smart and hungry for a new opportunity. You're also assertive, and I like that. I can teach someone retail, but I can't teach those personal qualities."

He sat back in his chair and folded his arms across his chest while he thought for a few minutes. "I'd like to make you the store manager here."

Store manager? That was like the sound of the cash register *cha-ching* to my ears. "That would be great!"

"I'm glad to hear that. I'm new to this district manager position, and I've got great ideas. I'm going to make this region the top district in the country. I think you're going to be a big part of that."

David reached across the desk, and we shook hands.

Finally, I had caught a break! David took a chance on a person with little direct experience and no college degree, but he had been intrigued by the one important question I asked: "Are you a good teacher?"

When David said "yes," I told him that I enjoyed being coached. I promised that if he would teach me, then I would learn everything I could about retail and leadership to prove that he made the right choice in trusting me to run a multimillion-dollar store.

I figured that I wouldn't get rich at Dollar General. Still, the salary and the health benefits would give me a steady income, making my networking revenue pretty much pure profit.

David kept his promise to teach me about retail. Within a few days of signing on, he sent me to Mayberry, North Carolina, for an intensive two-week management-training course. Mayberry, which is most well-known as the setting for *The Andy Griffith Show* in the 1960s was a small mountain town with a single traffic light. After spending most of my life in cities and college towns, small-town life was a new experience.

I spent my days working with a manager named Karen, learning how to run a store. She taught me some valuable lessons, but mostly I learned by doing. In the morning, I shadowed Karen while she worked. Then she would step off the floor for a few hours so I could practice. At night, I'd go back to the Days Inn to read over the training manuals. At the end of my two weeks, I got the keys to my own store.

Things were different in Carrboro than in Mayberry. Karen was an experienced manager in a small store that had been around for a while. My store, on the other hand, was brand new and in a more populated location, which meant I was involved in getting it ready for the Grand Opening and potentially large crowds. My first few weeks were a blur of unloading trucks, building displays, interviewing people, and writing schedules—basically, doing whatever had to be done. With my people skills and work ethic, it wasn't hard, just different. Soon after settling into Dollar General, I quit my security guard job, which made life easier. I wasn't exhausted all the time and could focus on running the store.

A few months after the Grand Opening, I was at the store before hours, completing some administrative work while things were quiet—no customers and no other employees. As I checked the displays in the toy aisle, I heard a sharp knock on the door. Frowning, I walked toward the front, the massive key ring jangling against my hip. As I got closer, I saw it was David, and I unlocked the door.

"Hey man, how are you? I didn't know you were visiting today," I said, resetting the alarm.

"It's an unofficial visit," he said, smiling despite how early it was. "I wanted to see how things are going." His eyes scanned the shelves and aisles.

"They're going well. I'm working in back, reconciling sales, and putting together next week's schedule."

We went to my office. It was too small for both of us, so we hovered outside the door.

David asked about employees and which merchandise was moving. I could tell he had more on his mind.

After a few minutes of chit-chat, he said, "Don, I've got something I want to run by you."

I nodded.

"Remember when I said I'd need your help making this region the top district? I wasn't kidding. You've done a fantastic job getting this store up and running. I'd like you to bring those qualities to all of the stores we're opening."

I could not pass up this chance to play a more vital role in the fast-growing company. I said "Yes!" Thus began my new path working as both the store manager in Carrboro and grand opener at new stores across the region.

My next two years were spent traveling around North Carolina and South Carolina opening new Dollar General stores. David saw my people skills as vital in getting a new store off to a strong start. At each location, I led the set-up team and then stayed on for a few weeks as interim manager. I'd interview and hire the whole staff, then hand over a fully operational store to the new manager. It didn't matter that I only had a few months of retail experience; what mattered is that I had years of people experience.

The effort made me a better manager when I was back in Carrboro. David taught me to get creative with scheduling and budgeting. The time in each new store was basically paid training. Just like I had done earlier in picking people's brains about their routes to success, I never said no to a learning opportunity.

Each trip also helped me grow my Amway network. During my downtime and breaks, I kept my Amway business growing—taking meetings at lunch, buying coffee for prospects during my fifteen-minute breaks, and maybe even running over to a dinner meeting after work. Getting paid to travel for Dollar General fit nicely with my overall plans. Opening a new store, I'd set up as many recruitment meetings as I could, which ranged from a couple people in small towns to daily pitches in larger areas. My day job supplied a steady income that covered the basic costs of living. In turn, my networking business expanded, providing me with the freedom to try new products, expand my territory, and have fun again.

David also prepared me for a higher-level position in his district. He saw me as a leader and partner, giving me added responsibilities and consulting with me on decisions. I appreciated his confidence and trust. Yet, at the same time, I hadn't planned to turn retail into my career focus. The hours weren't great, especially in the first few months of a store's operation when I pulled lots of night and weekend shifts that cut into prime Amway recruiting hours. I didn't see retail management as a clear path to the kind of success I wanted.

My work experiences led me to realize that I wanted a job that directly tied hard work to financial success. In sales, if I worked my butt off, I could earn commission, but in retail, my bonuses were tied to my employees' performances. In other words, my wallet was at the mercy of someone else's work ethic. I had excelled at being part of a team, from my athletic career to the Dollar General position, but this type of dependence just didn't work for me. What's the endgame in retail? Being a store manager? Managing multiple stores? I planned to be a millionaire, and that didn't seem like a realistic goal in the Dollar General org chart.

At the time, I didn't have the lens to understand that if I put in my time, I may have climbed the ladder at Dollar General. Who knows what might have happened if I had stayed with the company, but back then, I knew I had to play to my superpowers, which were sales and communications.

I knew I had to move on, but I wasn't sure what I wanted to move *toward*. In the meantime, I kept working hard and growing my network, looking for my next big play.

10

A NUMBERS GAME

I got home late one evening, a typical situation, after working a ten-hour shift at Dollar General, then meeting with a few potential recruits. While driving home, I thought through the cover letter I was planning to send to a pharmaceutical company that had a job opening. Once I'd decided retail was not my ultimate career path, I treated the search for a new position like it was my third job. The two fields I targeted were pharmaceuticals and technology. Those were the markets I believed had unlimited opportunities for growth—fields where I could learn fast, sell big, and make money.

When I heard the phone ringing, I rushed through the apartment door, hoping it was a call about a job. I took a deep breath. "Hello?"

"Don! It's Neil Clark."

Neil was a friend of mine through Amway. I'd known him for a few years. Now, he was a rising star in the tech industry. I'd contacted him early in my job search.

"Hey Neil, how's it going?"

I sat on the couch to untie my shoes. My feet ached after running the registers for the last hour. I had let the cashier leave early to help with our payroll budget.

"Good, thanks. How about with you? How's the job search coming?"

I laughed. "I'm not going to lie, man. It's slow. Very slow."

"Then I may have some great news."

I leaned back into the cushions behind me. "I love good news."

"I just interviewed with a company called Alphatronix. Have you heard of them?"

"Sure have. Sent my resume there a few weeks ago."

I'd gone through the yellow pages searching for every tech company in the Raleigh-Durham area and sent my resume.

Neil chuckled. "I should've guessed. I just interviewed there for a sales manager job. They didn't think I was the right person, so they offered me an inside sales job. I'm looking for a step up, so I declined their offer. But I also told them if they were searching for an inside sales guy, then you're their man. I think they'll be giving you a call."

I let out a laugh of delight and jumped up off the couch. "Neil, this is amazing! How can I repay you?"

Neil laughed. "No need to get dramatic. Just don't make me wrong. I told them you may not have the prerequisites on paper, but that if they trained you, you'd learn fast and make them some money."

"Thanks again. This is exactly what I need."

New Opportunity Nearly Trashed

The next several weeks passed quickly. Neil had recommended me to Alphatronix, along with Brad, another mutual friend. We'd both received calls from the company, resulting in interviews that included mock sales call tests. When I got offered the position, I put in my notice at Dollar General.

I imagined my new career in tech and fantasized about how I would climb the corporate ladder. In reality, though, I almost got fired before I started.

On the first day, Brad and I took a tour of the building and sat in on a few meetings to get a feel for the Alphatronix culture. The next day, we began training with Curtis, the new sales manager. He led us into a conference room in the middle of the building. The walls were floor-to-ceiling glass, so anyone who walked by could see in.

"Okay," Curtis said as we settled in on the stiff couch in front of a television. "You're going to watch training videos for the next few days before we get you started on calls. Any questions?"

When we shook our heads, Curtis popped a video in the VCR. "I'll check on you in an hour."

When Curtis came back, he found our feet up on the coffee table, the training worksheets untouched, and crumpled-up paper basketballs littering the floor around the trashcan. He stood there looking at us for a second. Brad and I just stared back at him.

Finally, after an awkward pause, Curtis said carefully, "It doesn't look like you've made much progress on the training module. Is there a problem?"

I tilted my head to the side. "Come on, man. You can't be serious with this stuff. We're Amway guys. We don't *need* this kind of training."

Curtis shrugged, "Well, you need to watch it and complete the worksheets anyway."

I laughed. "Come on, Curtis. If you give me a phone and a prospect, I can start making you money right now."

Curtis looked at Brad and then back at me. Later, I would realize he was a levelheaded guy—not easily ruffled. In that moment, however, he was angry. His tone reflected his irritation. Curtis must have thought he had made a huge mistake by hiring us.

"I apologize if you feel this is boring. If there's another opportunity outside this company better suited to you, let me know. If not, I suggest you complete the assignment. I'll give you both a minute to think on that."

He walked out of the room, shutting the door softly behind him.

Brad looked at me. "Man, I'm broke. I need this job."

I gulped and nodded. "Yeah, me too. I guess we'd better focus."

I turned back toward the television, picked up the workbook, and focused on finishing the training.

Curtis hadn't yelled, insulted us, or made a scene. Thankfully, he remained calm and didn't fire us on the spot. What a wakeup call!

All it took were a few words for me to realize how ridiculous I'd been. Curtis had taken a chance on us, and here we were messing around, sitting in a room where anyone walking by could see us. We weren't just making him look bad, we were being straight-up stupid.

I realized that as long as I was still struggling, looking for my big break, and asking others to share their experiences and knowledge, I had an obligation to be humble. My big ego was best kept in check. Curtis taught me a priceless lesson without taking the opportunity off the table. I needed to keep my head down and do the work.

A few hours later, Curtis checked back in. The room was spotless, we took notes, and our workbooks were complete.

Putting in the Reps

Since technology was a new field, I had a lot to learn. Alphatronix sold data storage for enterprise companies. Today, we save most things in the cloud, but back in the early 1990s, data was stored physically on disc arrays. Alphatronix kept copies of files offsite, sometimes in different states, that were accessible if a company's files were corrupted or physically damaged. Our customers were organizations who stored huge amounts of critical (and often top secret) data, including countless large corporations and the US Army and Navy.

My job centered on convincing decision makers that they needed Alphatronix's services. I had to convince people to use Alphatronix over other companies offering similar products. That's where my skills and experience came in handy.

Even though my day technically started at nine, I arrived at work before eight every day. The key to inside sales is to reach the important decision makers before their assistants come in and run interference. From what I learned, impact players in business get to work early and stay late, so I did too. Each day I said the same words maybe twenty or thirty times.

"Hi there, this is Donald with Alphatronix. Could I take up just thirty seconds of your time today to talk to you about the ways we've helped other companies protect their digital data?"

Repeating those lines could have felt tedious, but it didn't because I truly believed Alphatronix provided an invaluable service for its customers. There were a few different outcomes after my short intro. Either we'd part ways without them expressing any interest, agree on a callback time, or set an appointment. Appointments were the best outcome, but the prearranged callback was a step in the right direction as well. Even the hang-ups weren't that bad. I used each rejection as a learning opportunity. In sales, you expect rejections, but there were always more names on my call list, more opportunities for someone to say yes. So, I didn't dwell on the past. I focused on the future. I also asked Curtis for feedback. I wanted to be sure that each time I dialed I was doing a little better than the last time.

Although inside sales reps like me did most of the legwork, the appointments and deal closings were handed over to the outside sales team. Some people might have been bitter about this—people who didn't work any harder than I did were making intense amounts of money and spending half the day on the golf course—but I just couldn't see any advantage in that negativity. Instead, working with them motivated me. Many had specialized degrees and more bullet points on their resumes than I did, but I knew I could do that work and do it well. The product may have been different, but the basic skills were the same things I'd been doing all my life in one way or another. I stuck with inside sales for the time being, encouraged to know that one day I could make some real money in technology.

Less Than Paycheck to Paycheck

I'd been working at Alphatronix about a year when my wife became pregnant with our first child. Finding out I was about to become a dad motivated and energized me. I never doubted that I'd make it big one day, but now "one day" needed to come sooner rather than later. The nine-month deadline on my dream felt like a tall order, but I have always loved a challenge. I upped my game at Alphatronix—getting in earlier, making more calls, and scoring as many appointments as possible.

About five months into the pregnancy, my wife and I felt like we were ready to meet the newest member of our little family—or, at least as ready as any new parent can be. We'd just found out the baby was a girl, and we'd picked out a name for her: Moriah. Alphatronix had great health insurance, so we felt confident that my wife and the baby would get the care they needed. I was making more in commission than ever—my bosses were considering transitioning me to outside sales. Everything seemed to be falling into place.

Then I got fired.

One morning, I walked into the office, travel mug in hand, and had already scanned my call list for the day. As I entered the sales floor, I was prepared for the usual meet-and-greet, but today there were no waves or hellos from my colleagues. Instead, I saw people huddled in groups, some of them wiping their eyes. People in their cubicles were placing framed photos and knickknacks into cardboard boxes. They didn't even glimpse up as I walked by.

Maybe this has nothing to do with me, I thought as I sat down. *I'll just get to work, and everything will be normal. This is just another totally normal day.*

There was a sudden tap on my shoulder.

"Don." Curtis was standing behind me, looking grim. "We need to see you in the conference room."

I smiled and pointed to my headset. "I have a few calls to make first."

Did I think I could put off the inevitable? You're darn right I did.

"Don. Now."

In the conference room, our Human Resources representative, Suzanne, stood with about ten other salespeople. Her eyes were red.

"Alphatronix was acquired by a new company that already has a sales team in place. I'm sorry to announce that we're going to have to let you all transition to new opportunities."

I crossed my arms in front of my chest: "You mean we're being fired."

Suzanne looked at me, startled. Clearly, she hadn't been expecting a response. Clearing her throat, she said, "We're not using that term." Then she glanced down at the pile of folders she held and handed them out, trying to avoid everyone's eyes. "Just read the paperwork. It's all explained here."

I shook my head, "I'm not reading that."

"And why is that?" Suzanne asked, sounding like she didn't want to hear the answer.

"Because I'm not getting fired today."

Suzanne pressed her lips together into a thin white line before responding. "Donald, that isn't helpful."

Maybe it was an aggressive response, but with a baby on the way, there was no way I was going home to tell my wife I'd been fired.

Instead, I laughed and said, "I'm not reading the paperwork because I don't need paperwork. I'm not getting fired." I took a seat at the conference room table. "I think you need to talk to Brian. I'm pretty sure Brian will tell you I'm not fired."

Brian was the interim CEO. I figured that he needed to close as much business as possible and keep key customers happy while the transition occurred. He was motivated by the company's needs but also his own. Brian had to look good during the integration if he was going to have a shot at staying in the business after the acquisition was finalized. Dollars and deals mattered to him. He stood to lose plenty of both if I left that day.

Curtis chimed in, "Come on, Don. I know this isn't easy—"

I shook my head again, cutting him off. "I've got about $300,000 worth of deals in the pipeline. If I'm fired, I'll tell the customers not to go through with it. Go get Brian and see if he wants that money or not. My guess is that he does. He can't get it if I'm not here."

When I met with Brian an hour later, he was clearly frustrated that I couldn't just accept the situation and move on like everyone else.

"I understand you needed to see me?" he asked as I sat down.

"I'll cut to the chase," I said, crossing an ankle over my knee. "You know my wife is pregnant. I need income and benefits to cover us at least until the delivery. And you need deals closed. We both have things we want in this situation. I think the solution is pretty simple."

"I'm listening."

"Just don't fire me yet. I'll stay for a few more months, closing your deals and getting you money. And in that time, I'll be able to line up something else." I smiled. "Win-win."

In the end, I still got fired. But he had accepted my counteroffer, which meant I'd given myself a ninety-day head start on looking for a new job. Most importantly, I was able to secure health insurance for Moriah's birth. In this case, my creativity was driven by desperation. I didn't have a game plan for being out of work immediately, but I was confident that I could fix anything in ninety days.

I started sending out resumes and interviewing for a new role in technology sales, but I also wasn't in a position to be picky. I was out of a job, and to make matters worse, although I closed almost all of that remaining $300,000 in deals and received my commission, I didn't get the quarterly sales bonus for hitting my target numbers. That was $10,000 I'd been counting on, so not having it was a big financial blow. I decided that while I searched for a position that had real potential for growth, I'd take whatever short-term job came along first.

What came along was Mr. Cash.

In my rounds of calls, I'd left a message with Devon, who'd also moved to the Research Triangle around the same time I had. Even though he was still in my Amway network, he also picked up a day job. Devon was in sales at Consolidated Mortgage, affectionately known as Mr. Cash.

"I can hook you up here," he said when he called me back. "I'll talk to my manager. Unless you have any felonies that I'm not aware of, I'm 100 percent sure you can get in right away."

Devon was right. A few days later, I was on the sales floor at Mr. Cash, a subprime mortgage lender. I wasn't about to complain—I needed that paycheck—but I had to admit that this was far from my dream job. At Alphatronix, I had a position I'd felt good about. I was selling something I knew the customer needed: a product that made companies more secure. Even if I put the hard sell on folks, I didn't feel slimy because I knew that if they said yes, their business would be stronger.

I was more conflicted about Mr. Cash. We offered to help customers refinance, which gave them money in their pocket, the ability to pay a few more bills and clear up some credit issues. But those were immediate benefits for immediate gratification. When you took the long view, we were adding years to their mortgages and expensive interest rate points. Our computers generated lists of mortgage holders who were one missed paycheck away from losing everything they had. While a subprime mortgage would help them in the near term, it also set them up for potential long-term trouble.

Even under duress, I tried to find the learning opportunity. Some experiences I'd had helped me see all the good that was possible if I worked hard enough. Mr. Cash, on the other hand, was a master class in "How Not to Succeed." I gained valuable insight on how the financial system preys on the fiscally weak. Today, if I go into a bank and want to wire money or get a cashier's check, the manager will do it with a smile and a big "Thank *you*, Mr. Thompson." But the folks I called about mortgage loans didn't have those advantages. In truth, back then, neither did I. Like many of the customers I contacted, I had to *pay* to keep my money in the bank. My finances dwindled because I was being charged overdraft fees, low balance fees—the standard: "you're poor, so pay more" deal.

Our society rewards people who make it financially and treats them differently. Working at Mr. Cash helped reinforce my conviction that I needed to be on the winning side.

Even with my reservations about the company, I closed quite a few deals. I focused on the upside that people taking out these mortgages could use the money to get their financial lives in order. My problem wasn't making money for Mr. Cash. It was getting them to pay me on time.

At their core, the companies selling subprime mortgages were basically broke. They sold the loans they acquired to larger brokers and banks. Ironically, until those deals were funded, Mr. Cash was cash poor. When they got stuck holding too many mortgages, their own cash flow got tight...like a vise.

One day, a few months into my time with the company, our supervisor stepped onto the sales floor, announcing, "Your paychecks will be late this week."

I turned to Devon. "What's he talking about? Late?"

Devon shrugged wearily. "Yeah. That's normal. It happens every few weeks. If they get tight with money, they delay our pay. It sucks, but you get used to it."

My lifelong allergy to bullying flared up. I was convinced they had the money to pay us. They just didn't want to and thought they could use their power to get away with it.

"Uh-uh. No way. Nobody told me about that part," I said, pulling off my headset.

I marched across the sales floor and knocked on the door of the vice president of finance's office. Once he'd let me in, I stood in the center of the room and put my hands in my pockets. I wanted to start the conversation out casually, even though I felt like throwing the big brass paperweight on his desk out the window.

"About our paychecks being late," I said, keeping my voice even. "That's not going to work for me. I have no game plan for that. I need my check on time."

Describing my situation as "living paycheck to paycheck" would have been an understatement. Between credit card debt, COBRA insurance costs, and everything that comes with having a newborn, we weren't even making it from one paycheck to the next. It was more like "living paycheck to last month's expenses." Seems Mr. Cash and I had similar challenges.

He tried to explain the situation, beginning with cash flow difficulties and other problems at the bank. He told me that the company was under pressure, but I didn't care. I was under pressure too.

I crossed my arms. "Are you getting your paycheck?"

He stuttered a bit trying to dodge a direct response, but the answer was clear enough.

"I'll assume that's a yes. Okay. Here's a solution. You give me some of *your* paycheck, and then *you* wait to get paid."

"Now, Donald, I see your—"

I cut him off. "I'm not sure you're hearing me clearly. I did my thing; I sold my mortgages. Now I get my paycheck. That's the deal. If I don't get compensated for that work, I'm going to treat this like you—*personally*—are stealing from me, and we'll go from there."

Maybe threatening the VP wasn't the most diplomatic move, but it worked. I wasn't allowed to tell anyone else, but that was fine by me. I left his office with a check in my pocket.

Even though Mr. Cash was keeping food on our table and a roof over our heads, I wasn't achieving what I hoped. In the past, I'd always been able to keep myself focused with the gentle reminder that, even if I wasn't a big shot yet, I would be soon. Now, I found it harder to remain optimistic. With my job at Alphatronix, I'd been going in the right direction, getting ahead. Now I felt behind. I was still reinvesting every cent I earned from Amway back into the business. Even when they arrived on time, my sales paychecks were unpredictable. I never knew when a commission would come through.

One night when I came home from work, there was a piece of paper taped to the door. I frowned as I pulled it off and read the small print. It was an eviction warning—not a notice of eviction, not yet. We still had two weeks to pay our back rent. But if those two weeks went by, the landlord would contact the magistrate to initiate eviction proceedings.

I stood on the welcome mat at the front door of my home, staring at the paper, reading it over and over again until my eyes glazed over. Two weeks. I had two weeks to fix this. I *could* find an answer—payday was just two days away. Mr. Cash knew well enough now not to try to delay my check. But how could I have let this happen? I knew I was late with the rent this month, and now that I thought about it, we'd been late the prior month, and the month before that as well. I'd been so focused on the future that I hadn't seen what was happening in the present.

I figured that I could handle this immediate crisis, but what about next month's rent, and the next, and the next? I didn't have any new job leads. What made me think that thirty days from now would be any different than this moment I was in? My future started to look like an endless cycle of barely scraping by and trying desperately to catch up without ever truly getting ahead.

I closed my eyes, hoping the sick feeling in the pit of my stomach would disappear. When it didn't, I took one last breath then crumpled the note in my fist, shoving it into my coat pocket. I felt a pain deep in the pit of my stomach. This was my job, my responsibility. I would fix it. I was scared, but I knew I would find a way.

The next day at work, all I could think about was that terrible eviction warning. Normally, I started my calls with energy and excitement, no matter how unlikely it seemed that I'd get to the end of the long questionnaire we asked potential clients. Today though, every call felt like a test of my endurance. By the time I hung up, I felt wrung out and exhausted. I started thinking: *no matter how many sales I made, I wouldn't be able to pull myself out of this mess.*

Finally, I pushed back my chair, tossed my headset on the keyboard, and literally stumbled to the bathroom.

After I'd been gone from my desk for a while, Devon came into the bathroom and found me vomiting.

"What's wrong?" he asked, standing outside of the stall.

I wiped my face and opened the door. Feeling a little unsteady on my feet, I stood at the sink and splashed cold water on my face. "I'm working all the time. I never sleep. I'm doing everything right, but I'm still barely making it."

"It's not that bad, is it?"

"The job at Alphatronix was just ripped out from under me. It's gone, not because I was doing a bad job, but just *because*. I can't wrap my mind around it. Now, I can't get a leg up. Something has got to give." I wiped my face with a paper towel.

I believed in myself and the coaches, teachers, and others who had put their faith in me, especially my grandfather, whose words drove me. At that moment, however, I knew my life was out of balance. That eviction notice made me realize how steep some of the valleys would be in my journey. Without a mentor and feeling like my options were slipping away, I had to find strength in this chaotic moment. My faith had been shaken. I felt desperate and lost. I needed a solution.

"Why don't you just ask your folks for help?" Devon asked. "You know they'd do anything for you."

He was right, of course. Devon knew my parents. He understood as well as I did that they'd be more than willing to tide me over until I got back on track.

I looked at myself in the mirror, shaking my head. "Do you know what it does to a man to know he can't take care of his family? It's not supposed to be like this."

Devon handed me another paper towel. "You know I understand that."

Devon was also married and had a young child. He knew exactly what tolls the kind of life I was living could take. He was living it too. Seeing the concern on his face made me realize how grateful I was to have a friend like him.

I exhaled. "I'm okay. I'll be fine. I won't let this beat me."

I splashed more water on my face and looked back in the mirror. What I saw in the reflection was the product of two people who'd worked hard, who'd achieved great things, who'd made huge sacrifices so that my path would be much smoother. They hadn't raised me to dwell on the negatives or wallow in fear, the kind of behavior that leads nowhere. They'd taught me to see the positive, look at any situation, no matter how difficult, and find the opportunity within. What was I doing holed up in a bathroom paralyzed with fear?

No. This wasn't how things were going to go. I'd spent my life to that point learning through my parents' experiences and stories about persevering and seizing every opportunity. Now, I had to put all those lessons into practice. It was my time to step up.

I clapped Devon on the shoulder and forced a smile. "You ready to get back out there?"

As I let the bathroom swing closed, I vowed to leave the self-pity behind. Something good was around the next corner.

11

I'VE ALREADY BEATEN THE ODDS

"**D**onald Thompson?"

I placed the issue of *Forbes* I'd been flipping through back on the coffee table and stood up, flashing a smile. I extended my hand to the man standing in the doorway.

We shook.

"I'm Bill Riddick."

Of course, I already knew who he was. After Computer Services Partners had called to set up an interview, I'd spent the next two days trying to find out as much as I could about the company and its management team. A few calls out to my network had given me a thorough understanding of what CSP provided—remote and onsite monitoring of computer networks, plus data center services—and who the organization's movers and shakers were, primarily Bill, the company CEO.

I was determined to nail this interview. Over the last few months, I had sent probably one hundred resumes to one hundred companies in the North Carolina tech community. Finally, it paid off. I had a handful of interviews, but only two positions seemed promising: CSP and another local tech firm called I-Cubed. I hadn't gotten an in-person meeting with I-Cubed yet, so a lot was riding on this one.

"Great to meet you, Bill," I said, "I'm looking forward to the opportunity to talk today."

"Well, come on in and we'll get started." He smiled. I followed him into the office.

I looked around as I crossed the room, taking time to appreciate the view through the floor-to-ceiling windows. I liked the décor too, which included dozens of books. I could see myself in an office like this in the future.

Bill gestured for me to take a seat in one of the two leather club chairs across from his desk.

"I spoke with David at Alphatronix. He suggested I speak with you." Bill was friends and golfing buddies with the vice president of sales at Alphatronix. "He said a lot of great things about you and your work ethic. We're looking for that kind of drive and energy around here."

Bill told me about the history of Computer Service Partners, what they sold, and how they were a small, close-knit team. I listened carefully. Although I knew most of this from my pre-interview research, hearing it again reinforced my conclusion that this was a place where I could succeed.

Bill finished, and we went through the standard interview questions—accomplishments, strengths, and weaknesses. When we got to the "what can you do for us?" part of the conversation, I didn't hold back.

"I can make CSP a lot of money."

Bill chuckled, "Good answer."

After a few more questions, Bill leaned back in his chair, looking pleased. "Well, that about covers it on my end. Do you have any questions for me?"

"Tell me about my first year here. Can I make $100,000?"

Bill paused. I knew the figure startled him. He tried to hide his reaction. On my end, I was betting high. The largest salary I had ever earned had barely been half the number. However, that didn't dampen my determination.

Slowly, he shook his head. "I'm afraid not, Donald. But you could do very well in the first year. Based on your record, you could easily clear $60,000. With a little hustle, I bet you could make seventy, maybe eighty, if you put your nose to the grindstone."

He started to explain, but I held up my hand to stop him.

"I don't want to waste your time here, Bill. I'm going to have to pass."

This time, he didn't hide his surprise. "Don, you've just been laid off. You're working at a mortgage lender. Surely you can be reasonable about building your career and salary here over time."

As I reflected on the interview later that evening, I admitted to myself that Bill was right. I didn't have much in the way of bargaining chips. Most people in my shoes would have jumped at his offer. For years, however, I'd been going from one dead-end job to the next. This time, I was going to make sure the road took me where I wanted to go. I made a firm pact with myself that I wouldn't take another job where I couldn't make $100,000.

The number wasn't the real point, or all that important frankly, though it was a huge sum back then. I just wanted to ensure my next job would give me more than just a salary and include opportunities for growth and rewards for hard work. I wanted to work for someone who would tell me, "Yes, if you do XYZ, you can make $100,000." I wanted to work for someone with that kind of foresight, not for someone who immediately set barriers to success.

Instead of taking what was right in front of me, I looked ahead, willing to tolerate uncertainty if it meant I could keep myself open to a better opportunity in the future. I had learned this mentality from my dad. I thought back to when he didn't get the defensive coordinator position at East Carolina. He could have remained there as defensive line coach, which may not have been the role he wanted, but it was a good job and stable. However, he realized that ECU hadn't invested in him, so his opportunities for advancement were limited. As a result, he went to UNC, a chance to achieve his goals. By turning down Bill's offer, I followed what I had learned from Dad.

The same week I interviewed at Computer Service Partners, I also started preliminary talks with Ned from Integrated Industrial Information (I-Cubed): a small, startup tech firm. He was a former banker and business partner of I-Cubed's CEO, Grant Williard. They had engineers that built the product, but needed someone to sell it, so the sales position was extremely important.

Ned was fiercely protective of his business. Before he would even meet with me, he insisted that we talk on the phone, and when I say "talk," I don't mean a quick Q&A. I mean *serious* conversations. We had two 90-minute phone calls before even meeting in person. Everyone who knows me knows I love to talk, but Ned gave me a run for my money. His explanations about the company's work were so long-winded that I swore I could see the grass growing outside my window. Ned also asked complicated questions, rephrasing the same thing many different ways, as if he were trying to trip me up. Then, he would circle back to the original question. Those pre-screening discussions felt more like interrogations.

Finally though, we made plans to meet in-person. As I drove to lunch at Ragazzi's Italian Restaurant in Raleigh, I wondered what else Ned could possibly want to know. We'd been over every inch of my professional history at least five times. At that point, he knew more about me than my parents. Still, he seemed reluctant to either hire me or say, "Thanks, but no thanks."

Soon, I figured out why. Ned didn't like that I didn't have a college degree. It wasn't the first time someone had underestimated my potential because I didn't finish college—and it wouldn't be the last time either—but I didn't let it bother me. Instead, I focused on what I could do, who I knew I was, and what I hoped to accomplish. Ned knew I was interested in working at I-Cubed, but I couldn't let this dance go on much longer. Whatever the outcome, I'd decided this was the last interview I was going to have with Ned.

Despite our long business-based discussions, Ned wasn't much for small talk. As soon as the server walked away with my drink order, he plunged right into conversation.

"Don, there's something about you I like," he said, putting his elbows on the table. "I keep coming back to talk to you. But, there are also a lot of hang-ups on my end, because I'm just not sure about your background. It's not exactly what we're looking for."

"You mean my education?"

Ned slowly nodded.

I clenched my jaw as I quickly considered the best response. The intensity, the matching of wills, it felt like being back on the gridiron.

After a deep inhale and exhale, I said, "Well, it's true that I don't have a degree. But I think my sales record makes it clear that it hasn't mattered. What has mattered is that I make sales. I will sell your product better than anyone else you're going to talk to. I *know* how to do that. And for anything I don't know about the technology, I will glue myself to a book and work with the team until I know it backward and forward. I put my all into everything I do."

Ned didn't give any indication that a single word I'd said had sunk in. He just sat there staring at me as if he were trying to read my mind. I stared back. If Ned was a mind reader, that was fine by me. All he'd find out was that I was the best salesperson he'd ever met.

Nearly a minute passed in complete silence. I knew this was a great opportunity, but I was aggravated. Was I wasting my time? During this lunch, I could have been on the phone interviewing with someone else.

"Look, Ned," I said, letting a hint of frustration creep into my voice. "We're talking about a six-person company. I-Cubed isn't exactly IBM. You should consider opening your mind to a new way of doing things. I will make you a lot of money—more than anyone else you're considering. If I don't, you can fire me."

Ned nodded again, considering what I'd said, and then cleared his throat. "I see your point, and I know you have a great record. Let me be honest with you. How do we know we can trust you to follow through on our sales if you couldn't follow through and finish college?"

I took the napkin off my lap and placed it carefully on the table beside my plate. Then I said calmly, "I'm going to be selling a million bucks worth of products and services for *someone*. It can be you, or it can be your competitor, but I'm tired of talking about the same things over and over. I'll let you decide what you want to do. You can take a risk on me or not. But I promise that if you pass on me, I won't be available to you in the future."

I had my back to the wall—literally, because we were in the last booth—but I sat there convinced that the tide had turned. We had hashed through hours of conversation, but despite the risk, I said, "No, I'm not going to talk about this anymore." This was a defining moment. Then, I stood up and left.

Outside, I panicked, just for a moment. This was a huge emotional risk. Although I felt confident I didn't need a college degree to excel at this job, I also had no other prospects. I'd just turned down the offer at CSP. I was at the end of my line in terms of credit and past-due rent. Maybe I shouldn't have been so firm. I went to bed wondering if I'd made the right move.

Imagine my surprise when Grant Williard, the CEO of I-Cubed, called me the next day. He asked me to visit him to discuss a job offer. I kept my voice level and cool, but I couldn't help feeling proud of myself and impressed by Grant's humility. Even if the company only had six employees, the CEO got on the phone with a potential new hire.

Grant smiled, greeting me at the door with a firm handshake. He was about twenty years older than me, his hair just beginning to grey around the temples. "Thanks for coming in. Ned had great things to say about you. I'm pleased to finally meet you."

I chuckled. "You don't need to sugarcoat things. I know Ned had issues with my background."

Grant led the way through the small building to his office in the back corner. "Don't let Ned fool you. He's a pit bull of an interviewer, but he knows talent. He believes in you."

"Well, I appreciate that and thank you for calling," I replied as I sat in the chair that Grant had pulled over to the desk. "But I'm going to be totally honest. I've been interviewing for a while now and I'm currently considering more than one offer."

I leaned back in my chair, interested in how Grant would respond.

He studied my face carefully, taking his time to form an answer.

"Donald, your skills, personality, and toughness are what I need at I-Cubed. I have no doubt that you are entertaining multiple offers. But here, you'll grow in ways you never imagined. You'll learn things they don't teach salespeople at other places, because you'll be playing many roles here."

I was intrigued. The idea of not being boxed in by a particular job description was hugely appealing to me.

"You know," I replied. "I like what you're saying. I really do." I put my hands on my knees. "But let's talk bottom line."

"Right down to brass tacks, I like that. The starting salary is $43,000 base, plus commissions."

That wasn't what I'd been hoping to hear, but I wasn't ready to give up just yet.

"Look, I want to work for you, but I can't say yes to that number. I've got a family to support, bills to pay, and I need to make a good living. I've promised myself that I'll only take a job where I can make $100,000 in my first year."

The number hung in the air between us. Grant nodded, his brow furrowed.

"I understand. I really do," he replied. "And I admire the fact that you're doing your best to care for your growing family. That's what I can offer you right now."

My shoulders fell a little. I'd only spent a few minutes with him, but I could already tell he was someone I'd like to work for and with. But, if he couldn't give me the chance to meet my goal, those long interviews had been for nothing.

"But—" Grant continued, holding up his index finger. "I want *you* to understand that what you'll gain with this job isn't limited to money. You will be defining the sales role here. You'll have freedom to make decisions and to play the game the way you think is best. We can only grow from here. You'll be on the ground floor of that."

He painted a picture of opportunity that was only defined by how big I could dream. I liked the way it looked. "So you're not going to budge on the salary."

Grant nodded. "Right, but I'm also not going to limit how much money you might make here. I'm willing to create a bonus and commission schedule that will allow you to swing for the fences. It's simple—you sell more, you make more. No limits."

Now that was what I wanted to hear. I couldn't help but smile. This was the moment I'd worked for and hoped for—a chance to prove myself and grow without limits.

"And did I mention that we pay 100 percent of every employee's health insurance including family coverage?" he added.

Okay, now I was even more impressive.

"I-Cubed is not the Grant Williard show," he continued. "I need people like you to do the things that I can't do. You're an entrepreneur yourself. You understand what it's like to get interested in every new opportunity that comes your way. I'm the same. I see something new and shiny, and I want to pursue it."

I chuckled. I could understand that kind of thinking and why it was valuable.

Grant smiled, continuing: "I need help driving sales and growing this place into something we can all be proud of. Together, along with our great engineers, we'll add value to the technology community. I want to bring you along on that journey."

I had to admit; it sounded perfect. What Grant offered—an education, mentor, and seat at the table—was exactly what I'd been waiting to find. The lower salary wasn't ideal, but salespeople don't have to rely solely on salary. What he had essentially sold me was an opportunity to set my own salary by exceeding sales goals. That was a different story than I heard from other companies, which limited commissions and tried to manage my overall success. Grant told me "no" on the base salary, but convinced me that I was joining a team where I could be special. This was an organization that would get out of the way and let me soar. If you open the door a crack, I'm taking that opportunity. Grant gave me a chance. I was ready to seize it.

It helped to know that I-Cubed had a strong product that I'd have no trouble selling. If the only limit on how much money I could make was how much I could achieve, well, that wasn't a limit at all. He threw the traditional structure out the window.

Driving home, I replayed the entire meeting in my mind. It dawned on me that Grant had used some serious psychology. He sat there and got me, a sales guy who was low on cash and behind on bills, to take a job for less money than I'd been offered elsewhere. I was a master of the smooth sale, but today I'd been outplayed. Most amazing of all? I was certain I'd made the right choice with I-Cubed. Grant responded to my competitive side. Unlike other leaders that I had met or worked alongside, he heard a music that the world hadn't yet heard. Grant talked to me like a competitor.

Game on!

This was it; I knew it—my chance, my big break. Alone in my car, with an Amway motivational tape playing, I couldn't help but grin.

I signed the contract that night.

12

SEIZING OPPORTUNITIES

I started at I-Cubed by selling our data migration service to engineering and design companies. I easily understood why a company might need a service like ours. They were upgrading to new systems to manage all their engineering assets—basically, digital filing cabinets—and needed a way to bring legacy data and designs with them. Clients not only needed their data moved but also needed assurance that transferring wouldn't corrupt or damage their files. The digital information had to be intact and usable as it had been, though it was now housed in a new place. It was the technological version of hiring a moving company. You can't load up all the furniture and boxes by yourself, so you pay someone to help. You also want to know that your photo albums and favorite mugs will be all in one piece upon arrival.

The *why* of I-Cubed's product made total sense to me, and as in any sales situation, that knowledge made me better at my job. What I couldn't do was explain the *how*. True, I wasn't entirely responsible for that part of the pitch. The people on the phone wanted to hear from the actual engineers solving their problems, so if I could get someone on the phone who wanted to hear more, I would transfer them to Grant or someone with a technical background.

I had a lot to learn. Even though I'd worked with Alphatronix, also a tech company, what I-Cubed did was much more complex. I worked with people who had been studying these fields for their entire careers.

Grant was busy, but he worked with me to build my knowledge well beyond a superficial understanding. I didn't have to be an engineer, but I had to be able to answer a broad range of customer questions. If I couldn't, then I had to know the correct question to ask the engineers. Initially, Grant structured my days to include half a day of calls and half a day of reading and learning from the team. He walked through my doors with a stack of engineering magazines. "Okay, read these, highlight concepts you don't understand, and we'll talk about them over lunch." He didn't wait for an answer and walked out.

The magazines ended up heavily highlighted. After a while, I started to get the hang of it. At lunch, Grant explained the technical terms in detail and taught me how all the ideas related. He'd run the phone script with me, pretending to be a customer, and ask increasingly complicated technical questions. Eventually, I felt comfortable dealing with most of what he threw my way.

Would I ever be coding a bug fix? No. But quickly learning many of the intricacies of how I-Cubed moved and protected data made Grant more confident that I could handle customer calls for longer before handing them off to an engineer. As a result, I had greater freedom to get to know customer and company needs. What we began was a cycle of me making more sales than projected. Once I could get someone on the phone and keep them talking, I was good at identifying their hot buttons and then winning their business.

One of the first big deals I worked on was the La-Z-Boy chair company. I wasn't the first person who'd tried to close this deal. They'd kept I-Cubed in a holding pattern for more than a year.

When I went to talk to Grant about the account, he waved me into his office with his chin, both hands typing away at the keyboard.

"Just give me one second, Donald." I looked down at the paperwork I was holding while I waited. "And…" He clicked a key. "Done. What's up?"

"What's going on with the La-Z-Boy deal?"

Grant shook his head. "They keep saying 'yes,' but they never close. Don't waste your time on it. It's a dead end."

My competitive drive immediately shifted into gear. I didn't want to shy away from a challenge. In fact, La-Z-Boy suddenly felt like the most important deal in play.

"But this could be a good chunk of money." I waved the papers in my hand. "They have over 60,000 files that need to be converted to AutoCAD."

Grant nodded. "Yep. But they're never going to buy anything."

I smirked. "We'll see about that."

By the time I got back to my desk, I had a plan in mind. All I needed to know was why this company wasn't pulling the trigger. Once I knew that, I believed that I'd find a solution to their problem. I did some research and found out that there was a furniture conference happening in High Point, North Carolina, only about a three-hour drive from Raleigh. The La-Z-Boy VP was sure to be there. I gave him a call.

While his assistant transferred me, I thought through my strategy. What angle would I use to get my foot in the door? Ah, I'd play the "new guy" card, act like I was just familiarizing myself with our accounts. I wouldn't even mention the deal yet. Then, I'd throw in some subtle flattery. In the thirty seconds it took him to pick up the phone, I figured out what to say.

"This is Charlie."

"Hey, Charlie!" I kept my tone friendly without edging into over-eager. "This is Donald with I-Cubed. I'm just calling to follow up on your last call with Grant."

"Oh." Charlie suddenly sounded less chipper.

I quickly redirected the conversation. If Charlie thought I headed toward "where's our money" territory, I sensed he'd remember some "urgent business" that needed his "immediate attention."

"Listen, I'm new on the account, and I'd like to get to know you and your company better. Will you be at this conference up in High Point in the next few days? Maybe I could buy you some dinner, and we could talk in person."

"Yes, I'll be there." Charlie paused like he might regret giving me that piece of information. "But I don't know. I'll be pretty busy."

"Sure, sure. I understand. But, just so you know, the offer stands, whether you buy from us or not. It would be great to meet you and learn about your business. We love hearing about how hugely successful firms incorporate engineering excellence into their process."

And I meant it—flattery works best when it's true. Charlie could give me important insights into their operations and needs. If I closed the deal with La-Z-Boy, great. But if not, I'd be much better informed when I called up their competitors.

After a few moments, Charlie agreed to a dinner. The minute I hung up the phone, I jumped out of my chair, hurrying back to Grant's office with a huge smile on my face.

As usual, Grant's door was open. He liked employees to know that they could talk to him, that he was part of the team, not above it. I poked my head into the office, giving a little rap on the doorframe with my knuckles.

"I'm taking Charlie from La-Z-Boy to the Steak and Ale in High Point. I am going to close this deal."

Grant gave me a doubtful look. "I don't know, Don. We haven't made any progress with them in a year, and now you're treating the guy to steak."

"If it doesn't work, no big deal," I replied. "We won't have risked anything just by taking the guy out for a meal. But if it does work, we've made $75,000."

"Minus the cost of two steak dinners," Grant grumbled. "But fine. Let me know how it goes."

His tone spoke to his certainty. The potential client would avoid talking about the deal, the way he'd avoided our calls for months. He would enjoy a tasty dinner on our dime, then we'd never hear from him again. Risky, sure. Yet, in my gut, I knew that I could prove Grant wrong. In doing so, I would prove my worth.

At Steak and Ale's, Charlie and I sat in a dimly lit corner booth with wood veneer paneling. While we worked our way through the breadbasket and three salad bar refills, I didn't even mention I-Cubed. I let Charlie do the talking:

about the furniture industry, job frustrations, the vintage motorcycle he was restoring, and so much more. I listened, nodded my head, and asked short, prompting questions. It was a sales strategy, but it wasn't fake. As always, I genuinely enjoyed hearing other people's stories. The result is a strategy much more successful than pretend enthusiasm could ever be.

When the prime rib came, I decided it was time to start nudging the conversation toward business.

"Charlie, I'm new to this space. But I know enough to understand that you absolutely need to move your data. Your company is using archaic systems right now. It's time to upgrade."

Charlie didn't look up from his steak, but he nodded enthusiastically. "Oh, we definitely need to convert to AutoCAD. Without a doubt."

I frowned, my fork hovering over my plate. "Okay, well, I-Cubed is the best company out there to help you make that transition, and you keep avoiding us. Can you help me understand what's stopping you?"

"The budget." He shrugged. "I don't have $75,000 to spend on this right now, even though we need to do it." He reached for another roll, slathering it with butter.

Finally, I thought, leaning forward, "How much *do* you have to spend?"

"My quarterly budget is $40,000. That's the most I could get."

I thought about his predicament. He was hung up on the final number, the total cost, because his budget was allotted in three-month chunks. He wasn't saying no. In fact, he knew he needed to say yes. He was saying *I can't*. I sat in silence running some options through my head. The answer seemed obvious.

"What if we charged you $40,000 this quarter and then, in ninety days, invoice you for the remaining $35,000?"

Charlie looked thoughtful while he chewed a bite of steak, squinting his eyes as if he were doing some quick calculations. He started nodding. "Yep. That'll work."

This couldn't possibly be for real, could it? Even with my supersized confidence, this transaction seemed far too easy. But it was real all right. Charlie was ready to sign.

In a show of good faith, I offered to have the engineers work on migrating the designs as soon as the first payment cleared. Charlie walked away happy because he'd gotten what he needed for his company and he'd be getting it sooner rather than later. I walked away happy because I'd just closed my first significant deal for I-Cubed and provided the customer some incentive to pay quickly.

When I got to the office the next day, I couldn't wait to let Grant know that I'd risen to his challenge, even if he hadn't put one forth.

"Charlie from La-Z-Boy," I started.

"Oh, right. Your dinner meeting. How'd that go?" Grant asked, turning back to his computer screen like he was sure of the answer.

"We should be getting a check within the week."

Grant nearly fell out of his chair.

I explained how the whole dinner went down, and then watched Grant's face run a gamut of emotions. Finally, he let out a big laugh and stood to shake my hand.

"I like your thinking. You came up with a truly creative solution to that mess. But you know what I like more?"

I chuckled. "The money?"

"Well, definitely that too. But I like that you went after this deal even after I said it wasn't worth your time. You needed to see for yourself that it couldn't be done, and you proved me wrong. It's thinking like that that will continue to move us along. Nice job, Donald. Really great work."

Closing that deal was when I fully understood how significant the opportunities would be for me at I-Cubed. I realized that Grant respected what I could do and would give me the freedom to come up with creative solutions. He was honoring both my intelligence and people skills. I also noted that Grant's approach wasn't only about kindness toward his employees. It was a smart business move as well. Grant knew that giving me room to try out-of-the-box strategies made me happy. Like the smartest managers, he knew that happy employees do the best work. My satisfaction wasn't just good for me. It was good for Grant and the whole company.

His trust planted the seed of fierce loyalty to him and I-Cubed. Grant made all the I-Cubed employees feel like critical members of the team. As we got to know each other better, I learned his ability to bring people together came from his upbringing, just like my sales acumen. His father was treasurer and then vice president at Wake Forest University. His family lived on Faculty Drive and Grant's father would walk him to kindergarten on campus before heading to his office. Along the way, they'd run into employees from all over the university. Grant's dad spoke to them all the same way—with genuine interest in their lives and concern for their families. It didn't matter if the person cleaned toilets, trimmed hedges, or ran a huge research lab, Grant's father taught him that people are people and deserve respect and compassion no matter their perceived status.

Although Grant was closer to my dad's age than mine, we soon discovered that our fathers had instilled in us similar value systems. Just like my father reminded me that the team's victory was more important than my own, Grant's father reinforced in him that success at work did not define him.

Grant told me a story about going home for a family dinner well into the I-Cubed years and sharing the details of a significant success.

"Does that make you feel big?" his father asked him.

Grant, knowing the right answer for his father, said no, although he felt proud of his accomplishment. However, Grant understood the life lesson behind his father's question: be part of a team and don't let your ego get in your way.

It was from those early instructions in valuing people and being humble that Grant developed his leadership style. He led by example. I was receptive to his teaching. He took me under his wing, becoming my first business mentor. The more I learned about technology and business under Grant's tutelage, the more information I craved.

"Do you think I could expense about $25 at Barnes & Noble?" I asked Grant one afternoon. "There's a book the VP of General Motors suggested the last time we were on a call. It's about supporting design-based technology."

Grant didn't look up from his computer screen. He pointed a finger at me: "Don't you ever ask for money for books again."

My forehead furrowed. *Was he saying no?*

Looking up, Grant's face eased into a smile. "What I mean is, you never have to ask for money to better yourself. If you think you'll get results with that book or any other book you can find, then buy it. I'd never limit an employee who wants to learn more about what we do and how to do it better."

After that, I basically had an open tab at the bookstore. For a competitive learner like me, that was probably the best perk of the job.

All those books and learning sessions with Grant started me off on the right path. About a year into my work with I-Cubed, I'd been a part of closing several large deals. This experience came in handy when Grant decided to make a change.

I-Cubed employed a contract salesperson in Chicago. He'd been brought on to support Grant when the company was just starting out, but he wasn't closing deals as expected, and as my role grew, it became clear that I could do his job better. Still, there was too much work for me to do alone, so we kept him on.

I was knee-deep in paperwork for a bunch of deals when Grant knocked on my office door.

"Hey, Don. Can I talk to you a minute?"

I waved him in. "Of course." I started to get up and clear a spot on the chair, but Grant just piled the folders on another stack of paperwork and sat down.

"What do you think about…"

Before he could even get the sentence out, I replied, "I'm in."

This came from the same part of me that drove my high school teammates nuts—volunteering before I knew what I was volunteering for. But I didn't need to know. I trusted my coaches completely, and I knew they needed me. I felt the same way about Grant. I trusted his leadership. If he asked my opinion, it was worth doing.

He laughed. "You don't even know what I'm asking."

"Well, does it include more opportunity for me?"

"It does, but…"

"And can I make more money if I do what you're going to ask?"

"Yeah." Grant nodded.

"Done deal," I shrugged.

What I'd so impatiently agreed to was that Grant would let the Chicago guy go so I could take on a bigger territory. To help me stay on top of everything, he would hire a junior sales engineer to act as both my assistant and technical support. That way, I could get technical questions answered right away while I continued learning about our technology, thereby reaching a wider audience for I-Cubed. The new arrangement provided a less expensive alternative for the company and more opportunity for me.

I was expected to open up a whole pipeline of new opportunities. With Grant's support, an assistant by my side, and a growing level of comfort in the technology field, I finally found myself in a position to set my sights beyond my $100,000 dream. I was driven by my grandfather's belief that I'd be the family's first millionaire. Suddenly, seven figures seemed so much closer.

13

SUCCESS DOESN'T SNEAK UP AND ATTACK YOU

A t twenty-seven-years old, after two years working at I-Cubed, I made my dream salary and more. But, I continued being hungry for success, particularly after realizing that my dedication had paid off.

The networking business also grew, thanks to the efforts I put into constantly making new contacts. I made a modest monthly sum, but as a side project, my family benefitted from what I earned. Instead of just reinvesting, we were also putting some money aside in long-term savings.

We upgraded from our apartment to a spacious home. The extra space was a huge help now that we had a second child on the way. I looked forward to having a playroom—no more stepping on scattered building blocks walking to the kitchen each morning. The prospect of having a real yard was exciting too. With our hard-earned financial security, I could even pay someone else to mow it. I needed to use my time efficiently. Having a Saturday afternoon to read or build my Amway network was worth way more than the fifteen dollars it cost to hire a neighborhood kid with a lawnmower.

Of course, we weren't completely free of financial worries. Even though I'd paid off most of the credit card debt, there was still some left, as well as some financial repercussions like high interest rates and loan refusals. Yet, for the first time, money problems weren't suffocating our chances to grow. We didn't have to choose between paying our bills and improving our living conditions. Plenty of people would have rushed out to buy a new Mercedes-Benz as soon as they hit the $100,000 threshold, but I'd learned my lesson. I wasn't going to hurry to buy anything (not even a tracksuit). That meant, even though we were pushing the money needle in the right direction, it took a little while to decide that renting the house, instead of an apartment, was the best idea for our family. I made a sound decision.

At work, I made steady progress, learning more about the field, and bringing in correspondingly larger deals. That advancement resulted directly from the qualities my parents instilled in me (tough work ethic, perseverance, thirst for knowledge), plus some of the ones that had exasperated them, like my inability to accept the word "no." Grant's mentorship, however, gave me the chance to show what I could do with all that drive, as if my father's lessons were placed on warp speed.

Grant served as my first business mentor, but the relationship didn't start out with that in mind. In the first few years I worked at I-Cubed, he simply taught me the basics of the technology we sold. He watched my progress, critiqued my performance, and celebrated my successes. Whenever he sat down with me, I knew I'd always learn something new, perhaps about engineering or business strategies. That's when I learned what a difference a mentor can make on a younger person's career.

As our relationship progressed, I found that the information exchange wasn't always one-sided. Grant was one of the smartest people I'd ever met, and even many years later, when I became comfortable in the technology sphere, he continually opened my eyes to new ideas. But like me, Grant was never closed to new knowledge. No matter how much he knew, he was always searching for more. He saw that he could learn from me as well.

"Don, you know my father was a trained accountant, right?"

Grant's face reddened in the chilly wind as we strolled across the courtyard. He liked to get out of the office and walk around Centennial Campus, the section of North Carolina State University where I-Cubed and other technology innovators rented space. It wasn't cheap, but it meant we were close to some of the best resources and thinkers in the nation. The walking trails were an added bonus.

Grant did this walk-and-talk with many people, but I was a frequent companion, mostly because he liked to hear how our projects were trending. His approach generally focused on "trust, but verify." I owned the sales targets, but he always wanted to be in the loop about closings.

During those walks, I learned so much about technology, leadership, and business. I also learned to buy rubber-soled shoes. When I finally started making money, I had allowed myself one small luxury and bought a pair of leather Cole Haan loafers. I thought those shoes were about as slick as they came—until I wore out the soles walking around with Grant.

I nodded to Grant's question about his father, even though it was rhetorical. By this point, Grant and I had spent a lot of time together. Like me, he credited his upbringing for his success: his parents' commitment, drive, and humility had made him the leader he had become.

"Well, accountants don't deal with 'gray areas,'" he continued. "In our family, things are pretty much black and white. There's the truth, and then there's lying. Do you see what I'm getting at?"

"Is this about the call I was on this afternoon? With the automotive supplier?" I asked a little more sheepishly than usual.

Grant nodded sharply. "I wouldn't have told them we're working on that software fix because, technically, we're not."

I thought I knew what Grant would say when he heard about the call, but I wasn't worried. I had followed a strategy on that call, and I had a strategy now.

"Are we *planning* to fix it?" I asked, falling into pace with Grant as we rounded a corner.

"Yes, but not now," Grant said, frowning. "And saying that feels dishonest."

"It's not dishonest. I never promised a delivery date. I didn't say how we're fixing it. I said we're working on it. I gave them a message that communicated our intent and gave us a path to discussing details when we had more information. If we're planning to fix it, then we're working on it. The planning stage is part of the work cycle."

I grinned as Grant shook his head.

"What you're saying is, don't let the facts get in the way of a good story."

"I wouldn't put it quite like that," I shrugged, but my grin widened even more. "I was giving the client a vision of what the product could do for them."

Grant let this sink in. "That makes sense. Just remember, our industry is small and relationships matter. A creative stretch is fine, but only if it helps us help customers meet their goals."

"I agree. I like to sell people on the future, but we have to deliver that future. I wouldn't have promised anything our team couldn't handle."

We kept walking, making the circuit around the cluster of buildings and little green spaces. The conversation moved on to other business topics—delivery date problems, new markets, and the like—but in my head, I kept coming back to Grant's response. I thought I'd be able to bring Grant around to my way of thinking. It was fair to the customer and good for the company. I hadn't anticipated, however, that he'd be willing to shift his viewpoint.

I considered Grant to be one of the smartest people in the room. I learned more from him each week than I'd learned in my entire time in college. Knowing he was willing to learn from me was a good feeling. The small window of openness he showed that day gave me confidence that I could discuss critical business ideas with him. The relationship we'd developed reinforced the way I'd felt when I took the job. Here, walking around this frigid office park with a blister on my heel, this is exactly where I needed to be.

Vice President of Giving Grant Breaks

A lot of people spend their working lives avoiding their bosses. They think staying quiet, doing their job, and not calling attention to themselves will keep their jobs secure and drama free. But I'm not built to blend into the woodwork. If I have a question, I'm going to ask it. If I have an idea, I'm going to share it.

At I-Cubed, especially in those early days, I wanted Grant to know that I was open to learning everything I could. Whenever I got time with him, I'd soak up what he said and pepper him with additional questions. If I had a solution for a customer problem, I'd poke my head in his door and run it by him. If Grant had a book on his desk, I'd go buy it. Then I'd mention what I'd learned from it in conversation.

We worked with a lot of intelligent people—mechanical engineers, computer scientists, and MBAs—who wrote code to solve complex engineering problems. However, most of them place didn't themselves in a mentee role with Grant. They knew a lot of the same stuff he did, or at least they thought they did. Many had advanced degrees in difficult fields. Perhaps they thought they knew enough. We'd often end up in meetings that I privately referred to as games of "Who's the Smartest?"

On the other hand, I didn't have a degree, so nothing stood in the way of acquiring more knowledge. If other employees thought they didn't need mentorship, well, that just meant more for me. I took every opportunity to pick Grant's brain. I made sure I was always available as a sounding board for new ideas. Projects that were probably earmarked for other people ended up coming my way because I was open to the knowledge and too stubborn to get out of the way.

As I listened to Grant, got to know I-Cubed, and discovered what we were capable of as a company, I realized the way I'd been selling our data migration services wasn't as efficient as it could be. With the help of my technical assistant, we'd been selling to companies individually. But I soon saw that we could bundle our product with another company's and get them to make the sale for us.

I identified a software firm in Boston that had hundreds of salespeople and sold millions of dollars of software. I set my sights on getting to know their team and explore the idea of partnership.

"Hey, Greg, it's Donald at I-Cubed…"

Click

"Hey, Dave, it's Donald Thompson at I-Cubed…"

Click

"Hi, Jeff, it's Don at I-Cubed…"

Click

And so it went. But I knew I just needed to connect with a couple of the three hundred salespeople, and it would all be worth it.

"Hey Lawrence, it's Donald Thompson from I-Cubed."

"Yeah?"

That was a good sign. No dial tone.

"I know you're busy. Can I take up two minutes of your time to talk about bundling our data migration services with the software you're selling? Once those engineering companies upgrade their software, you know they're going to need to migrate designs to a new server. Why not have that solution in place and built into the package you offer them?"

"How much?"

A lot of these salespeople were ex-athletes or ex-military. I had noticed that along with that pedigree often comes a certain amount of aggression. Is that a stereotype? Sure, but I had plenty of experience that revealed it was frequently true, and I'm including myself as a prime example. I could play the same game, and if it came down to sheer grit, I knew I was going to win.

"We'll want seventy-five grand. You could charge whatever you want for the package."

Lawrence scoffed, but he didn't hang up. He must have had a few extra minutes in his schedule and decided to use them to try to intimidate me. Which, of course, is exactly the kind of environment I love. There was nothing he could dish out that I couldn't handle. Let the sparring begin.

"Donald, was it? Why would you think I'd be interested in a deal like this? I have a $10 million quota. I'm pretty sure that talking to you isn't going to help me meet that."

"I understand you're successful, Lawrence. May I call you Larry? But the thing is, Larry, if you keep an open mind, we can explore not only how to secure your quota but also how to create a dominant position with your customer while still building trust."

Larry didn't answer. He didn't want to give me any credit, but I knew he was interested. I forged ahead.

"You see, when you displace your competitor's technology platform, your customer is going to be concerned about how their mission-critical data will be safely migrated from the old system to the new one. We have a patented technology and the expertise to eliminate this concern. I'm calling you now because it's in both our interests to bundle I-Cubed's products with your services, and the news should come from you, their trusted advisor. If I call the customer directly, which I will—" I paused to let this bomb drop. "Well, then I'm just afraid it will seem like you hadn't done your homework on your client's needs."

I counted to five, giving my words time to sink in. I imagined Larry's face—somewhere between furious and dumbstruck—and enjoyed it.

"Wouldn't you like to control that conversation," I continued. "Rather than be the topic of it when I call them?"

Larry cleared his throat. "Assuming I wanted to hear more, let's get to the bottom line. What's in it for me?"

"I'm not sure what I can do for you personally, Larry, but I know what we can offer your customers. Fast, reliable, secure data transfer. We work with some big names in engineering and design, and they'd be happy to sing our praises if your customers have any questions."

"Fine. We can try this with a few of my smaller deals, and if you support my sales the way you describe, maybe we can make some cash together."

"Perfect. I'll reach out to your assistant and get a call set up for early next week, maybe try to get one of our technical engineers on the phone too. Looking forward to doing business with you, Larry." I didn't wait for him to object before saying goodbye and hanging up.

Generally, if I could get that far in the discussion, I'd be able to get the salesperson to agree to a partnership. Each of the salespeople at that Boston firm had ten to fifteen accounts. My relentless calls and ability to spin refusals into possibilities eventually led to partnerships with two or three of the people on that team. As a result, I got I-Cubed services into the hands of more than fifty new customers each quarter.

These deals grew out of the lessons I'd learned from Dad's coaching and my own football experience: a team is more powerful than an individual. I learned not to think small about who I included on my team. I couldn't have gotten I-Cube's software and services into some of those major companies alone. We were just too small. Being open to all types of partnerships that would help to close the deal meant our team had more opportunities to win.

After just a few quarters, I became the highest producing salesperson Grant had ever worked with. In response to the way I amplified the company's presence in the engineering and design tech world, Grant promoted me to director of partner relations. The role hadn't even existed before, but Grant created it based on my strengths and the value I brought to the company. It came with a nice little raise, some stock options, and a whole lot more opportunity.

I didn't foresee it back then, but ultimately, this move would pay off big time. The lesson I learned is that, whenever possible, it makes sense to take less money but more options in a growing firm. Ownership matters.

One of my first priorities was to figure out a way to grow that didn't include expanding our workforce. Instead, I wanted our engineers and technicians to be working on projects that stoked their passion, challenged them, and kept them engaged.

After about four years at I-Cubed, I'd formed strong relationships across the tech industry. These connections helped build the brand and let customers know that we could do more than just migrate their data, including creating technical solutions. I established strategic partnerships with other software companies in which we built out certain pieces of technology that they added to their products. Again, someone else was doing the sales portion for us, saving us both money and time. As long as we were embedded in other products, we stayed relevant and successful.

Bringing these relationships to the table had advantages externally for the company and for me specifically. Some of Grant's business burden eased. He was more interested in engineering work than in the hard, smooth talk that sales required. Giving Grant creative freedom was a huge benefit for both me and him. I could handle the sales and marketing load, while he spent more time inventing cool stuff. This new role felt like the perfect blend of my core strengths. I was working as a teammate to build I-Cubed, while using my sales and marketing skills to make myself indispensable.

Of course, as in any relationship, Grant and I had some differences to work through. Each of us had habits the other couldn't stand. From Grant's perspective, my sheer stubbornness caused was aggravating. From my perspective, it seemed like Grant had a tendency to wade too deep into details that other people should have been handling.

Like good partners though, Grant and I worked together to solve problems and create opportunities, despite some style issues. Before it sounds like I'm complaining, let me say that I cannot overemphasize Grant's sheer generosity. Not only did he offer us all health insurance at zero cost. he also made sure the plan he offered was best for absolutely everyone at I-Cubed. For example, the company had planned to switch insurance plans while my wife was pregnant with Ciera, our second child. Realizing it would cost us much more money, Grant postponed the change until after the pregnancy care and birth.

Many other people also benefited from his care, intention, and thoughtfulness. At one point, we had a technical writer who was battling cancer. When her treatments started to impact her ability to keep working at the intense pace required by the job, she approached Grant, thinking that she might have to leave the business. Together, they made the decision to part ways, but instead of letting her go with no support, Grant kept her on for three more months while she looked for a less demanding position. Then, he paid her salary for another six months and kept her on the company insurance for more than a year until she transitioned to her new employer's plan.

Grant never advertised the lengths he went for this one employee. Doubtless there were many others. I only knew because, by that point, he and I were discussing most of the significant business decisions.

Realizing Grant would go that far for an employee only increased my loyalty to him. He wasn't a pushover by any stretch, but he also knew how to lead with compassion. He understood that to manage effectively, he should get to know his employees as people. I saw that trait in him every morning when he stopped by my desk to say hello. We'd check in about sales and partnerships, but he always asked about my family and folks—all of whom he'd met at social events.

When I transitioned to my new role, I spent time considering what I needed to do to help Grant become more comfortable giving up the reigns a little. Once I had a plan, I decided I'd bring it up next time he got bogged down in details.

One day, Grant knocked on my office door and walked in. "Hey, Don, I need you on a new project." He took a seat facing my desk. "John Deere is looking for proposals, and I want us to submit something."

I flipped through my Rolodex. "I've got their lead sales guy's number right here."

"Great. Here's what I think we should do first..."

As Grant outlined the plan, I unveiled my new strategy.

When he paused for breath, I jumped in. "Before you get into that, can I ask something?"

Grant looked up, startled and slightly thrown off his groove. "Yeah. What's up?"

"I want to make sure I have something straight. Is this the kind of project you want to be deeply involved in? You driving...me along for the ride?"

Grant frowned. "Well, no. You're more than capable of handling this."

"Great. Here's what I'm going to do. I'll draft a quarter of the proposal and run it by you. That way I'm not so far along that there's no turning back."

Grant nodded slowly. "Yeah...yeah. That's perfect." He warmed to the idea as he realized what it meant. "You check with me with the overview, and I'll let you know if it's going in the right direction."

"Sounds like a plan," I said.

Grant beamed. "Excellent." He slapped the desk as he stood. "Well, I'll let you get to it, then. Good talk."

Once I heard Grant's footsteps fade down the hallway, I let out the chuckle that had been building while we talked. The plan had worked. Grant would get oversight, but I'd get a chance to work with the team and gain some new experiences. From then on, I used that strategy for most new projects.

I'd find out what kind of project we were starting and break it into delivery points for Grant. The strategy made me more productive, while also keeping Grant updated.

I made sure to always approach him with several options. Rather than simply letting him know there was a problem with a deliverable or telling him about an unhappy client, I explained the issue and then suggested three or four ways we could solve the challenge. Giving him options let him spend less time trying to come up with fixes from scratch and also gave him ideas on which solutions to build out.

The experience taught me yet another important lesson: when you take weight off your manager or boss, you become exponentially more valuable. Because I knew I could do my job well and that Grant didn't need to be involved in every step, I got projects eighty percent complete, then brought him in to finalize that final twenty percent. My work meant he didn't have to do it all by himself anymore.

Once I showed how much I could bring to I-Cubed, Grant invested in me more, gave me greater responsibility, and consulted me on more critical decisions. The more I gave him in productivity, the more he gave me in opportunity.

Eventually, I was promoted to vice president of business development. I heard about the promotion in a meeting with Grant and Ned, but I wasn't the first person to find out. The day before he talked to me, Grant had told one other person about the promotion…my dad.

I wouldn't find this out until later, of course. When I called my dad to tell him the news, he responded in a tight, constrained tone, not like him at all. I expected him to be more excited and couldn't understand the subdued reaction. I pressed him and, at last, he burst out laughing, telling me he already knew.

"Hang on, what? How could you have known?" I asked, frowning as I tried to sort it out.

"Grant called," he replied, still chuckling softly. "He said he wanted to tell me first."

"Really? That's…"

I didn't know what it was. Then I decided. It was cool. Grant knew how much I felt I owed my folks and wanted them to share the big news. Yeah, it was an incredibly cool move.

"That's awesome, Dad."

"At first I didn't know *what* was happening. I thought for a minute—" Dad laughed again at the memory. "Like it was going to be like old times, and he was calling to say 'Mr. Thompson, come get Don. He's selling candy at the office!'"

For a while, neither of us could get a word out as we laughed. Finally, Dad caught his breath.

"But then Grant told me you were going to be vice president. Said he was so comfortable leaving things in your hands that he was going to take his first vacation since he started the company." Dad cleared his throat. "I'm proud of you."

I smiled. I took a breath. I kept smiling. We didn't have the kind of relationship where we shared our appreciation all the time, so this expression of approval meant a lot. Even though we didn't say it, I was sure we both were thinking of all we'd gone through together. My decision to leave school had hurt my parents deeply. I knew that winning would be the only way to heal that disappointment. Today, I'd won big.

"Thanks, Dad. I've got so many ideas for this company. Gonna make Grant a lot of money."

"Oh, yeah? And what plans are those, Mr. Big Shot?"

My smile widened. This was more familiar territory.

"See, I was at Costco last week, and I saw a *great* deal on Jolly Ranchers—"

I couldn't even finish the joke, we were both laughing too hard.

And so, a little more than five years after I started at I-Cubed, at just thirty-one-years-old, I became a vice president at a fast-growing technology company.

I also became a dad for the third time. That was the year our son was born. We named him David, after the hero of my favorite Bible story.

"A slayer of giants," I said as I held him for the first time. "Just like his dad."

Good Cop, Bad Cop, and Riding Shotgun

As I-Cubed's second in command, I started to feel like Grant's partner. For those first five years, I had been constantly learning under Grant's mentorship. As vice president, I became a more prominent voice. Grant and I balanced each other out. Where one of us had a weak point, the other was strong. Together, there was almost nothing we couldn't handle.

When we had to, we even did a little "good cop/bad cop" routine. Once, not long after my promotion, I had a phone call with an account rep for an automotive company in Germany. The guy was so furious that he couldn't keep his languages straight. He yelled in English and then in German. When that failed, he launched into a hybrid of the two. It didn't matter that I didn't have a translator. I understood exactly what he was saying.

While he shouted, I held the phone away from my ear, waiting for him to take a breath. I knew this was a multimillion-dollar account and that we'd had problems meeting their expectations in the past. I also knew that what he was complaining about was something for which we hadn't yet found a fix.

When he finally paused, I jumped in fast before he could get revved up again. "I'd like to get Grant on the line to help us understand the specific technical issues and possible fixes. Would you mind holding?"

"I will hold as long as it takes to fix this piece of—"

"Okay, great."

Grant sighed as I finished describing the conversation so far. "I'll talk to him. I mean, he's right though. It doesn't work the way it's supposed to work for them."

"What are you going to say?"

Grant looked down at the blinking light on his conference phone.

"I'll figure it out in a second." He lifted the phone receiver, pressed the hold button, and said, "This is Grant."

From my seat, I could hear the guy lighting into Grant, just like he had with me. Grant pressed his lips together, clearly aggravated that he couldn't get a word in.

Finally, the client paused, allowing Grant to cut in. He responded, saying, "Well, when you're up to date on your royalty payments, we'll fix what's wrong." Then he slammed down the phone.

I practically had to lift my jaw off the ground. A bug in our software was holding up a multimillion-dollar order for our partner. Though his cursing was a little over the top, he had legitimate reason to be angry.

"What just happened?"

Grant shrugged. "The software is broken, and I don't know how to fix it right now. I needed more time to figure out what we're going to do. If you had any better ideas than me hanging up on him, you should have chimed in earlier."

"Fair enough," I laughed. "I didn't have anything in mind. But if that guy was mad before, just think of what he's going to be like now. I'm going to have to do some serious damage control."

"I know," Grant said, looking apologetic. Then he shrugged again and grinned. "But that's what you're good at—smoothing things over. Meanwhile, I'll get with the engineers and figure out a way to fix this."

The outrageous thing is that the plan worked. I repaired the relationship, while Grant and the team fixed the software. We learned to divide our work. I worked with people. Grant worked with product.

At that stage in my career, being the number two fit me. I supported Grant and learned by observation. In addition, I felt some security knowing that the buck had to go one more person up the chain. If something didn't work, if a project tanked, those results would be pinned on the leader, not me. As second in command, I got most of the freedom and control I wanted without having to shoulder the same burdens as Grant. It was one thing for me to have wanted that control on the football field as quarterback, but it was a whole different thing to have it in business. Football has rules. Business is all trial and error. Some errors could cost everyone in the organization their livelihoods, and that's a lot of pressure. As big as my ego was, I knew I wasn't ready for the number one spot.

As Grant's right-hand man though, I realized that, for the first time in my working life, I could settle into one position. I didn't have to keep multiple irons in the fire, waiting to see which prospects worked out. As a result, after six years in the business, I moved away from Amway. In the past, I'd assumed it was going to be my golden ticket to success, but after becoming vice president, I saw that my future was in the tech sector. Amway had been good to me and taught me many skills. However, I had a responsibility. I needed to be one hundred percent focused and not get distracted by the effort it took to maintain a side business.

A few weeks later, my life veered once again when I got a call from Adobe. They were accepting proposals for a new partnership program that would concentrate on manufacturing. Adobe executives believed I-Cubed might be a good fit. The rep wanted to know if I was interested.

"Sounds good," I said. An intriguing prospect, but I didn't give it much thought. "We'll put something together for you."

And with that, our collaboration began—one that would have a huge impact on I-Cubed, Grant, and me.

14

THE OPPORTUNITY OF A LIFETIME

"Well, thanks so much, Jeff. You've given us a lot to think about. Don and I will talk with the rest of the team. We'll reconnect with you after the weekend."

Grant reached over to the office phone on the table between us and ended the conference call. His hand sat still on the table for a minute, as if he were too stunned to move. Then, he looked up at me, and we stared at each other in silence.

After a minute, I said slowly, "Did you hear that?"

"Of course I did." Grant sat so far back in his chair that the springs creaked.

"And?" I asked. Grant always let silence linger when he was deep in thought.

Suddenly he stood, his chair bobbing. "Let's get going. We've got work to do!" He jogged toward the door.

"Whoa. We need to talk about that." I pointed to the phone. Lowering my voice so no one else could hear, I added, "Adobe wants to buy us out."

"I can't think about that right now," he said, waving me away. "I told them I'd consider it, and I will, once I run that authentication login through beta testing."

"All right, all right. When you're ready to figure this out, you know where to find me."

I watched him walk down the hall toward where the engineers worked. Grant was still hands-on when it came to the technical side of the business. The suggestion from our contact at Adobe had clearly thrown him for a loop. When he wanted to get his mind off something, he liked to dive into the complex technological details.

On the other hand, I couldn't stop thinking about Adobe's offer. This was a huge deal, especially for our little company. Adobe hadn't even fully vetted us as a partner, but apparently they'd decided that they wanted to own—not just borrow—what we had to offer.

I walked down the hall to my office, only vaguely aware of what was going on around me. When my coworkers smiled and greeted me as usual, I basically responded on autopilot. My mind was miles away, considering all that their offer presented. If Grant decided to sell, I-Cubed would become part of a huge corporation, a brand that was an industry standard and household name. I could hardly get my head around it. What would that mean for us? What would that mean for me?

I sat at my computer and opened the email I'd been working on before the Adobe call. After typing the same sentence three times, I closed it. I needed to think.

When I'd first started working on the partnership with Adobe, both companies had laid out clear goals. Grant and I wanted the stability, visibility, and of course, money that working with a huge company might bring. Adobe wanted our expertise in engineering and manufacturing to help get their products into new markets. In our initial talks, we focused on ways they could use our engineering heritage and map that with their PDF technology enabling clients to move and manage design-based data.

My strategy had been to get our products included in other people's deals. Basically, I wanted them to do the selling for us. To be included in Adobe's suite of tools—well, that was the dream for a small tech business. On our end, we'd get brand exposure and reach more clients than we ever could on our own. On Adobe's end, they'd get our product and additional sales and marketing support. We'd write white papers and work with their sales team to help them reach the right clients with the right message at the right time.

Adobe liked that we came with a solid reputation in the areas where they were trying to grow, but that didn't mean they were just going to jump into business with us, no questions asked. As is typical of big and well-respected companies, Adobe didn't partner with just anyone. They had spent much of the past year doing their due diligence about I-Cubed, Grant, and me—researching and getting to know our company and our team on a personal level—but they had made no decisive moves.

Over that span, however, the factors influencing Adobe's decision had shifted dramatically, altering the course of our relationship. The first major change seemed like it could be a promising development: Adobe had discovered Grant's side project in digital rights management. This technology would enable engineering and manufacturing firms to password-protect documents, track who opened documents, and trace unauthorized attempts to access information. They were immediately interested, understanding that Grant's work would be attractive to the engineering and manufacturing firms they courted. The technology could prevent prototypes and designs from being leaked to competitors. The more they learned about this side project, the more interested they became—to the point that they were hardly paying any attention to the data migration technology they had originally wanted.

The second change was less encouraging. For the last few years, I-Cubed had been working with a technology firm in Massachusetts. Every year, the company doubled the amount of work we did for them until they became about 85 percent of our business. It probably wasn't a smart business move, eggs in one basket and all, but the steady increase in revenue was easy to justify. The steady and ever-expanding business was a drug that kept us growing at a nice clip each quarter. We were addicted. Since we didn't have another source for that drug, we weren't in any hurry to replace them as our biggest client.

Then, without warning, everything changed.

One afternoon, Ian, our contact there, called and told us that they'd found a group in India who did what we did for ten cents on the dollar. We were being replaced.

Of course, it wasn't as simple as just cutting ties. The company had been so deeply involved with I-Cubed for so long that a lot of their projects used our technology. To find a way to go on without us would take them some time.

That phone call with Ian started the complicated process of our biggest customer slowly taking its business away from us bit-by-bit. Instead of the three-year contracts we were used to, we ended up with a series of ninety-day contracts. When one expired, they'd see if they still needed us. If so, they'd renew for another three months. If not, we were done.

This gradual withdrawal was tough, but not nearly as difficult as it would have been if the company had pulled the plug all at once. At least this way, we had time to figure out what we were going to do to replace their business. Grant and I pooled our brainpower into looking for new ways to keep I-Cubed solvent—new customers, new packages, and new budget strategies.

But the answer was in front of us. Once Adobe knew about Grant's side project, they'd gone from lukewarm potential partners to eager buyers over the course of a few weeks. They launched negotiations to buy the digital rights technology. Their initial price was a great start.

Our major challenge was that Adobe didn't want the rest of our company—and by "the rest," I mean "almost the entire thing." The digital rights management project was still in its early stages, not even factoring too heavily into most of our business, so even if the Adobe buyout solved our cash flow problems, it left us with another dilemma. Without our biggest client, how would the remaining company stay in business?

Grant Makes a Decision

"Why wouldn't they want the most profitable part of the business?"

The day after Adobe called with the acquisition offer, Grant and I were sitting on a bench by the Oval, the main quad on Centennial Campus.

"Because they like your technology," I shrugged. "It fits exactly into their business model." I pulled my coat tighter around me as the wind whipped and the temperature dropped.

North Carolina was inching toward winter. Grant and I had been walking the campus trails nearly an hour. I wasn't complaining—I'd tolerate anything short of frostbite to help make this decision—but I secretly wished Grant did his best thinking in a heated office.

"But all they want is the digital rights program…the four people who worked on it and me," Grant explained, again dragging his hand through his hair for the fiftieth time. "It seems like they're missing the bigger picture." He put his elbows on his knees and stared aimlessy out at the browning grass.

I knew the deal caused Grant to lose sleep. He wanted a perfect outcome, but that isn't how business deals usually work. I knew it and so did he. Grant needed to hear that his employees would be okay—even without him—and even without I-Cubed.

My perspective was different. Everyone on the team was smart and capable. Otherwise, they wouldn't have been there. We would be fine. Personally, as much as I didn't want this chapter of my life to end, I knew I'd land on my feet. I had gained experience and wisdom working day-to-day with Grant. This was a priceless education. For me, there would be more opportunities now than ever before.

"Grant, you know I'm fine with this deal."

He sat up and looked at me with a puzzled expression. I continued: "You do what you need to do with Adobe. I support your decision no matter what."

Grant smiled and put up his hand, shielding his eyes from the sun. "You wouldn't want to come to Adobe with me, would you?" he asked. "I could fight for you to be part of the deal."

"We can worry about those details later," I laughed. "First, we need to focus on what you're going to do."

"You're right," he said, nodding. "I just need a little more time. I'll have a firm answer by the end of the day—promise."

That evening, I knocked on Grant's open door. He smiled and waved me in. "What's it going to be?"

For a minute, Grant didn't say anything. He just sat behind his desk with a blank expression on his face, twisting the cap of a pen he had in his hands. I let the silence drag on, figuring he must be gearing up for something. I was sure we had both reached the same conclusion. He placed the pen on the desk and rested his hands in his lap, staring down at them. When he looked back up, his expression was calm, resolved.

"Donald, you know this company means the world to me. I grew it from nothing. It's my baby." He sighed. "But I've decided that it's time to let I-Cubed go. I've had a good run here, but now it's time for me to try something else. And of course, I'm going to make sure that you all are taken care of."

"It's the right thing to do, Grant." I nodded toward the phone. "Do you want me to call Adobe?"

"I already did," he said. "They're coming in two days."

Grant's New Boss

The post-offer visit didn't take long. Adobe had already done all its research and was ready to jump on the deal. A few of the people from their new manufacturing division flew in one morning, we all had lunch, and then we sat down in the conference room to begin signing papers. The transaction turned out to be straightforward. Adobe would take the digital rights technology, the engineers, and Grant. All of this would happen in three weeks. After the uncertainty, tension, and hope leading up to this moment, simply signing a few papers felt anticlimactic.

But the deal wasn't settled quite yet.

During the signing, Grant seemed concerned. He stood by the whiteboard at the front of the room with his arms folded. He looked on as Pete, who'd be his new boss, skimmed several documents a final time.

"What do we do with the rest of the people at the company?" Grant asked. "I can't let twenty people go right before the holidays."

Pete stood up, holding a pen for Grant. He shrugged. "You'll need to decide how much severance you want to give them. If you're generous, you'll give two months. If you want to maximize the deal, you'll give two weeks."

Grant took the pen and sat down to sign the documents. After all the congratulations, handshaking, and backslapping, Grant prepared to accompany the Adobe team to the airport. He ushered them to the door. However, before he left, he turned back and whispered.

"No way," he said in a low voice and keeping one eye on the door. "I'm not treating our people that way. Meet me here when I get back."

While he was gone, I racked my brain for solutions. In the end, I had decided to turn down the offer to join the team in San Jose. Suddenly, I was in a vulnerable position, but more importantly, I didn't want to see my fellow I-Cubed employees without jobs.

While I considered different options, Grant came back with a bounce in his step. "Okay Donald, I have a plan," he announced. He rolled up his shirt-sleeves, explaining, "If we're going to pull this off, we've got a lot of work to do. Are you up for it?"

I grinned…"I can't believe you have to ask."

"I've been mulling this over for a while now," he said. "I think I have a way that I can hand my company over to someone I trust."

"What do you mean?" I frowned. "Did you get another offer?"

"No, I didn't *get* another offer," he countered. "I want to *make* an offer. To you. I want you to own the company. But not just you—all our core employees. I'm going to sell it to all of you. And it's not going to cost you a dime."

Over the next week, Grant and I wrote up a plan for an employee-led buyout of the majority of the company that Adobe hadn't purchased. Grant had always owned most of I-Cubed's stock. As the company grew, though, he had looked for ways to get it into employees' hands. First, we transferred all the stock he still owned to the core employees who weren't going to California. With that transfer and some fancy money maneuvers, as well as Grant's continued generosity, sixteen I-Cubed employees were able to buy the company for business profits. We'd pay nothing out of pocket and would pay Grant back over three years until we owned the company outright.

Even after the lawyers had been over the paperwork and finalized the agreement, I still could hardly believe it had actually happened. Not only had Grant kept the company together, but he'd also figured out a way to allow us a true stake in the business we all loved. I was riding high on the knowledge that, in a few years, I wouldn't just be working *for* I-Cubed—I would be an *owner*. At that moment, I couldn't imagine how life could get any better.

A New Chief

"Don, there's something I want to talk to you about," Grant said. He held his napkin loosely and dabbed at his mouth.

We had taken a lunch break, going out for pizza at a restaurant with a covered patio. As I knew all too well from our walks, Grant liked to talk business in the fresh air.

"Okay. What is it?"

"I've been thinking a lot about the structure when I leave—"

"Grant," I interrupted. "I told you, don't worry about that now. You have more than enough going on. We'll figure it out later."

Grant was a lifelong North Carolinian, but in just two weeks, he had to hit the ground running in San Jose. Everything was changing so quickly that Grant's wife Laura, who did I-Cubed's bookkeeping, was staying in Raleigh to work on the transition.

Grant shook his head. "I know you can handle it, but I'm not going to feel settled out there unless I know there's a plan in place. I want to make sure the company is in good hands. I've thought about it a lot, and Don, you were instrumental in building this company and in figuring out this deal. I think you'll continue to help us grow."

I chewed slowly on my bite of pepperoni pizza and searched Grant's face for a clue to where he was going with this.

"There are plenty of people at I-Cubed who are very talented—people with impressive resumes who have a lot of experience leading engineers and developing products," he explained. "But the more I've thought about it, I don't believe that's what it's going to take to lead the company into the future. I think it's going to take someone who can think differently about the potential."

He paused...looking me in the eye: "And I think that person is you. I want you to take over as President and CEO."

I froze mid-chew!

For a second, all the ideas that usually kept my mind running in overdrive screeched to a halt. I wanted to say something—anything—but I couldn't seem to remember how to make words come out of my mouth. I just stared.

"You're speechless!" Grant laughed. "I should get a prize for being the first person to ever leave Donald Thompson at a loss for words!"

The joke jolted my brain back into motion. I swallowed hard, shaking my head. "This is mind-blowing. I never imagined running I-Cubed. I always thought, as long as I was with the company, I'd be working for you. Working *with* you." At just thirty-six, I knew the future had great things in store, but part of me couldn't believe it was all happening so soon.

Grant tilted his head and gave me a disapproving look. "Come on. You've been a great number two, but you know that's not your future. This is your time, Donald."

As I tried to process the news, Grant continued: "I wish I could tell you exactly what you're going to need to do and what you're going to face. But I can't. I'm so excited about your future and to be able to offer you this opportunity. And of course, I'll always be available if you have questions or want to bounce around ideas."

I had a sudden flashback. I was four or five, skinny, and squirmy, standing with my father on the dock of a swimming pond near our house. We watched the other kids splash and scream.

"I can swim, Dad," I said confidently.

"Son, you can't swim," he said patiently. "You've never even been in the water."

"Yeah, I can though, Daddy. I definitely can."

He sighed and picked me up. "You can?"

I nodded.

"You ready?"

I nodded.

He tossed me in.

Splashing, coughing, and sputtering. A minute of kicking, sinking, and kicking again. Then, thankfully, my father's strong hand on my skinny bicep, pulling me up out of the water.

"You can swim, huh?"

I spit water, coughed once, and brushed more water from my eyes. Then I looked up at my father. "Yeah, I *can* swim. I just need a little more *practice.*"

Throw me in that water, Grant. I got this.

We shook hands, sealing my new position—the biggest opportunity I had ever earned. Ten years before, Grant had bet on me, and I had bet on him. Although he hadn't paid what I wanted at the time, I had the sense that under his mentorship, the possibilities were limitless. I knew we had both placed a bet and both won.

With my support, he'd sold his technology for top dollar. With his backing, I was holding the keys to the kingdom.

Now I just had to make sure I didn't mess it up.

15

SHARED RISK, SHARED REWARD

Monday morning. 2005. Just two months after Adobe called Grant offering to buy part of the company.

I woke up suddenly, feeling a jolt of panic. Had I overslept? Was I late? Why wasn't the alarm going off? I reached over to the bedside table and pulled the clock toward me, squinting at the blurry neon numbers. No, I wasn't late. I was early. Even earlier than usual. It was 4:15 a.m. My alarm wouldn't go off for over an hour. Everything was dark and quiet. No birds chirping, not a car on the street, and no kids arguing about the bathroom.

I lay back on my pillow and stared at the ceiling. Maybe I should try to close my eyes for a little bit longer. Last night, I'd been on the phone with Grant until almost midnight. Now that he was in California, the three-hour time difference meant our calls had to happen early in the morning for him or late at night for me. After that, I spent some time going over numbers before going to bed. Even then, I hadn't been able to get to sleep for what felt like hours. It wasn't that I was nervous. I mean, yes, I had some new-job jitters, but it was nothing serious. In a few hours, I would be walking into the same place I'd been going for ten years. I'd see the same faces, minus the several who were now living in Silicon Valley.

No, the feeling that had kept me from sleeping that night and woken me so early in the morning wasn't nerves. It was more like determination. *I have to get this right. I will get this right.* There was so much riding on my success as head of I-Cubed. My performance would impact my career, of course, and the well-being of my family, but I was also now also responsible for a whole company, *their* careers, and *their* families. Also, I thought about my responsibility to Grant. He'd entrusted me. My job hinged on leading the team we'd built together.

The importance of the moment was on my mind too. I finally had my chance to be a business leader. This idea wasn't lost on me. If I blew it, I might not get another shot.

While I had spent the previous evening planning and studying, I also took the time to call my father. I just wanted to hear his voice, talk about football, and get a break from the pressure. He was encouraging, but as I should have expected, he also gave me some real talk. In his coaching career, he never lost sight of the reality of what it took to be a Black man in a high-pressure, high-prestige job. The opportunities were harder to get, so when he got a chance, he knew he had to work twice as hard and be twice as good.

My position wasn't all that different. I was a Black CEO in a field where almost no one looked like me. And what's more, I didn't have a typical CEO pedigree. I realized the need to prove myself would probably never end.

As I lay there going over my to-do list, schedule, and the conversation I had with my father, I could feel the weight of what stood before me. It was heavy, but not more than I could bear. This would be my biggest test yet—my personal David and Goliath moment. I felt ready.

I glanced at the clock again. 4:45. The day still hadn't begun, but clearly I wasn't getting any more sleep. Might as well get up and get a jumpstart on the day.

I'm not a big clothes guy, so picking out my outfit was fast and easy. After a final glance in the mirror, I gave myself a quick thumbs-up. "*Looking sharp, Mr. CEO.*" Then I shook my head, laughing. It was good to know that even with a fancy new job and title, I could still be completely ridiculous.

The drive into work was quick at this early hour. Only a handful of cars were on the road. Alone with my thoughts, I remembered the struggles early in my career—living on bulk sale potatoes, barely making rent, the mountain of late payments, and even the uncertain feelings about how I would support my family. Now, I was a CEO—It didn't seem real.

When I arrived, the office was dark, except for the few lights that stayed on overnight. I waved the key fob and let myself in. The walk down the hallway felt familiar yet different, like when you rearrange the furniture in your living room—it's still your stuff, but the place feels new and bigger. I stopped in the break room to get the coffee started…my usual job. The engineers had always complained that I made it too weak, but I didn't care. In fact, I jokingly worked out an equation that proved by eliminating a mere one scoop per pot, I saved us a solid chunk of change over the course of a year.

However, as I reached for the filters, I paused and thought about what was happening in that moment. *I was the CEO—should I still be making the coffee?* I immediately tossed that passing thought into the mental garbage bin. Maybe some people thought a leader shouldn't brew coffee, but I wasn't one of them. There were many aspects I'd have to learn about this job, but one thing I knew for sure was that I wasn't going to do anything just because it *looked right*. That wasn't I-Cubed culture, nor was it my style.

Once the coffee had brewed, I poured a cup and continued down the hallway. When I got to my office, I didn't burst right in. Instead, I stood listening to the street coming alive outside. Pausing again, I took a breath.

As soon as I stepped through the door, it would begin. I sat my briefcase down, letting it fall against the wall. Instead of going through the door, I turned on my heels and continued down the hall. Stopping at the familiar door at the end of the hallway, I noticed the nameplate still affixed to the wall: Grant Williard, CEO.

Grant's old office was empty and dark. It took on a new feel. I remember thinking that the window blinds were drawn, which had never been the case when he was in. I didn't stay long, just took a quick look, and then headed back to my office. It felt surreal knowing that Grant wouldn't be arriving later, asking about my family, tinkering with new projects, or giving me grief about a deal that had been taking too long to close. For a decade, we'd spent so many hours together—every day, Monday through Friday, plus quite a few weekends when we had big projects on the line. I'd miss Grant. He was my boss, mentor, and friend. At the same time, though, I couldn't hide my excitement at the chance to make my mark on the company we both loved.

By the time the lights in the other offices started snapping on and people trickled in, I'd set my big picture reflections aside, already deep into the day's work. As my colleagues—my *employees*, I corrected myself—walked by my office, they waved and greeted me as usual. Some stuck their heads in to congratulate me and ask how it felt to be in charge. A few even gave me some good-natured teasing. Did I take the corporate jet to work this morning? Would I be having lunch in the executive dining room? I laughed. I knew that the team respected me and what I had been able to accomplish thus far.

Amid the familiar hum of the office springing into action, I reviewed my calendar. Unsurprisingly, it was packed. I was glad I'd carved out some time to myself before the day started at full tilt.

First on the list: "Company-wide meeting." I'd scheduled this meeting weeks ago, as soon as all the paperwork had been signed. I wanted ensure that the sixteen team members at I-Cubed came together before the holidays so that no one left for vacation feeling like there were any unknown factors in the way of their work. I had already thought about some changes for later, but first I needed to get my bearings. While I did, we would continue, business as usual. I also wanted people to know that the I-Cubed fundamentals—the adventurous spirit, close-knit team, and the value that leaders placed on every employee—weren't going to change.

After that meeting was "Leadership Team Lunch." Then the whole afternoon and into the early evening was a solid block of back-to-back client calls. The Adobe deal had happened so quickly. Considering that we were still such a small company, no one in my former role. While I now had all the responsibilities of President and CEO, I also had all the same duties I'd had as VP of Business Development. Clients weren't going to stop calling with problems or presenting new partnership opportunities just because of the leadership change. Keeping that reality in mind helped me get through some of the difficult times during the transition. I couldn't get too caught up in the craziness. I had a job to do. Nothing would get done if I froze or choked. I had to keep moving forward.

The final item of the day made me smile: "Dinner with Dad and Larry Hines." Nearly twenty years after we first met, Larry, ECU's sports psychologist, had become my best friend. When I'd told him about the promotion, he had insisted on taking me out to dinner. Naturally, he invited my father to join us. I could already imagine the battle we'd have over who got to pay the bill, but I was determined to win that argument. After all these two men had done for me, it was the least I could do.

The promotion was a huge deal for my whole family, a real game-changer. I imagined that the path I'd be able to make for my children would be even smoother than the one my parents had made for me. But that didn't mean the change was easy. Sacrifice now for a big payoff later, that's what I always said. The sixty- and seventy-hour workweeks would be a distant memory when I was able to send my kids to college with their tuition checks in hand or do special things for my granny, still living down in Bogalusa.

I sighed, but then turned my attention back to the calendar. There was one item that didn't have a scheduled time: "Call Grant."

I reached for the phone and then glanced at the clock. It was only 6:30 a.m. in California. Grant would definitely be up. He had said to call him whenever I wanted. It was his first day at Adobe, so I figured he'd be caught up in preparations, just like I had been this morning. Then I thought—maybe I'll just let him call me when he gets the chance. As much as I wanted to chat, get his engineering perspectives, and maybe even argue with him, I also wanted to show him that I could do this on my own. I wanted to prove it to myself too.

I put down the phone and sent him an email instead. I told him how strange it was to be in the office without him, that I had a few thoughts to bounce around when he had time, and that I was looking forward to talking later.

In the meantime, I had a little window of time left before the company meeting. I pulled the files for the latest deal out of my backpack and started to read them over. This task was no different than it had always been, except that this time I couldn't pass the paperwork off to anyone else. *I* would finalize the deal and approve it. The buck stopped with *me*.

That thought interrupted my reading. It was funny—every time I thought I'd gotten my head around this promotion, I'd then experience a fresh wave of realization of what the job actually meant. From now on, it would all be on me.

I placed the contract on my desk and stared out the window. I was used to being part of a team—from football to sales to being Grant's lieutenant. I'd always worked with other people and we created solutions together. Even though I dreamed of leading a company, being alone at the top would take some getting used to.

So, I did what I'd done most days for the past decade. I pushed my chair back, left the office, and took a walk. Not a walk outside though—it was December and freezing. I wasn't going out in the cold unless I was making a direct path to a heated building. I'd been willing to follow Grant just about anywhere, but he and I didn't agree about what constituted "good" weather. *That's one perk of being CEO*, I thought. *Total walk location discretion.*

Instead of heading to the quad (and the cold), I went walked around inside the building. I stopped at cubicles and asked about people's families. I knocked on office doors and chatted about holiday plans. Then, with a grin on my face, I returned to my office ready to make some executive decisions.

Service with a Sneaker

There were many hurdles getting through the first few weeks. I went from working closely with Grant daily to talking to him just once a week. He commuted into San Jose, so he'd call while he was on the train. Often, he'd have to yell to be heard over the automated announcements, the rumbling rails, and the other Silicon Valley commuters. Sometimes, there was static and interference or the call would drop. It wasn't the best way to conduct business, but for a while, it was all we had. Grant was busy. Though he offered as much guidance as he could from the other side of the country, he was understandably focused his new role.

If there were a bonus to the distance, it was in providing me with time to think about the changes I wanted to make. As much as I had respected Grant, I had my own way of thinking. I realized it was time to put my ideas to the test and see if we could be successful.

Grant was a product person: an engineer at heart. His goal was to build and sell technology. On the other hand, I focused on service. I believed we could make much more money in a shorter time frame by offering services, such training and consulting. The problem with putting all our eggs in the product basket was that we could sink hundreds of thousands of dollars into building something that might fail when it went to market. When Grant ran I-Cubed, we were primarily a product company, although we did offer some services. During my early tenure, I decided that we would flip that dynamic and transition into a consultancy business.

The key to being successful is not to do too many new things all at once. We had a loyal customer base in the engineering and manufacturing fields, so we stuck with what we knew. Tech consulting isn't a new idea, but we had to find something that made us unique, something that gave us a competitive edge. For I-Cubed, that something was using engineers as consultants. We could send someone in to make tech recommendations, then that same person could come back and implement the recommendations. Once we got the word out to our customers, we started generating interest.

Of course, even the best-laid plans face some hiccups.

Several weeks into our rebranding effort, I'd convinced the team at the Hyundai KIA Motor Corporation to listen to what we had to offer. I brought James, one of our best engineers, to the meeting. He was young and super smart. I was sure he'd do a first-class job on anything that had to do with our technology. However, before we left for the meeting, a little voice in the back of my head suggested I might want to check with James before we left. He wasn't a salesperson, after all, so I wanted to make sure he was prepared for communicating with actual people, rather than computers.

A few minutes later, James knocked on my door and stepped into the office.

I took one look at him and shook my head. "No."

He tilted his head to one side. "No? What do you mean, 'no'?"

I pointed at his shoes. "Seriously, man? I mean, I love Adidas, but not for a business meeting."

He dug the toe of one sneaker into the carpet and sighed, "Yeah. I don't have any fancy shoes."

"Or clothes, apparently." It was a little harsh, but this was an important meeting. I didn't think I should have to tell an adult how to dress for work. "You couldn't even find nice slacks?"

He brushed some imaginary lint off his cargo pants. "I thought these were nice."

I grabbed the keys off my desk. "Come on. If we leave now, we can stop at a department store and pick up something more professional. At least some khakis and a polo."

To be fair, the office dress code was fairly casual. Most of us wore jeans. Still, it was an odd thing to have to teach someone how to dress for a client meeting, especially after my years in the sales world. When I'd started the engineers-as-consultants initiative, I'd known there would be a learning curve, but it wasn't until this moment that I understood the challenges wouldn't be only about sales training. It wasn't enough to teach the engineers how to pitch to clients or give them the right promotional material. I had to figure out how to lead employees who were much different from the salespeople I usually worked with and who felt very different than me.

The engineers at I-Cubed weren't aggressive and thick-skinned like the typical sales rep. For the most part, they were quiet, cerebral, creative, and really, really smart. They didn't think about what they looked like to the client because, in programming and development, no one cares how polished you appear. They only care how well you know your stuff. These people knew their stuff better than just about anyone else in the industry.

In the end, I didn't make a huge fuss about what they wore, as long as they were presentable. We let the customers know that our consultants generally show up wearing khakis rather than suits, but they could make much more effective tech recommendations because they knew the products inside and out. I did, however, draw the line at shorts.

The shift to a consultancy business took off within the first four or five months of my tenure as CEO. I'd taken what I learned under Grant and amplified it in a way that reflected my skills. Since I knew what I could do with five consultants, which is what the company had under Grant, I figured we could double the business with ten. The consultants interviewed customers to find our what kinds of products they built and what requirements our new technology would have to meet. Information—such as the number of employees at a customer's company, where and how they stored their data, how many subsidiaries they had, and whether any or all of those subsidiaries had in-house IT—all went into our analysis. We then offered up a portfolio of options that would meet their needs. Not only could we suggest the direction they should go in, we could also come back and implement the changes. We were proud of these new services: pleased with the comprehensiveness, quality, and innovation.

All this careful strategizing and implementation meant that I-Cubed had an extremely profitable year in 2006. The success felt well deserved, both for the company and for me. My leadership was the culmination of everything my family had given me and everything I'd had to hustle to earn myself. All those night shifts, all those go-nowhere sales calls, and all those peanut-butter-and-jelly-sandwich dinners—they finally paid off.

16

PLAY TO YOUR STRENGTHS

"So, Donald, how does it feel now that you've got a year under your belt?" Grant asked over the phone.

It was early January 2007, the first day back after the holidays—or at least, the first day back for most people. I'd taken Christmas Day off, but for most of the last two weeks, I'd been here working while the rest of the office was dark and silent. At least the buzz of the overhead lights kept me company. The time had been useful, giving me the chance to catch up on tasks that fell by the wayside during the normal rush. I'd also been able to talk to Grant more than usual.

Unlike me, he had taken the holidays off. Well, he could afford to. Adobe was a huge company. Certainly, it could run for a week or two without him. But I could also tell that he was getting a little restless, eager for the spontaneity and control he didn't get as just another employee in a big corporation. That probably accounted for the more frequent check-ins.

"It's amazing," I yelled back, hoping Grant could hear me over the noise of the train. "Did you see the numbers?"

As the sole member of the board, Grant received our year-end statement showing how much I-Cubed had accomplished in 2006.

"I did, and they look great." He paused for an announcement over the loudspeaker. "But remember, good times don't last forever."

"What? Those aren't 'good times don't last' numbers. They're 'completely crushing it' numbers."

Grant chuckled. "You're doing well, I'll give you that. Cash is king though. Just make sure that you always have money in reserve. You're still paying off the business, so try to hold off on accumulating additional debt."

"Not a problem. There's nothing in the pipeline that's going to need extra cash."

"What about ECF?"

Grant had a point. Although, normally, I was all about the services I-Cubed offered, recently I'd decided to invest in developing a new product called Enterprise Connection Framework, ECF for short. The idea was fantastic—middleware that could connect two different technology systems. Grant and I had talked about it at length. He'd approved the expenditure, and so we'd taken several of our consultants off the road and bringing them back into the office to be fulltime engineers on the project. I was sure we'd get a significant return on our investment, even though the project had just begun and we'd have to invest substantial time and money to finish it.

"Okay," I admitted. "The bank account is going to take a little hit on that but only for two or three months, tops. Then, we'll make a couple million from it at least."

"Right, but a verbal agreement to buy something isn't cash," Grant warned. "When they transfer funds from their bank account to yours, only then is it revenue. What about putting two people back into consulting and slowing down on ECF? Just to make sure you've still got money coming in."

"I don't know. I mean, I see what you're saying, but we can—"

There was another announcement, and Grant broke in.

"Sorry to cut you off. I'm at my stop. We'll talk about this more later, and in the meantime, give my suggestion a little thought, okay?"

I told him I would. For a few minutes after the conversation, I sat thinking. I knew Grant was trying to be helpful, but come on. I understood the difference between a promise and actual cash in the bank. Yes, ECF involved some risk, but every project does. My experience taught me that the greater the risk, the greater the reward. Without taking risks, I-Cubed would never grow, never change.

This was the right move. I was sure of it. But I guess it wouldn't hurt to talk things out with someone here in the office, closer to the situation. Grant was probably just uncertain because he didn't have the whole picture. I took a quick walk. As I rounded a corner, I saw a few people leaving Tony Pease's office. Once they'd gone, I ducked into the open door.

Tony had become vice president of business development when I became CEO. He'd questioned ECF from the start, so I asked him to talk to the two engineering leads on the project to get a better sense of what we were trying to accomplish. Since they'd all met a few days earlier. I figured Tony would now see things my way. After all, I was sure this project would turn out to be the beginning of my CEO legacy.

"Got a minute?" I asked Tony, who was erasing the whiteboard.

He checked his watch, "Just a few. I'm on a call at eleven."

"This won't take long. I just wanted to ask about your conversation with James and Al. Did you get a chance to check in?"

I leaned against the doorframe. No point in sitting down. I was going to get a nice dose of "You were right all along, Don!" and then I could get back to work, confident that we were on the right track.

After a short pause, Tony nodded. "Yeah, I talked to them."

I waited, but he didn't follow up with the reassurance I was expecting. Instead, Tony scowled.

"And?" I pressed him. "What did they say?"

"They have lots of ideas, and they're working hard, but it doesn't change my opinion. ECF is a good concept, but it's too ambitious right now. I don't think we should be pursuing it."

"But you just said that the engineers are on board!"

"Of course they are. They're engineers. They're all fired up about this cool, new idea that you're asking them to explore, and they're telling you what's possible. But Don, they're telling you what they *could* do, not what they *can* do. There's a big difference."

"I'm aware of that," I said, my face flushed. "But I trust our team. We're not just doing this thing on a whim. We have data that says it'll work. What data do you have to say that it won't?"

Tony shrugged one shoulder. "None. It's a gut feeling. But this is a huge risk, especially since we're still paying for the company. And I don't know why we're putting all this money into a product anyway. I mean, that's Grant's thing. You're a service guy, and you're good at it. Why not play to your strengths, right? You don't have to do things Grant's way to do a good job."

I clenched my jaw, drawing slow breaths. Once calmer, I said, "Look, I appreciate your honesty. You're a smart guy. You're still new to business though. I don't think you understand what we're going for. I may be new as CEO, but I've been in this industry a long time, and I think this is the right call. Unless you can give me some hard numbers on why ECF won't work, then I see no reason not to go ahead with it."

We stared at each other for a few beats without speaking.

Then Tony shook his head. "Well, it's your call. You're the boss."

For the rest of the day, I replayed the conversation in my head. Every time, I was more convinced that, in a few months, Tony would come around. He just didn't have the experience to see this thing from the right angle. Yes, it was a risk. I acknowledged that in every conversation I'd had with Tony and Grant, and even in my own mind. But we could take risks and still be smart about money.

I was sure I had everything under control. But I didn't.

Down at Halftime

A few months into the project, it was clear that the ECF plans weren't working out as I'd envisioned. The development process was not going as quickly as it should, and there was another, bigger problem. The software didn't work. On top of that, the people we had working on it weren't making the company any money. If they'd been on the road consulting, they could have been billing customers. Instead, we were spending money that would never be recouped. Between that and the cash that was going to pay off our debt to Grant, I-Cubed had developed a major cash flow problem.

In other words, Grant had been right. Cash *was* king. The realization came with an ugly feeling of déjà vu. The whole situation reminded me too much of the warning about credit cards my father had given me almost two decades earlier. In both cases, someone with more experience had offered me strong financial advice. In both cases, I'd been too sure of my own ideas to listen. Now, like then, I had to pay the price.

When I'd gotten those credit cards and racked up debt, only my family suffered. That had been bad enough. Now, my decisions had a ripple effect that extended far beyond my family. As the financial situation at I-Cubed worsened, it became obvious what I had to do. I spent a few sleepless nights wrestling with the problem, but that didn't change the outcome. If I wanted to save the company, I had to take drastic action.

It was nearly 11 p.m., and I was still at work. I was almost always the last one in the office, but this was late even for me. For the last few hours, I'd been going over the numbers, running the same calculations again and again. Before I made this decision, I'd wanted to check one more time, just in case there was money I'd somehow missed. But the numbers didn't change. They reaffirmed what I already knew.

I dialed Grant's number.

"Hey, Grant," I said when he answered. "Do you have a minute? Are you on the train?" I didn't want to have to shout through this conversation.

"No, made it home before eight for once. What's up?"

I took a deep breath. "Well, actually . . ."

I'd run through about a dozen ways to say this before I'd even picked up the phone, but no amount of rehearsing would make it easy.

"I screwed up, Grant. ECF—it's a total failure. All this time and work, and we don't have anything to show for it. It doesn't work, never has. We're losing money so fast I can barely keep up with it." I sighed. "You warned me about this. I should've listened."

I wanted to keep talking. Justify my choices. Explain myself. Instead, I said, "I'm sorry."

There was a long pause that made the knot in my stomach even tighter. Finally, Grant spoke.

"Well, it'd be easy for me to say, 'I told you so,' and part of me would like to. But that wouldn't be fair. I warned you about keeping an eye on the cash, but I thought ECF was a good idea too. I can't say that, in your shoes, I wouldn't have tried it."

"Thanks, Grant. That means a lot. But I can't help feeling like I let you down." I swallowed hard. "Because if you *had* done this, maybe you would have done it right. Maybe I'm not as good with products as you are."

To my surprise, Grant laughed.

I frowned. What could be so funny?

"Of course you aren't! How many times have I heard you say, 'Grant, you focus on the tech; I'll focus on the people'? More than I can count, and I'm an engineer, so I can count pretty high."

I chuckled. Even a bad joke was a relief right now.

"My point is," Grant went on, "You aren't a product guy, and that's fine. Because you're the best services guy I know, and that includes all these big shots in Palo Alto. Donald, there's a reason I left you in charge. But you can't try to do things the Grant Williard way. You're going to have to figure out how to lead I-Cubed your way. The Donald Thompson way."

I shook my head, smiling. "That's a good halftime locker-room speech, coach."

Grant laughed again. Then there was another pause, but things felt less tense this time. "All kidding aside, you have work to do, and we both know that the next few months aren't going to be pretty. But you can do this. I wouldn't have chosen you if I wasn't one hundred percent sure you could."

Mr. Cash Flow is King

In May of 2007, I-Cubed laid off—*I* laid off—seven people. These were seven people who had goals and dreams and families, who depended on me to steer them in the right direction—seven members of my team.

That Friday afternoon, as we called them one by one into the human resource director's office, the weight in my chest grew heavier and heavier with each conversation, until I could barely breathe. After the last meeting, I hurried down the back stairwell, almost jogging, bursting into the courtyard. It was a perfect day, warm and cloudless, but I couldn't enjoy it. A beautiful day felt wrong right now, when seven people were packing their belongings and getting ready to leave our offices for the last time.

I stood for a while, blinking in the sunlight, and taking in big gulps of air. I hadn't felt this bad since that day in the bathroom at Mr. Cash when I was facing eviction. But, there was one important difference between that scene and this one. Back then, the pain had come from the fact that, no matter how hard I worked, I couldn't get ahead. I'd felt like I was failing, but through no fault of my own, which had been deeply discouraging. Now, though, I was in charge. As bad as it felt to say, "This is my fault," there was power in that statement. If my choices had steered us in the wrong direction, then I believed that my new strategies could get us back on track.

Back inside, I called a company-wide meeting. I dreaded the idea of facing my remaining employees, but the alternative—letting them go home for the weekend to doubt their job security and me as a leader—was much worse. People assembled in the conference room in complete silence. They sat down and watched me with uncertainty in their eyes.

"Today, we had to let go of seven great people." My voice wavered. I cleared my throat and started again. "You all know that I-Cubed isn't a big company. And with today's events, we lost thirty percent of our team. This is not a shining moment for the business or for me personally."

I paused to look around the room. They looked like they'd been through it and back, and I felt the same way. In a company with only twenty-five employees, we all knew each other's names and enjoyed hearing about each other's families. The layoff would affect each and every one of us, not in the abstract but in concrete and measurable ways. I took a breath and went on.

"Of course, the bad news is the loss of our colleagues. That hurts all of us, and I won't try to insult you by sugarcoating it. But, for those of you who are still here and still willing to stick it out, I promise you that we will make this right. We've worked with Laura and consulted with the accountants, and today's layoffs will make up the difference in a fairly short time. We'll be profitable again in a few months."

Al Martel raised his hand. He was an engineer who wrote nearly flawless code. He was a big guy, gentle and soft-spoken as they come. He asked simply, "So…you're going to fix this?"

"Yes. I'm going to fix this," I nodded slowly, looking him straight in the eyes. "This will never happen again at I-Cubed."

Al nodded and sat back in his seat. "Well. Okay then."

With that, the remaining eighteen employees agreed to do their part in keeping I-Cubed moving forward. Nobody quit or deserted the ship, even when it looked like it was in danger of sinking. They stayed on, helped the company grow, and taught me to be a more careful leader.

By the third quarter of 2007, we broke even. We ended that year with a three percent profit. To get there, I started watching the money very carefully. Each day, I poured over spreadsheets and accounting forms.

Even though I was working long hours to make sure I kept I-Cubed progressing, I was also needed at home. David had started playing Little League baseball. At seven, he was still a little uncoordinated and struggled to compete, especially when at the plate. He had lots of people rooting for him, but he was also perceptive enough to know that he wasn't a superstar. Though David was a pretty confident and easygoing kid, that realization hurt.

If anyone knew about believing in yourself despite seemingly impossible obstacles, it was me. David was a lot like me. I knew if I could give his skills a boost, he'd find his confidence. He just needed to put in the work. In response, night after night, I'd come home as early as I could and throw the ball to him in the backyard. We'd stay out there until it got dark: me tossing pitch after pitch, David making swing after swing.

Over time, he got better and better, making consistent contact with the bat. Every time he did, he'd say, "Quick, throw another one, Dad." He worked to make them automatic: the right batting stance, handgrip, and hip rotation. He went from feeling down about his abilities to figuring out how he could get better.

In the last game of the season, David was up to bat with players on first and third. If just one of them scored, David's team would win. All he had to do was not strike out.

The first pitch came. David swung and missed. I took a deep breath and tried to concentrate for him. "Eye on the ball," I muttered to myself. I'd moved from my seat in the bleachers to stand along the first-base side, my fingers gripping the fence in anticipation. When the second pitch came, David's bat made contact. It was just a little dribbler into the outfield, but that didn't matter. The runner on third came home to score.

After the game, his teammates hoisted him over their shoulders and chanted, "David! David!" He was a hero that night. But most importantly, he learned that it's not about where you start out, it's about where you finish. He also figured out something I'd been working on as a rookie CEO. You don't have to be good at something the first time you try it, but if you want to get good, you've got to put in the work. The work always pays off.

It stuck with me, my work with David—how sharing my own hard-earned knowledge helped him and what a difference that one small victory made in his life. Soon, I was taking a stronger mentorship role with my own employees, trying to encourage the confidence, experience, and skills they needed to take the big swings when it counted. This mentorship not only helped my employees perform, it also helped me form strong relationships with them, relationships that made the company stronger as a whole.

But that didn't mean they always agreed with me. Early on, I had to make plenty of decisions that weren't popular. David's struggle to get better and his end-of-season victory was a story I told myself frequently during those first few years. Sometimes I had to make decisions that weren't popular with the engineers and others who'd been at the company a long time.

One of these decisions came during the 2008 recession.

I was finishing an email to a partner when Tony stormed into my office. "I just got off the phone with PTC. They want to lower our rates!"

I got up and closed my office door. This didn't sound good. It wouldn't help to have the whole office listening in to the conversation. I gestured for Tony to take a seat. He sat there with crossed arms and blazing eyes.

"Okay," I said, "Now back up and tell me what happened from the beginning."

For the next few minutes, he recounted his conversation with PTC, one of our large partners. Earlier in the week, Tony's counterpart there had asked for a meeting. PTC, like many businesses during the Great Recession, struggled during the financial crisis. They informed Tony that they simply weren't going to be able to pay what our contract stipulated. Instead, they lowered the rates they'd pay for consulting by about $8 an hour.

"It's outrageous!" Tony concluded, his face turning bright red. "After all the work we've done for them, after all the time and energy, never mind money we've put into this partnership, they want to lower our rates?" He shook his head. "Uh-uh. Not a chance. I'm going to call Dennis and see if we can get on the phone this afternoon to go over the contract, but I don't need to talk to a lawyer to know that they don't have a leg to stand on. We can fight this…"

I let Tony rant for another minute. When he ran out of steam, I nodded slowly, folding my hands on the desk in front of me.

"I see where you're coming from. Obviously, I'm not happy about this either. And yes, we could fight it. But that's not the only option. Think about it. Imagine you work at PTC, and you're calling all your partners to tell them you're going to start giving them less money. How do you think those partners are going to respond?"

"I don't have to imagine," Tony said with a bitter laugh. "They're going to be furious."

"Right. Every one of their partners is going to come at them swinging— yelling, demanding money, threatening lawsuits for breaking contracts. Maybe some of those partners will get what they want, but some of them won't. And even if they do get what they want, their relationship with PTC will be seriously damaged. What if we take the opposite route?"

"They're not going to hand over the money without a fight, I can tell you that," he scowled. "Asking nicely isn't going to work."

I shook my head. "That's not what I'm suggesting. I'm saying we don't ask for the money at all."

"What are you talking about?"

"Look," I explained. "PTC is hurting. Everyone is hurting right now. So instead of getting angry, we take the opposite emotional reaction. We call them up and we say, 'Hey, we get it. Times are hard. Thanks for letting us know.' We tell them that we can be flexible and assure them that we are going to be the best partner they have."

Tony paused to figure out what he wanted to say. Then he exploded.

"Are you kidding? We agree to take less money? We act like violating our contract is no problem? I'm sorry, but that's totally senseless."

I smiled. "I know it's unconventional. But consider what we could gain in the long term. PTC is going to lose other partners over this. If we agree to stay at a lower rate, we'll gain their trust. Eventually, the economy will improve. Their financial problems will blow over. When that time comes, they're going to look back and see that we stuck by them. And who are they going to want to do business with then—us, or the people who abandoned them?"

"Donald, it's a nice idea, but this is business. Accepting this rate cut will just make us seem weak. PTC isn't going to appreciate our graciousness; they're going to realize they can walk all over us."

"Maybe you're right," I nodded again. "But let's try it this way and see what happens."

Sacrifice now to win big later. I believed in that idea. I'd witnessed the principle and lived it my whole life, starting with the sacrifices my parents had made to create a better life for our family.

Tony stared at me for a few seconds, as if he were waiting for me to tell him this was all a silly joke. When I didn't say anything, he shook his head.

"Well," he said. "I guess I have a phone call to make."

"If it doesn't work out," I added, as he walked toward the door, "I will be totally willing to admit that you were right." I smiled. "I'll make a company-wide announcement."

Tony talked to PTC, taking the approach I advocated. As I'd predicted, PTC was so grateful not to have to fight with us that, as time went on, we became their preferred partners. They ended up consolidating their business with us. For years after that, our partnership showed thirty to forty percent growth, quarter after quarter. I never had to make that announcement.

Tony wasn't the only one who questioned the way I responded. But I wasn't concerned with what people thought of me. I focused on cash flow, learning my lesson that some cash now was better than the assurance of more cash later. Like Grant said, a promise isn't cash, only a transfer of money is. I protected those transfers like my livelihood and the livelihoods of eighteen employees depended on them…because they did.

17

EVERY PROBLEM IS A LEADERSHIP PROBLEM

As the aftershocks of the layoffs settled down, I set my sights on other areas of improvement for myself as a leader. I didn't have to look too far for signs of what my employees wanted from me. Or rather, what they didn't want from me.

In the same way, my aggressive nature had served me well throughout my career. Of course, I knew how to take a softer approach with clients, as I had with PTC. But, when it came to my internal team, I typically used tactics that had motivated me on the football field. That didn't work always work when leading a company full of technologists, people with more creative, intellectual perspectives.

"Jack, I'm examining this product report. Some important information is missing." I sat the report on the table in front of me.

Jack, one of the senior engineers, ran a hand through his hair and laughed uncomfortably. "And what's that?"

"Well, I know who's on the team, what the product update will accomplish, which parts still need to be coded, and where we might run into some implementation trouble," I paused, giving Jack a hard stare. "But I don't know when it's supposed to be finished."

"Uh, well, see, if we get started next week and don't run into any problems..." Jack squinted at the ceiling, as if he were calculating on the fly.

My frown deepened.

"End of May?"

I tapped the paperwork with my index finger. "Okay, add that to the project specs and I'll agree to it. You think we can get this thing off the ground in less than a month?"

"Yeah. Definitely," Jack said.

Then, a month passed with no finished product.

I hung up the phone with one of our international clients. Their data migration had gone smoothly, but there were minor bugs in some of the newer software versions. Several weeks before, I'd told their CEO not to worry because we were working on a resolution. Now I had to backpedal, explaining why we weren't going to be able to deliver on time. I was more than ready to take responsibility for anything that was my fault, but I hated looking like a liar because someone else had given me bad data. After crashing the receiver into the cradle hard enough that the phone nearly fell off the table, I took a few seconds to compose myself, then marched out of my office.

I walked into the cluster of cubicles where the engineers worked.

"When is this thing going to get finished?" I demanded. "Because I'm promising a whole lot of discounts on it at this point. I'm getting tired of giving clients free stuff just because we don't seem to know how to use a calendar."

The engineers were alarmed. Jack cleared his throat: "Uh, well, we found another glitch, so we're trying to work that fix into this patch."

"So you're saying the project is going long because you're adding to it? Did you think to consult someone before doing that?" My voice got louder. I didn't bother to soften it.

"Well, no, but…"

"No! No, you didn't. Do you know where my office is?"

Jack looked around at the other engineers. They were studying their shoes with apparent fascination. "Yes."

"Okay, do you know my office extension?"

"Yes."

"Well, that's a relief. In the future, if you decide to add to the scope of a project in a way that increases time, budget, and risk, you let me know. Email, phone call, invisible ink message, carrier pigeon—I don't care. But you need to let me know." I folded my arms in front of my chest and stared, jaw set and nostrils flaring. "Now. When will this project be done?"

After a silence, Jack finally said, "Let me run what we have through QA, and we can probably send the original version out tomorrow."

"Fine. I want to know the minute it's ready to go."

I left their space and headed back to my office. As I did, I noticed people glancing up at me from their cubicles. Some gave me little closed-lipped smiles like they were trying to get on my good side without annoying me. Others just lifted their heads and then ducked back down to work.

I rolled my eyes as I neared my door. People here were so sensitive! I wasn't that scary.

Was I?

Back in my office, I stared at the contract I'd been reviewing without actually seeing it. I was angry at the developers for not delivering, but soon, another kind of anger surfaced. I was mad that they had made me mad. I didn't like losing my cool. Being unable to control your emotions makes a leader weak, especially when it comes to negotiation. But I had to ask myself, was it the developers' fault that I was mad? We'd been having the same conversation for weeks, but it takes two people to have a conversation.

Clearly, our communication needed work. Adding to the chaos, I didn't have an assistant—yet again. I'd gone through four executive assistants in the last few years. None of them had stayed longer than eight or nine months. Most of them left crying. Maybe I did need to tone it down a little.

In fact, in recent months, I'd already begun to adjust my communication style. You may have read how President Obama liked to work alone late into the night. His staff got used to finding emails he had sent at 2 a.m. I did the same thing. So, when my employees showed up for work at eight, I'd be ready to dive into the tasks I'd outlined or the questions I'd asked in those late-night emails. I had to learn to remind myself that I couldn't expect even the most dedicated engineers and salespeople to work the same long hours that I did.

I also had to rethink the way I worded my communications with them. In my early days, those emails came off as too aggressive or harsh. Over time though, I learned to structure my critical emails this way: open with a compliment, move on to the critique, then add a few coaching points.

I thought back to the looks on the engineers' faces. Even though my engineers were fiercely intelligent adults, they weren't trained to consider the bottom line. They had gone to school, gotten multiple degrees, and spent years practicing to make the best products possible. That's exactly what they'd been doing on this project. Plus, as intensely creative engineers, they'd never be satisfied with the end product. There were always more tweaks and improvements in their minds. If I'd let them add everything they wanted, we'd never get a single product out the door.

Okay, I thought, getting up to pace my office (maybe those walks with Grant were more productive than I realized). *The engineers have one perspective. Now what is mine?* Easy. We needed to make money, which meant we needed to deliver products and services. We needed to be able to work iteratively and get projects completed. We could always come back to a product if it needed updates, but we couldn't keep delaying the release while trying to achieve perfection. Those two viewpoints weren't completely at odds, but there was some disconnect between my worldview and the engineers' that caused a communication breakdown.

Obviously, they didn't like confrontation. They were uncomfortable when I raised my voice or made them agree on hard deadlines. Because their work involved so much of their creative perspective, they took product critiques personally. I needed to find a way to communicate that took emotions out of the equation. I wanted everyone to be able to speak to each other objectively, without any hurt feelings. But how? It seemed as if every time I left a meeting, someone thought I was angry at them.

As I usually did when I needed to learn something, I turned to books. I scanned the shelves in my office. My eyes landed on *Six Thinking Hats* by

Edward de Bono. When Grant was CEO, he had suggested that everyone read it. The book focused on teaching people a system of communication that asked them to speak about just one aspect of a project at a time. I grabbed the book off the shelf and thumbed through it.

"This might actually work," I muttered to myself as I skimmed.

For us to implement the system, everyone would need to read the book, get training, and commit to following through. We ordered books for everyone in the office, talked through the six-hat system during several all-staff meetings, then began implementing the language from the book.

In de Bono's method, each color of hat represents a different style of thinking. During a meeting, if the facilitator introduces something new and wants to encourage critical thinking, they might say something like, "Okay, wearing our blue hats, what do we know about this product?" The blue hat represents operational and organizational thinking, so while "wearing" this hat, teammates discuss how the project might impact the company and the brand. The white hat is for data, information, and facts. The yellow hat signifies positive views about the topic. The black hat means it's time to think about potential risks and downsides. The red hat is the emotion hat, and green hat time indicates creative work and brainstorming.

It took a lot of work to get everyone on board with using the language, but it made a huge difference in our interactions. The team learned comments and critiques weren't personal attacks. I learned to lead and communicate with people who were very different from me. It also showed the employees at I-Cubed that I was committed to changing what didn't work and that I respected their input and their feelings. Together, we could talk about projects and ideas independent of emotional connections and come to better, stronger decisions.

Growth and the Art of Surprise Interviews

My first five years as CEO were a whirlwind. We paid Grant for the company, changed the business model, and continued to grow and thrive despite the financial crisis and brutal economic recession. In fact, we became extremely profitable as we learned to adapt to the changing business landscape. Even in a tough economic environment, we grew revenue by thirty to forty percent while remaining profitable and debt-free.

At one point, as I was going over another great quarter's numbers with Tony, he asked: "How is this happening? Why do things always seem to work out for us?"

"Belief," I answered, without hesitation. "When you believe you can win, you punch to exhaustion, because you know it will be worth it in the end. Doubt decreases your punching power. We don't doubt, so we keep pushing long after others quit."

Of course, we also maintained growth by recruiting the right people, those who had a broad range of experiences. Some of the folks I recruited already had successful careers in tech and business. That made them expensive, but the people I wanted to work with were worth the cost. For example, years ago I'd met Lewis Kennebrew, a stellar engineer in product life cycle management. He worked for PTC when we met, and we couldn't afford him, but I let him know that, once the company had grown, I was going to come calling. Now I made good on that promise and added Lewis to our team. Eventually, I convinced him to move his family down to Raleigh, which meant a lot for a die-hard Chicago guy like Lewis.

I-Cubed also recruited people whose careers had just begun by developing a strong internship program. The Millennial generation came out of the recession ready to work and wanting big responsibility right away. I understand that thinking. I had been the same way. If someone gave me a chance, I'd run away with it. I respected the ambition of the young people in the market, and we used their drive to our advantage.

However, attracting these new members of the workforce was a constant challenge. There's nothing sexy about data migration. So, instead of drawing them in with the appeal of the product, we sold them on the dream. We'd tell possible recruits, "Hey, IBM is probably a great gig. You'll get your cubicle and your business card, but then you'll spend eight years in an entry-level position while you go through all the bureaucracy of trying to climb the corporate ladder. Did we mention that I-Cubed is small and promotions are performance-based? We care about what you can do *and* deliver."

The strategy worked. We recruited a lot of talented recent grads and interns. They were attracted to the adventure of growth and building their careers on their own terms, just as I had been over a decade before. The success of the program meant we had many employees without much experience, but I wasn't concerned. We could teach people about our technology and sales strategies, but we couldn't teach the drive and commitment that would make them a good fit with the tight-knit team and high-octane atmosphere at I-Cubed.

We also sought talent in lots of places. One example is my old friend, Devon Wilkins. Returning to my office after a meeting one day, I checked my phone and saw I'd missed a call from Devon. I smiled. It had been a while since we'd talked. I was busy with my job. He was living in Greenville and working in broadcast media. But it was about time that we caught up again. I listened to the message. Devon had been on an interview here in Raleigh. They had offered him the job on the spot. He wanted to let me know that they might call me for a reference.

I started to think about the possibilities. We had a lot of new potential partnerships coming up, opportunities I was sure Devon could make the most of. He didn't have experience in the technology world, but I knew he could sell anything. Anyway, I'd known almost nothing about the tech world when I'd started and things had worked out pretty well for me. It was all about the right attitude and personal qualities. Devon definitely had those.

I called Devon immediately, told him I'd be happy to serve as a reference, then asked if he was still in town. He said he was just about to head back to Greenville, but I invited him to come by the office and take a quick tour so we could catch up. He sounded excited and said he'd be over in just a few minutes.

That didn't leave me much time. I hurried over to Tony's office to strategize, then headed downstairs. When Devon arrived, I met him in front of the building.

"Man, it's so good to see you! It's been too long," I said, shaking his hand and clapping him on the shoulder. "Come on in. I'll show you around."

"Nice space," Devon said as we got off the elevator. "I mean, it doesn't compare with Mr. Cash," he added with a grin. "But it's not bad."

"Well, you've gotta have something to aspire to, right?" I laughed.

I took Devon around the floor, introducing him to the salespeople and engineers. When we got to Tony's office, I rapped on the half-open door with my knuckle.

"Hey, Tony," I said, pushing the door open. "I'd like you to meet someone."

Tony stood to shake hands as Devon approached his desk. "Good to meet you, Devon. I've heard a lot about you."

Devon gave me a sideways glance. "Good things?"

"Of course!" I said. "Now, I have to take a quick call, so I'll let you chat with Tony, okay?"

I didn't give Devon a chance to object. I turned and ducked out into the hallway. As I walked toward my office, I chuckled to myself. I'd just invented a new recruitment strategy: the stealth interview.

Fifteen minutes later, Devon poked his head in my door.

"I'm going to head out. Thanks for the tour."

"Hang on a sec," I said, hitting save. "I'll walk you out."

As we crossed the parking lot, I asked, "How was your chat with Tony?"

Devon frowned slightly, seeming to choose his words carefully. "I'm sure he's a great sales guy. And he's definitely smart and qualified."

I nodded, pressing my lips together to keep from laughing. I imagined the hard time Tony had just given Devon. Tony could be a bulldog in an interview. And, after all, Devon didn't even know he was being interviewed in the first place.

We got to Devon's car. "Well, thanks for coming by," I said as we shook hands again. "Let me know the next time you're in town."

Tony was waiting for me in my office when I got back. I raised my eyebrows in a silent question.

"You were right," Tony said. "He didn't back down an inch. And when I started telling him how tough it is in tech sales and not everybody's cut out for this work, he let me have it. He said whatever I was doing, he could run circles around me. And then he walked out."

We both laughed. Then Tony announced, "Let's hire him."

I grinned and dialed Devon's number on my office phone, putting him on speaker.

"Hey, man. I've got Tony here, and we wanted to talk to you. Got a minute?"

"Sure." he said, his tone was light and friendly, but he was obviously confused.

"Well, Tony tells me that you two had a pretty good conversation. Said you were tough and confident. I told him this morning that you'd make a good addition to I-Cubed, and now he agrees. We want to offer you a job in our sales division. I guarantee that you can make more money and go further here than you would in radio sales."

Devon didn't say anything for a few beats.

I could imagine that the whole experience had thrown him for a pretty good loop, so I added, "I know it wasn't easy to have us spring this on you all of a sudden, but that's how things are here. It's fast-paced: lots of changes and surprises. I wanted to make sure you could handle that kind of environment."

Devon started laughing.

"I should have known it wasn't just a visit. You always have something up your sleeve."

I grinned. "You know it. So what do you say? You want to come work with me?"

It was 2010 when Devon Wilkins started working in sales at I-Cubed and opened up a new recruitment strategy for me and the business. I didn't stop there. I liked being surrounded by people I trusted—people I knew shared my values. That same year, I hired my sister, Amie, as sales operations manager. She is one of the smartest people I know, so when the company took off, I wanted her to oversee our sales staff, helping them reach their revenue targets. We were both raised by a successful college football coach, so I was sure, like me, she knew how to motivate a team. On top of that, she's a strong, polished professional who can shut down my ego with something as simple as an eyebrow raise.

Paying it Forward

As I spent more time with the young workforce at I-Cubed, I realized how intense the entrepreneurial spirit was within this generation. Everywhere I turned, I heard about some new twenty-something entrepreneur who was starting a successful business. I met with many of these bootstrapping founders. Usually, the meetings came about when a friend said something like "Hey, my niece is starting a business. Would you be willing to talk to her?" I'd hand them my business card, and tell them to pass it on. If they called, that was great. If not, that was okay too. But when I did, I really enjoyed offering my insights and advice.

In other words, I fell into mentorship gradually. One guy I worked with, Bryan, actually began our relationship by pitching me at I-Cubed. He was a graphic designer and wanted to work on our website.

His pitch was terrible.

When he finished presenting, I leaned forward and rested my chin on my hands. "Your work is good. But that was the worst pitch I've ever heard. I would never pay you $20,000 to do this for me."

Clearly, I was still working on my communication with creative people, but to Bryan's credit, he nodded thoughtfully. "Really? Well, what was wrong with it?"

"For starters, you're telling me I only get a few revisions, but if you're the one doing the work incorrectly, then why do I get penalized for your mistakes?" Then I listed some other issues I had.

Bryan listened quietly and waited until I was finished. "I want to run a successful business. I'd love to learn more from you."

I considered his statement, then offered: "Why don't we meet for breakfast in a few weeks? Say, the fourteenth at 7:30?" I figured anyone who would agree to an early morning meeting was driven enough for me to at least chat.

Bryan agreed. "Any time. Name the place, and I'll be there."

Sure enough, Bryan showed up. We talked business over scrambled eggs and hash browns. Over the course of that hour, we developed a good rapport. I ended up as a business advisor to his digital ad agency for the next year and a half.

My commitment to mentorship wasn't confined to young entrepreneurs I happened to meet outside of work. Like Grant, within the company, I was drawn to working with people from nontraditional backgrounds, like me, who'd made their way to the top through hard work and a desire to succeed.

Devon, for example, was doing great at I-Cubed—so well, in fact, that within his first few months, he was working on a $200,000 deal. I had complete confidence in him, but just to make sure he had support while he was still adjusting to this new sphere, I asked him to meet with me so we could discuss the deal before anything was finalized.

Over lunch, Devon walked me through his work with the company. I listened carefully, scanning his words for any details that might indicate there was still money left on the table.

When he was finished, I complimented him, saying, "Devon, you've done a great job with this. And if we get $200,000 out of the deal, that'll be great. There might be a chance, though, that we could do more for this customer and expand our relationship. Here's what I want you to do."

Using some questions and strategies we developed, Devon went back to the company to find what we might have overlooked. In that conversation, he realized that in addition to their need for data migration, the company needed consulting on their content management system. To complicate matters, they had serious time constraints. If the system change wasn't completed on time, they'd end up losing a huge amount of money every day. Devon and I checked with the engineering team and worked out a plan. We offered them additional consulting services, plus an accelerated schedule for delivery and implementation. The client was more than happy to accept our offer and pay the higher fees that it entailed.

And just like that, a $200,000 deal became a $1 million agreement—Devon's first ever. Once it had all gone through, he came to my office to thank me, but I shook my head.

"It wasn't a favor, Devon. Yes, I helped you, but we were also helping the company. And don't forget that you helped yourself, too."

Devon frowned. "What do you mean?"

"Well," I said. "You could have tried to show how talented and smart you were by doing it all on your own, but that attitude would have limited you—limited us. Instead, you grew this deal by five hundred percent because you were open to other people's perspectives and to being mentored."

"Of course I'm open to being mentored! The bigger commission on a bigger sale doesn't hurt, either," Devon said with a laugh. "All jokes aside though, I'm new to tech, and I'll take all the advice I can get. Plus, mentorship from Don Thompson?" He smiled. "You'd have to be foolish to turn that down."

18

THE BEST IDEA WINS

I-Cubed was doing well, so I could have pulled back a little on the demanding schedule I'd kept in my first couple of years as CEO. Instead, I kept at it, full throttle. That was the only speed I knew, and it was the reason the company continued to grow by thirty percent intervals. I also knew that my time was the most important asset I had, and it could be used much more effectively if I wasn't constantly hiring new executive assistants.

When yet another assistant quit, I decided this time I would find someone who fit with our company *and* with me, no matter how long it took. I wasn't always easy to work closely with, so I needed someone who was up for a challenge—someone who, like me, had extremely high standards and was motivated by being told "no." I'd been able to bring the company together by learning to communicate with engineers productively, so I was sure I could use those same skills in finding an assistant.

Before I started my search, I had to look inward. Why *was* I going through so many assistants? I already knew compensation was a problem. I wanted to be supported by someone who saw themself as a partner, who wanted to build a great company, and who shared in the dream. My former assistants had viewed their position as "just a job"—somewhere to be from 9 to 5. But I was there from 8 to 8 every day, putting me 20 or 25 hours ahead of them each week. If I wanted an assistant who was also a partner, I'd have to pay for one.

This introspection also revealed that, while I was right to have high expectations, I wasn't being realistic. Previously, I'd unconsciously expected to find a person who knew exactly what I needed, when I needed it, how it should be done, and who could learn to do all of that without direction. In short, I'd been searching for a mind reader. This time, I vowed to spend significant time on training. My commitment to learning had to extend into guiding the person who was going to work so closely beside me.

Most of all, I needed to find someone tough. I'm not known for a soft, gentle approach. My blunt feedback had driven away more than a couple assistants. Although I was working on my communication style, I knew I'd always be the kind of guy who says what's on his mind without sugarcoating it. I needed someone who was mentally and emotionally prepared to work with me, who could take criticism without taking it personally.

I first interviewed Jackie in late 2010. My finance manager, Julie, had been her colleague and recommended her. Jackie's resume looked promising, so we set up a meeting at a local deli. I'll be honest, at this point in my search, I felt pessimistic. I knew from the start that I had to determine her toughness and ability to handle my style. Her actual credentials and capabilities were secondary to her character traits. If she had the right attitude and personality, I could teach her any tangible skills I needed her to master. It is much harder—often impossible—to teach adults to be thick-skinned and perseverant.

At the meeting, we started with introductions and some preliminary questions. Then Jackie handed me a portfolio of work from a marketing campaign she'd led at her current job. After flipping through the folder, I put it on the table and sat back.

"This campaign," I said, tapping the stack of papers. "Do you think it's good?"

It was an intense interview tactic, but my point wasn't to insult her work. From my glance at the papers, it seemed like she'd done a good job on the project. I just wanted to know how she'd respond to tough criticism. While I saw my feedback as direct, some saw it as mean or harsh. They saw my comments as a personal attack, not criticism of the work itself. Those were the people who didn't make it at I-Cubed.

Jackie shifted in her seat uncomfortably. For a second, I thought she might be getting ready to leave. But then she cleared her throat.

"Well, as I mentioned, it was a very successful campaign, and I will say that I'm proud of the work my team and I put into it." She paused for a second. "But I'm always looking for opportunities to improve, so if there are areas you think could have been more effective, I'm definitely open to your suggestions."

I smiled, "Good answer."

I wanted to hire Jackie right away, but then she told me she couldn't start work for a little while. She was buying a house and wanted to get final approval before changing jobs. I didn't want to wait. Would she disappear on us before she could begin the job? As great as she seemed, wouldn't it be better to settle for someone less qualified who could start right now like I wanted?

Disappointed, I told Jackie I needed someone who could start immediately. I had already been without an assistant for too long. We parted ways and I hired a different assistant, someone I'd been interviewing simultaneously. The woman was smart and qualified, but I didn't have the same confidence in her ability to deal with the demands of the job.

Two months later, she quit.

I didn't know it at the time, but Jackie had told her friend Julie, "Let me know if the next one quits." The same week my assistant left, Jackie reached out to say she'd like to resume her candidacy. I was relieved. I thought I'd be wasting time waiting for her, but my impatience had actually cost me more time in the end.

All right, Don, I told myself as I responded to her email and invited her to come into the office to talk. *From now on, this is your motto: The right people are worth investing in. Got it?* It was another good reminder that, despite my good work and progress over the last five years, I still had plenty to learn about being a leader.

Jackie's commitment as my assistant made a huge difference in my day-to-day schedule. She took on many of the tasks that ate up my time and worked with my leadership team on several projects, freeing me up to focus on fulfill-ing my vision for I-Cubed. I also had more space to expand the work I was doing outside the office. I was on the lookout for new investment opportuni-ties and new advisory roles. That meant networking.

Networking had always been important to me, and that didn't change just because I was the CEO. Although the people I leaned on now were different than the ones I turned to for help in my early days at Amway, the same prin-ciples applied. The more people I connected with, the more knowledge and resources I had available to help me when I needed that extra boost to get a few steps ahead.

Time and time again, I'd seen how the strength of someone's network could be a make-or-break factor. After all, a "network" is just another way of describing the people with whom you share ideas and spend time. My parents had taught me the importance to choose that group wisely.

People either add value to your life, or they don't. As someone with a growing responsibility to the North Carolina business community, I wanted to surround myself with people who could help make a more significant impact. I applied to join the Young Presidents' Organization (YPO), an international group of business leaders who met certain qualifications, such as achieving leadership status before age forty-five and running businesses of a certain size or volume. I was accepted and began attending events. I wanted to connect with even a small fraction of the tens of thousands of high-achieving business leaders who were also members.

The people in YPO didn't keep secrets. They believed in the wisdom of their peers, in crowdsourcing answers to nagging questions, and in finding support for upcoming projects. When you're crowdsourcing with people who run multimillion-dollar businesses, you're bound to get some great ideas.

Not long after I joined the group, I contemplated leasing some new office space. I-Cubed was expanding, and we'd been looking at a floor in a building on the other side of town. The leasing company had sent over the documents, but after a few minutes with them, my eyes glazed over—pages and pages of legal jargon. I knew they were trying to catch us in loopholes, but I didn't know enough about real estate to identify the challenges.

That night at a YPO meeting, chatting over drinks and hors d'oeuvres, I met a leader in commercial real estate. I mentioned the impending lease.

"Why don't you send me a copy and let me take a glance at it?" he said.

"Is it that clear I've never done this before?" I laughed.

He clapped me on the shoulder. "It's not that. There are just some key things in these types of agreements that you should watch for. You probably wouldn't think of them unless you'd been around the block a few times. Send it over, and I'll check. It'll take me thirty minutes, tops."

Sure enough, within an hour of my sending it, he had it back to me with notes and a list of things I should keep in mind for any future leases. His help saved me close to $100,000 when I negotiated with the landlord. Talk about added value from your peers.

Of course, knowledge isn't one-time use. You can pass it on while keeping it for yourself. Not long after signing that new lease, I took the information I'd learned from the commercial real estate connection and used it to help one of my side projects grow. In addition to some other advisory roles, I was serving on the board of a digital marketing company. When they grew from two to eight employees, they started looking for new office space. Once they had a potential lease, I reviewed it, searching for the things my YPO friend had pointed out—and yep, there they were.

The experience reminded me of a time in fifth grade when a bully named Wes was body-slamming this other kid named Danny. Wes held Danny over his head, literally shaking money out of his pockets to steal. I stepped in to stop it back then, and I also stepped in to stop it now with this young marketing firm, passing on what I'd learned about commercial leases.

As result, this small but steadily growing business saved substantial money. In the bootstrapping economy, that amount of money makes all the difference between paying employees or going belly up. Helping them out was a great feeling, all thanks to a simple question to the right person.

The Good Goodbye

I-Cubed's consistent success under my leadership gave me the freedom to branch out during my free time. I was still aware, however, that growing into the role of a leader was an ever-evolving process. While Grant was a lead-by-example, get-his-hands-on-everything kind of CEO, I saw my role as a coaching position. I'd dig into the fine details of a project *if necessary*, but I preferred a style of leadership that focused on empowering my employees to lead from their strengths. I organized, planned, strategized, posed questions, and offered solutions, but I didn't insist that my way was the only way. In fact, I always hoped I'd have at least two employees who could do it better than me. I believed in using all the talents of the people on my team. I wanted to hear every idea.

"Where are we with the company in Paris?" I asked. I was sitting with the leadership team in our conference room, going over a recently-sold data migration package.

"All the software is ready."

I smiled. "Excellent. Anyone have any questions about how we're moving forward?"

Silence.

"Okay," I continued after a beat. "The executive in Paris I talked to was pleased. What do you all think has made this project successful so far?"

I looked at each individual, but I knew there would most likely be more silence. A lot of people, even those like the smart, competent ones on my team, are hesitant to ask questions or make observations in a group setting. Even though I'd learned to work with that behavior, it wasn't one that I identified with. I was raised with little fear, so I never had any hesitation about offering my suggestions, questions, or comments when they were called for… and often when they weren't.

But a few meetings with too many awkward silences had taught me that not everyone feels the same way. Most people aren't praised for challenging authority as children or as adults, which makes it difficult for them to speak up. That's why it's crucial for a leader to encourage the sharing of new perspectives and ideas. I'd learned that, if I wanted to hear from everyone on the team, I often had to ask the same questions in a few different ways, then leave plenty of long pauses for answers. By asking open-ended questions, I could encourage both collaboration and leave room for necessary instruction.

I tried again. "Well, how about anything we could have done better? Or differently?"

I sat back in my chair, letting the silence swell, and took stock of people's reactions. A few members looked like they had something to say. For example, Rick, who was new to the team. I guessed he wasn't sure if he had the right to speak up yet, so he half-raised his hand, letting it rise a few inches then pulling it back down when he seemed to lose his nerve. I nodded.

"Uh, well, sometimes," Rick began, clearing his throat. "We have a hard time communicating with the Paris team. We don't speak French, and even though they speak English, their meaning isn't always clear. We went back and forth a lot in the planning stages trying to get things right, but I'm still not sure we're 100 percent there."

"What do you all think of that?" I asked.

Heads nodded all around the room. Patricia from the sales team added, "I agree. Everyone's done a great job of trying to figure out what the customer is looking for, but it's been difficult. I think, in the future, we need to secure a translator just to provide quicker service."

There was more nodding and words of agreement.

"Translators on big international projects? Easy enough," I said, jotting a reminder in my notes. But I wanted to get deeper, so I kept going. "If you had a magic wand, what new strategy would you implement immediately?"

The team glanced around the room. They were familiar with my habit of asking off-the-wall questions, but some of them were still uncomfortable responding to such undirected invitations for feedback.

"A new software install process," Al suggested.

Everyone looked at him.

I smiled, not sure where Al was going but happy to be along for the ride. "And why is that?"

"Well," Al pointed at the project workflow on the board. "A lot of things have to happen before we actually do the work—contracts and all that. But if I had it my way, I'd *show* the customer exactly what they were getting with a beta software install. Migrate a few files up front, and let them make their decision. Then, once they gave the go-ahead, we'd be ready to hit the ground running."

I nodded. "Thanks for sharing, Al. Anyone care to comment?"

As it turned out, Al's pie-in-the-sky idea rubbed a few people the wrong way. The room erupted into a fast-paced, back-and-forth conversation about the logistics of giving services away for free. I watched with satisfaction as the team forgot their usual, reserved behavior and had an open, honest dialogue instead.

As the debate died down, I stepped in. "I think we've all heard some interesting opinions here. I'm not sure I'm convinced either way. Al, is this something you'd propose we start doing in the future?"

"I think it's worth a try. Obviously, there are some things we'd need to consider first, like what happens if the client doesn't go with our solution. But I think there are enough advantages to make it worth exploring."

"That's fair. Listen, if you think this is something you'd like to run with, put together a team to explore the idea. I'd want a report that includes input from every department—finance, product management, engineering, and customer service. But your first priority is this project. Don't switch your focus until your work here is done."

Al nodded. "Tomorrow, I'll figure out whether this idea is worth pursuing and let you know for certain."

I clapped my hands together. "Thanks, everyone. Nice job today. Jackie will coordinate another status meeting in a couple of weeks."

As I walked back to my office, I replayed the discussion we'd just had. A few years earlier, I might have walked out of a meeting like that without any new insight into the ways we could improve. Today though, we'd gotten below the surface to find ways we could make a good project great. I didn't have to poke and prod my employees to get the information. I didn't have to be at every meeting with the client and see the problem for myself. In most cases, the solutions were right there, in the team of talented, creative people we'd assembled. I just had to give them the space to bring their best ideas to the table.

Getting employees to share what was on their minds wasn't always a smooth process. Sometimes, the answers took a long time to show themselves, too long for us to implement them effectively. At other points, I had the opposite problem: meetings that didn't make any headway because everyone had a thousand points to make, usually naming problems and not solutions.

Then there were the times when people were willing to share what was on their minds, but I had a hard time listening because it wasn't what I wanted to hear.

After lunch, I walked by Chris's desk to check about progress on a fix for a bug. There was a cereal bowl sitting by his workstation, but the milk was dried up and the few remaining Frosted Flakes were stuck to side of the bowl. It had probably been there since yesterday. Chris was nowhere to be seen.

"Hey, Doug. Have you talked to Chris?"

Doug lifted one of the huge headphones off his ear. After I'd repeated the question, he shook his head. "Not today."

I looked at my watch. "It's one o'clock."

Doug clearly had no idea how to respond, so he just stared at me to see if I had any more questions.

"If you see him, tell him I'm looking for him, okay?"

Doug nodded and returned to his work.

Back in my office, I sat down heavily and rubbed my temples. This situation was getting a little out of control. Chris was a developer on a key project. He was the only person who could solve some of the tricky technical items required by one of our customers. He was good at what he did. Of course, he knew that too, and to show me he knew that *I* knew how good he was, he'd often come into the office whenever he felt like it, kick his feet up on the desk, and spend the afternoon coding away. At first, I'd been able to write off his behavior as run-of-the-mill tech genius eccentricity. I figured he'd settle into the job and get on board with the whole "adult work schedule" thing. But he hadn't. Now, his erratic schedule was starting to impact productivity.

A little while later, I heard a few light knocks on my door.

"Hey there, boss," Chris said, entering my office and sweeping his dark hair out of his eyes. "You wanted to talk to me?"

"Well, good morning. Or should I say afternoon, Chris? Glad you could make it in today. Please, have a seat."

He draped himself across the chair.

"I spoke with some of your colleagues. They said there have been some scheduling conflicts. When the team is ready to collaborate, they're not sure where to find you. That you won't commit to certain meeting times."

Chris nodded, a small grin creeping across his face. "Yeah. I mean. I know they can't do it without me, but I just don't always know when I can make it in, you know?"

I shook my head. "No. I don't know. You're going to start being here during regular hours so you can collaborate with the team. You're not working on this thing solo. You need to maintain a more predictable schedule."

Chris raised an eyebrow. "Look, Don. I'm sure you know this, but I want to say it aloud so we're both clear on the facts. I'm the only one who knows the code. I'm the only one who can fix bugs for these customers. Keeping customers happy means we make money. Therefore, the job I do keeps customers happy so that we all keep getting paid. Which means I'm pretty much in charge of things, and I'll keep coming in when I feel like it."

I folded my hands together on the desk in front of me and breathed deeply. What he said was not untrue. We didn't have anyone else who could do the work he did. I swallowed back the "you're fired" that was on the tip of my tongue.

Instead, I said, "Well, Chris, you make some good points. I will certainly take them into consideration as we move forward. But I also suggest that you take what *I've* said into consideration."

Chris stood and saluted me. "Aye aye, captain."

As soon as he stepped out of my office, I called a few of the other developers in. We created a plan through which they'd get up to speed on the code base that had been Chris's territory. It meant extra work, since they'd still be keeping up with their other projects, but they were motivated. They were careful about what they said, but it was clear they didn't like depending on Chris any more than I did.

Four months later, I was standing by Chris's desk waiting for him to arrive. It was two o'clock in the afternoon when he glided in, a Big Gulp clutched in one hand and the hood of his grungy sweatshirt casting a shadow over his eyes.

"Hey," he nodded, sliding into his ergonomic chair and booting up his computer.

"Chris, buddy," I said with a gigantic grin. "I think it's time we had a little chat. Join me in my office, will you?" I turned and made my way down the hall.

Soon, Chris was sitting comfortably in the same spot where we'd had our previous enlightening conversation. "What's up?"

"Well, I wanted to take the opportunity to thank you," I said.

He yawned widely and slouched farther down in the chair. I guessed he thought I was about to hand him a gold star. "For what?"

"You taught me something important about leading a technology company," I explained, my face still bright and friendly. After all, it was true. He *had* taught me an important lesson. "I mean, I'm always open to ideas, no matter where they come from, but I was not expecting the insight I had after our last conversation."

Chris smirked. "And what was that?"

"I realized we cannot have a single point of failure. It's bad business to have just one technologist supporting any service or product we offer without a backup plan. Over the last few months, I've had the rest of the team expand their code knowledge. And now, they're doing great. They're all trained up."

"Really?" he asked, confused and surprised.

I got the sense he didn't believe me. "Yeah. Totally. In fact, I think this means we need to wrap things up."

Chris's eyes, which had been focusing on the zipper of his hoodie he was pulling up and down, suddenly snapped up to meet mine. "Wait, 'wrap things up'? What does that mean?"

"It means today is your last day here."

Chris and I both learned something the hard way. Chris learned that brains and talent don't earn you a free pass. While I learned never to have one employee I couldn't live without. It was too risky. Moreover, it went against the principle I'd operated on since little league baseball. Success isn't about being a superstar. It's about achieving something great. Like Dad had taught me, it doesn't matter how many homeruns you hit if you're not helping your team win the game.

19

A TOAST TO BEGINNINGS AND ENDS

After eight years as President and CEO, I could say without hesitation that the business was thriving. Each year, we showed strong growth and became more efficient. I-Cubed was future-focused and on track to be successful for a long time. There was only one thing holding us back.

"What do you mean 'too small'?"

I was on the phone with the executive vice president of our key technology partner in Boston. We'd done lots of successful work with them in the past and had just put in a bid to take on a multimillion-dollar project. They rejected it.

"Listen, Don. We enjoy our current relationship with I-Cubed. You are always on the ball. We just don't think your company can handle the scope of this project." I tried to object, but he continued: "The truth is you just don't have a big enough workforce. I mean, consider it from our point of view. If we gave you the contract, and your team fell short, we'd have to bail you out and eat the losses. If we give the project to a bigger firm, and they screw it up, at least they can afford to absorb the losses. It's not personal, Don. It's about risk. I-Cubed is too small for this deal, period."

I tried again. "But you know I-Cubed has always delivered in the past—and delivered on time. A bigger project won't change that. Let us just draw up a proposal, and you'll see…"

"I'm sorry," the EVP broke in. "We've already made our decision. I-Cubed isn't getting this contract from us. But we do want to maintain the relationship we have on the smaller projects and continue to grow our partnership."

"Of course," I agreed. "Those were never in question." I frowned, trying to come up with a last-minute fix. No great solution appeared. "There's no way to convince you we can handle this project?"

He gave a short laugh. "Sure. Get Jim to sign off on it."

I dropped a few mental expletives that I managed to keep to myself. Jim was the CEO. He'd already said no to us twice. Our odds were less than zero. I had to deal with the reality of the situation.

We said a tense goodbye and hung up. Immediately, I opened the spreadsheets I'd been studying over the last year. Not getting a project was bad enough, but even worse was that this was becoming a pattern. The phone call I'd just finished was the fourth one like it in the last six months. *We're happy with the work that I-Cubed has done. We want to continue our relationship at that level, but your company is too small for us to hire you for anything bigger.* The same story, over and over. I was getting tired of it. I needed to do something, but I wasn't sure about the solution.

The bottom line was that we needed to grow. Of course, we'd grown plenty since I became CEO, from 16 employees back in 2007 to 125 in 2012. But that had been steady, incremental growth. To meet these new challenges, we'd have to compress a decade of expansion into just a few months.

I saw a few ways to make that happen. Over the last quarter, the leadership team and I had been discussing options for fast-tracked growth. We thought about acquiring debt to expand quickly and build out a larger team. Although that plan had the advantage of keeping the company's structure and leadership intact, it wasn't ideal because it would mean having to repay substantial debt. Also, getting money from private equity firms introduces oversight from outsiders, which can be good but can also slow the decision-making process and would probably lead to culture changes, like the removal of our one hundred percent funding for employee healthcare. Ever since we'd paid back Grant, I-Cubed had the autonomy to make its own decisions. We weren't eager to change that.

Our leadership team also considered acquiring another company. In that scenario, we wouldn't have to seek out a whole new workforce because the new company would deliver one, already trained and ready to go. But merging two companies of similar size is difficult. How do you form cohesive development teams? Who gets laid off in sales or accounting or wherever there are redundancies? What will the leadership look like? The best situation would have been for I-Cubed to acquire a company whose CEO was ready to step down, but we couldn't find anyone in that position.

As for me stepping down, well, if we could find a new CEO as fierce about winning and protecting our people as I was, then yes, I could see myself willing to let that person take over. I had more than enough side projects to pursue. And having a new leader would allow me to focus on my family—a focus that was needed more than ever in those days. But there was no way I was going to leave I-Cubed in the hands of someone who wasn't stronger than me. When I looked at the leadership of the companies we could afford to acquire, I didn't see anyone I was certain could do the job better than I could. They probably felt the same about me. In the end, a possible merger of equals just didn't work for us.

The third option was one I'd put off thinking about in much detail. We could sell to a larger company. There were lots of benefits to that option, especially for my employees, who would be able to take on new types of projects that would challenge them and allow them to grow as engineers and consultants. The negative side of selling, of course, was that I-Cubed would eventually cease to exist. It would no longer be ours. I would no longer be CEO, and our team would be swallowed by a much larger organization. No matter what role I was offered after that, it would be a significant change.

So, every day, on top of running the company and managing all my other business commitments, I scrutinized the numbers, trying to determine the right way for our little company to grow so we could take on bigger projects. As always, I relied on my network for advice. Word got out in the business community that we were exploring options for growth. The phone started to ring, but all the initial discussions fell well below our expectations, to put it mildly.

"Hello, Donald, this is Chad from Prime Time Investing. We'd like to discuss acquiring I-Cubed. How about $10,000 and some Skittles?"

Okay, so maybe they weren't that ridiculous, but the initial offers were insultingly low. I ignored just about everything, still trying to figure out a way to make it work so we could all keep our jobs *and* stay independent *and* grow the company. We weren't in fire-sale mode, by any means. I-Cubed was still growing. We had plenty of projects to keep us busy, and we had no debt whatsoever. But I had to think about the future. We had double-digit revenue growth annually, even through the worst years of the banking crisis in 2008 and 2009. But, if we couldn't take on bigger projects, that growth would eventually slow and ultimately stall. In a service business, you are constantly growing to build momentum and maximize margins, which requires expanding your deal size. No one wants to pay a premium for a firm that isn't growing.

After months of research, calculations, phone calls, and meetings, I had to accept that there was only one viable way forward. I realized I was looking for a solution to our size problem that didn't involve any change, but that wasn't possible. Nothing grows without changing. True, change can be painful, but the longer I deferred, the longer I kept my company stuck in the status quo. In business, especially technology, the status quo is a heartbeat away from going backward. That wasn't who we were. We built a team that met challenges and rose above. As a leader, you need to predict problems in advance so you can be ready when turbulence arrives. The issue was clear: we needed help to scale our firm. Resisting change was no longer an option.

Over the next few weeks, I held several conferences with the board about the current state of the company and the best next step. After many long discussions, the board members and I made a decision.

We voted to sell I-Cubed.

Options and Reflections

A parallel play was also happening in my personal life. While I was contemplating this major shift at work, my wife and I were realizing that we had grown apart. After careful consideration, we also realized that resisting change was not an option. We came to a mutual decision. It was time to go our separate ways.

Even in the early stages of that process, the end of 2013 became a period of reflection on what I'd come through and, simultaneously, a preparation for the challenges I would face in the future. I was now moving through two major changes in my life: selling my company and ending my marriage. While I knew these changes were for the best, they were each difficult enough individually. Together, they were nearly too much to handle.

During this transition, I leaned even more on my family. Amie still worked with me at I-Cubed. Seeing her at the office each day helped me remain positive. Besides serving as a source of personal support, she was also a strong business partner who gave great advice on all my key ventures. Amie has a brilliant mind for business. When it was time to make big decisions, I listened to her.

In addition to all she brought to the company through her sales and management skills, her presence also kept me humble. Of course, Amie expected a certain level of aggressiveness from me, otherwise she might have wondered where her brother had gone. But sometimes, when I had to make a tough decision or provide critical feedback, I imagined my sister calling up my mom and telling her I'd become some power-hungry, out-of-control business leader. That image ensured I gave every decision extra thought and looked for less intense ways to talk to employees about their work.

I also spent more time with my parents during this difficult time. They weren't directly involved in my work, but that didn't mean they weren't a huge part of my success. Although they had divorced a few years earlier, they were both always present at important events, both for me and for my kids. I was quick to give them credit for what I'd accomplished. When I could, I included them in big company functions so they could see firsthand what all their hard work and sacrifice meant for me—and my whole team. This year, I was especially glad they were both attending the company Christmas party. As I got ready for new chapters in my life, I appreciated their steady support.

We held the 2013 I-Cubed Christmas party in a hotel event space. It wasn't the grandest ballroom in Raleigh, but it was still pretty classy. Each table had a poinsettia arrangement. Evergreen garlands with twinkle lights hung over each window. In the corner was a majestic, decorated tree. I had to smile when I thought of the contrast the scene made with my first holiday party at the company, which was basically seven guys in a conference room with fruit punch and a grocery store cake. This felt like success.

The best part of what I saw from the stage wasn't the fancy venue or even the amazing desserts. It was the people. This wasn't just a group of people who all happened to work in the same place. We were a team, focused on always doing far more than was expected of us because we each believed I-Cubed was a dream worth fighting for. There had been hard times. There had been tests I'd failed. But, at that party, I felt only proud. I'd led this team to a point where we could stop working, gather together, and share the fruits of our hard work with our families.

I looked over at the table where my own family sat. My mom and sister were deep in conversation with Devon's wife. Dad caught my eye. I smiled, and he winked back.

"All right, everybody," I said loudly. "Now that you've gotten something to eat and drink, I'd like your attention for a minute."

The noise died down. People turned to face the stage.

"I see that they're about to bring dessert out, so I promise I won't take too much of your time because there's a slice of cheesecake with my name on it." There were some soft chuckles around the room. "And, as you know, the accounting staff needs to be at work early tomorrow to prepare your bonuses, and I am the last guy to make anybody wait when it comes to getting paid."

The laughs were louder now. I saw Devon shaking his head. I knew he was thinking back to me and the VP of Mr. Cash.

"But, I want to take a couple minutes to acknowledge what we're doing." I paused and scanned the room. "We're celebrating. Not just the holiday season—we're celebrating our team and all our many successes. We don't do that enough. When one thing is done, I'm always ready to push on to the next project. But it's important to pause and reflect on what we've achieved—as individuals and as an organization. I want to recognize all the work every one of you has put into this company. It's your dedication that's gotten us where we are today. And more personally, I want to recognize my parents."

I held my hand out to their table. "Because it's *their* dedication that got *me* where *I* am today. Thank you, everyone, for a great year. I'm looking forward to a lot more like it."

There was a big round of applause. No one clapped harder than my family. Mom beamed. Her face lit up with pride. Dad's expression was more subdued, but I could tell he was just as pleased.

I had jumbled emotions. Seeing the faces of all the people who had helped us reach this moment was uplifting, but a voice in my head reminded me that this might be my last Christmas as leader of I-Cubed in its current form. While it was true that 2013 had been great, it was far from wonderful for me on a personal level. As I looked ahead, it seemed as if things were already shaping up for it to be the best year and worst year, all rolled into one.

"Alright, alright," I said after a minute. "That's enough from me. Let's enjoy the rest of the evening!"

I left the stage and made my way back to my family's table. Lewis—who was enjoying the North Carolina winters more than the ones in Chicago, though he'd never admit it—was sitting in one of the extra chairs. When I approached, the whole table was laughing.

"What's so funny?" I said, taking the chair next to Amie and pulling a piece of cake toward me. "I hope you three haven't been telling Lewis embarrassing stories about me."

Lewis raised his eyebrows. "Well, they haven't so far, but now I'm curious. Any good ones?"

Dad glanced at his watch. "How much longer does this party go? I don't know if we're going to have time for even the top ten."

We all laughed again.

"Actually," Lewis said. "I was just telling your parents about how you got me to move down here from Chicago."

I grinned. "I have to give some of the credit to your wife."

Lewis turned to my mom and dad. "I'd been working remotely for a couple years, and I guess Don finally decided he wanted me here. So he sent me this email that said 'I want to revisit the idea of relocation.' I forwarded the email to my wife, and she sent a message back. You know what it said? 'Let's start packing.'"

Amid more laughter from the table, I shrugged and said, "Well, she's met me, and she knows I don't mess around. She's a smart woman."

"That's true," Lewis said nodding. "And I also knew that I loved working for I-Cubed more than I loved living in Chicago. And that's saying something."

After a few more stories, Lewis told my parents how much he enjoyed meeting them then headed back to his seat.

"What a nice man," Mom said as he walked away. "And he obviously thinks very highly of you, Don." She put her hand on my arm. "It's so good to see how much your employees care about you. I know you can be tough, but I can tell they know you're just pushing everyone to do their best, and they appreciate it."

"It's like football," my dad reflected. "When you're recruiting, you see things in people they didn't know were there. Then as a coach, you push them further than they thought they could go. Some of them won't like that, and they'll quit, but the ones who stay—well, now they're not just a bunch of talented players. They're your team."

Dad looked over at me and gave me a nod. From the outside, the gesture didn't seem like anything remarkable, but I knew exactly how much it meant.

"Thanks, Dad," I said. "I'm glad you all could come tonight. This year has been—" I paused, trying to think about how to sum up twelve months full of such big highs and lows. "Well, it's been intense. And there are about to be even more changes."

"Change is good," Mom said. "That's how you learn things, explore places you haven't been before. Just think—if your father and I had been afraid of change, we never would have left Bogalusa. But as tough as it was, we faced those challenges head-on. And look how blessed we are today."

She raised her glass. "To the coming year. And all its new adventures."

I lifted up my tea. Mom was right. There were new adventures on the horizon. And when they came, I'd be ready.

20

BIG DECISIONS

The knock was soft, but it startled me. For the last two hours, I'd been reviewing the financial data, making sure I knew exactly what we expected for the quarter. Even nine years later, I was still haunted by the impact of having to cut staff because I'd failed to manage money. I never lost sight of the fact that cash on hand is critical for a bootstrapped firm. I looked up from the spreadsheet and saw Doug, the CFO of I-Cubed, in the doorway.

"Hey, Doug," I said, waving him in. "What's up? Want to have a seat?"

He shook his head as he walked forward. "I only need a minute," he said, resting his hands on the back of the chair across the desk from me. "I just wanted to let you know I got a call from an investment broker representing a company in India. The company is planning to acquire a project life-cycle management firm, specifically one working with manufacturing. Are you interested in talking to them?"

"What's the company?" I asked without much enthusiasm. We'd gotten a few acquisition offers since I started spreading the word, but they'd all been pathetically low. These offers weren't a reflection of I-Cubed's actual worth. Our cash flow, customer portfolio, and technical expertise all positioned us to receive offers that were significantly higher. It was just a question of finding the right company that appreciated our value.

"They're called KPIT," Doug replied. "A technology services company out of Pune, India. Guy on the phone sounded like it was a name I should recognize. I thought maybe you'd worked with them before."

I shook my head. "Never heard of them." I turned to my computer screen and typed the name in the search engine. "When are you calling the broker back?"

"I told him I'd let him know by day's end."

I looked up sharply. "The end of the day? That doesn't give me any time."

Doug shrugged. "I figured you'd just give a flat out 'no' like you usually do."

"I keep saying no because all the offers so far have been completely ridiculous. I'm not turning people down for the heck of it."

"You're right. The offers have been bad," Doug agreed. "I only hope you haven't backed off from the idea of selling just because the right offer hasn't come along yet. They sound like they might be worth talking to."

"Okay," I said. "I'll do some research and get back to you."

Doug nodded and headed back to his office, allowing me to comb through the articles I'd found. I discovered that, like I-Cubed, KPIT offered a combination of products and services and focused on clients in manufacturing, transportation, and energy. In fact, they worked with many of the same companies we did. Of course, our projects with those clients were much smaller. Even though I hadn't heard of KPIT, that didn't mean they were some rinky-dink operation: their revenue was upwards of $500 million.

Even more interesting about them was that twenty-five years after KPIT had been formed, all four founders were still with the company. I was impressed. A lot can happen in more than two decades—new opportunities, acquisitions, and professional or personal conflicts. Four people maintaining dedication to a shared vision over that length of time was quite an accomplishment. They clearly valued their work, and more importantly, they valued their team. I told Doug to ask the broker to send us more background information.

The materials he sent looked good, but I still wasn't sure. KPIT might value their own team, but would they value ours? One significant question in the lead-up to an acquisition is whether the cultures of the two companies will be a good fit. This query is also the most difficult one to answer. Often, you can't tell what a company's culture is really like until you're part of it.

KPIT looked great in many ways, but they were a huge organization and likely had a rigid, hierarchical structure. That wasn't necessarily a bad thing. It just wasn't the way that I-Cubed operated. Our team worked well because we believed that the best idea should win, no matter whether that idea comes from the CEO or the newest intern. Could that bootstrapping philosophy survive getting sucked into a large machine?

I wanted to think about the idea a little more. But the next day, I found out that Doug had also talked to Mark Winnie, our technical fellow and a member of the I-Cubed board, about the call. That meant Doug was serious about KPIT, and he thought they were serious about us.

I called Mark and Doug into my office.

"Listen," I said as Doug shut the door behind him. "I understand you want to get moving on this sale, but we need more time to think about this whole thing. If I meet and tell them about our team, our projects, and our future, they're going to want to buy us. And I just don't know if we're ready for that."

Mark just stared at me, exuding calm. He was a man of few words. I knew he wouldn't respond until he had thought through exactly what he wanted to say.

"Don," he said after a few quiet moments. "You have an obligation to shareholders to explore legitimate exit opportunities."

"Stop clouding this discussion with facts, Mark!" I laughed. I knew he was right. I sat silently then turned to Doug. "Okay. Book the meeting."

Doug nodded. "Will do," he said and headed out the door.

I rubbed my face with one hand and let out a long breath.

"I know what you mean."

I looked up to see Mark's sympathetic smile.

"I know this is what we need to do," I said. "And you were right to remind me of that. But even though I know that in my head…" I trailed off.

"You don't want to let go of what we're building," Mark finished. "Neither do I."

We were silent, letting the uncertainty, hope, and resignation we were both feeling drift between us, unspoken but understood.

Mark shrugged. "Well, you do what you've got to do."

"And we both have plenty to do before this meeting," I agreed. "So let's get to work."

Thinking Too Small

A week later, I was in the Marriott restaurant at Washington Dulles Airport, drinking bad coffee and waiting. Kishor Patil, KPIT's CEO and one of its co-founders, happened to be in the States on business. He flew into Dulles to catch an international flight back to Pune. I'd flown into D.C. the previous night and got to the lounge an hour before our meeting, just in case his flight from Boston was early. That way, I'd be relaxed when Kishor arrived, like this whole thing was no big deal—as if I talked about multi-million-dollar acquisition deals for the company I loved on a daily basis.

Kishor showed up at eleven o'clock on the dot. He paused at the entrance, scanning the room. When I raised a hand in greeting, he smiled and waved. I watched him as he made his way to the corner booth I'd chosen. He had bright white hair and dark eyebrows. He looked energetic and excited to get started. Despite my uncertainty, I found it hard not to like him right off the bat.

"Don, it's so good to meet you," Kishor said as we shook hands. "Thanks for meeting me here. I know the location isn't ideal. How's the coffee?"

"I've had worse," I replied, smiling and thinking back over stale pots brewed at some of my less impressive jobs. "But then again, I've had a lot of bad coffee."

He smiled and signaled for the server. "Ah, well. It can't be worse than what they have on the plane."

Kishor was easy to talk to—thoughtful, relaxed, super smart—and we had plenty in common. Although we both worked in the tech world, neither of us had formal training in the field. Kishor and Ravi Pandit, one of the other founders, had both been accountants before starting KPIT.

"The accounting and back-office support is where we started, but my love is helping people develop new skills and building products," he explained with a shrug.

I nodded appreciatively. "Sounds like we'll get along just fine."

Kishor spent a little time telling me about the history of KPIT. Of course, I'd also read the official version of the story online, but it was good to hear it directly from him. The company had grown fast. Within ten years, it had gone from nothing to a $400 million enterprise. For a company that didn't have the name recognition of an IBM or Infosys, they were crushing it.

He also wanted to know about the history of I-Cubed and my vision for its future. We talked about how I grew the company by focusing on services, not just products. I spoke about the lessons I'd learned regarding cash flow and not depending too much on one project or one person. I also told him about losing out on some projects because we were small. Mainly, we chatted about what I hoped we'd be able to achieve if we could grow past those challenges.

It wasn't often that I was asked to recap a decade of business experience in five minutes or less. When I reflected on those points, the story sounded pretty good. If I'd been in his shoes, I definitely would have bought the company. Finally, after a lot of getting-to-know-you and high-level talk about company vision and direction, I asked the question I always like to ask people I respect.

"Kishor, let me ask you something." I placed my forearms on the table and interlaced my fingers. "You've obviously spent a lot of time researching I-Cubed, and we share some of the same customers, so I'm sure you've reached out to them to find out how we work. Now that you've gotten to know me a little, I'd love to get some feedback. What are some weaknesses you see in my thinking about my company or business in general?"

Kishor swallowed his sip of coffee and shook his head. "There's nothing wrong with the way you think about business. You just think too small."

Before I had time to process what he'd said, a wave of annoyance rushed through me. *Too small?* I thought.

He barely knew me, but without hesitating for a second, he'd cut my lifetime of ambition to the quick. He'd said the words as if they were nothing. As if it were clear as day to him that I wasn't thinking big enough.

After a pause that was just a few seconds too long, I cleared my throat. Curious about his perspective, I asked, "Too small? What makes you say that?"

Again, Kishor didn't seem to have to think about his answer at all.

"It's the progress of your work. Small thinking keeps people focused on the day-to-day or even year-to-year goals. To think big, you have to think way beyond that. You can't look at what's right in front of you and make plans. You have to imagine possibilities that are totally outside your grasp and make plans to realize them."

Wow! He was right.

I wanted to be irritated at his evaluation, but I couldn't. Kishor had made a quick analysis, and he had the experience to back it up. I'd done well. No one could deny that. Compared to KPIT though, I-Cubed was tiny. Our size was the reason I sat in an airport hotel hundreds of miles away from home. My company wasn't big enough to achieve the goals I had for it.

As the initial shock dissipated, I realized a more important point. Kishor wasn't criticizing me personally. He wasn't saying that my team and I weren't smart, ambitious, or creative. He was only saying that we hadn't scaled up our talents and skills for a global stage. That was the difference between our two companies. That difference wasn't bad or good. It was just the truth.

I was impressed that Kishor could so quickly and accurately assess the potential acquisition. He and his partners were able to do the big picture thinking that was necessary to take a business to the next level. Simultaneously, he and the KPIT leadership team were able to maintain a unified vision. I realized I could learn a lot from them.

We wrapped things up, decided to touch base later in the week, and each headed our separate ways. As the airport shuttle rumbled over the parking lot, I thought about the meeting. I pulled a little notebook out of my bag and jotted down some thoughts—issues to follow up on, pros and cons, and people to call. There were still a few outstanding questions, but I knew if

KPIT eventually made an offer (and it was a good one), I would seriously consider it.

In the days following the meeting, however, I felt more conflicted about the decision to sell. Even though I had mentally prepared for the challenge of seeing someone else in the driver's seat, I knew the transition would be tough. I'd have to acclimate to a much different life. Part of me knew that selling I-Cubed, whether to KPIT or another company, was probably the best move for our business. Yet, part of me wasn't at all ready to accept that.

I spent a lot of time alone during that period of my life. There were only a few people I could talk to because the whole process had to be confidential. Actually, KPIT wasn't even close to making an offer. My meeting with Kishor had been all about getting to know each other, not about signing any long-term deals. I spent a lot of long nights at the office, eating fast-food dinners, and examining every possible way this thing might turn out.

Eventually, I moved past my reluctance and accepted that, if it happened, it happened. Selling meant facing a new phase of my life, but as I reminded myself more than a few times, Mom had been right. Change is good. It's a chance to grow.

Then, without warning, KPIT went silent.

"Rumor is they're looking at other companies," Doug said at the end of a meeting one afternoon. "I guess they think we're too small and they can find another company who does what we do but with a bigger workforce."

I couldn't help but laugh. "They knew we were small—that's why we were talking to them in the first place!"

"Yeah, but that's the way business works," Doug said with a sigh.

"Sure," I conceded. "And you know, if they decide not to make an offer, then you're stuck with me. It's a win-win!" I grinned and gave Doug a quick pat on the shoulder. "One way or another, this is going to work out. I'm not worried."

And that statement was true. I didn't like being kept in limbo, but nothing great in my life had ever come to me immediately. I could wait. First, it meant I held onto I-Cubed that much longer. Second, as Doug had said, that was just the way business worked. Companies had to conduct significant due diligence.

Six weeks went by before KPIT reached out again. Kishor and one of the other KPIT presidents were going to be in San Francisco at the Oracle OpenWorld Conference. They wanted to meet with me while they were in the country. I traveled out to San Francisco to have dinner and get to know them over the course of a few hours. As I had after my meeting with Kishor, I left feeling good about KPIT as a company and excited about all I could learn under their leadership.

Again though, we were out of contact for a month. As time rolled by, I kept reminding myself of what I'd said to Doug. KPIT would do their research and make a decision based on what was best for them. Back to my old lesson about self-interest—this deal proved that point all over again. I was certain that I-Cubed *was* the best, but if KPIT didn't think so, it was their loss.

Then, one day in late October I got an email from Kishor. He wanted to schedule a call to follow up on the conversation in San Francisco. KPIT was interested in taking steps toward a possible acquisition. At the end of the subsequent call, he proposed that we talk regularly to help us both decide if we wanted to move forward with the sale. I agreed, seeing it as confirmation that they were getting serious. In our weekly calls, we talked about I-Cubed's history and my leadership. After several of these calls, Kishor said that KPIT was committed to beginning the process of acquiring the company.

"We've drafted up a letter of intent. I'll email it. You'll want to get with your team soon to pull together the information we're requesting. It's all laid out in the letter."

He kept his voice at an even tone, while I felt a complicated mixture of emotions. I couldn't decide whether I was more excited, nostalgic, anxious, sad, or just relieved to finally have a clear direction. I took a deep breath.

"That's great news. I'll tell the team, and we'll get back to you soon."

India? No. Pancakes? Yes.

In 2005, I had worked closely with Grant during the sale to Adobe, so I thought I knew how the process worked. But the view from the driver's seat was very different. As I gained more experience in mergers and acquisitions, it became clear that getting that letter of intent didn't entitle me to do a little dance of joy, sell the company, and ride off into the sunset with my cash. In a deal with a large global company like KPIT, the letter of intent isn't the end of anything. In fact, for me, it was the beginning of one of the wildest periods of my life.

That letter was a formal indication that KPIT was interested in acquiring I-Cubed at a price that I knew truly reflected the value of what we had created. But before we continued, they had to be sure no skeletons were lurking in our closet. As in the option period when you're buying a house, a company does due diligence to make sure they're actually getting what they pay for. KPIT didn't mess around. They needed every detail about what we'd done and how we'd done it, from major deals with clients to the money allocated for petty cash. While our accountants and lawyers looked over the letter and started crunching numbers, Doug and I gathered the information Kishor and his partners had asked for. The process grew tedious, but finally, we delivered all the files and data they wanted.

"Everything looks good. We're happy with what you've sent," Kishor said on a phone call about a month after the letter of intent. "Next, we'll send over our deal team. It's made up of lawyers, accountants, and high-level managers."

I frowned. "That sounds like a lot of people. How big of a team are we talking about here?"

"Oh, it's not that big—maybe ten or fifteen people."

"Fifteen people?" I said with a short laugh. "How are we supposed to keep this a secret if we've got that many visitors?"

The few people at I-Cubed who knew about the deal—primarily, members of the core leadership team—were sworn to secrecy. I had let them know in frank terms that if they leaked the information, and we pinned it on them, they would be fired immediately, regardless of whether the deal went through. A group of fifteen strangers wandering around the office looking through files and chatting with developers would definitely start rumors.

"Don't worry," Kishor assured me. "We can work offsite. We'll get a conference room set up at a nearby hotel and interview people there. Also, a lot of the financial stuff can be done remotely. We'll just need a secure workstation to access your records."

I nodded as he described the arrangements. It all seemed like a big production, but clearly, KPIT had this down to a science.

"Well, I look forward to meeting more of the KPIT team."

As soon as we hung up, I went into action. For a week, I ran back and forth between the office and the offsite deal rooms. I did everything from sitting in on integration planning meetings and helping people dig through financial records to ensuring that there were absolutely no breaches in confidentiality. I also had to make sure that none of my regular tasks went by the wayside, so I could keep I-Cubed profitable. If the business tanked while I was distracted, there'd be no deal, and we'd be left with a damaged company.

The investigation period between the letter of intent and the final days of the deal were long and difficult, to say the least. I barely slept.

If there was anything positive about this endless stack of work, at least it gave me something to focus on while my wife and I were still keeping our marital separation private. My life felt pulled in so many directions all at once. It was the perfect storm of pressure and responsibility—to my kids, to my employees, and to all of I-Cubed's stakeholders—but, I worked hard to stay optimistic. On the other side of these enormous challenges, there was definitely something better and worth moving toward.

Then, in what seemed like the final hour, just as we were poised to close the deal, KPIT brought a revised offer to the table. They wanted to purchase only the product lifecycle management part of the business. They didn't want the digital marketing company we offered.

"I'm totally confused," I told Kishor when he proposed the new plan. "Why wouldn't you want the most lucrative part of the business? This part of the business more than doubled its revenue in one year. You've seen some of the clients we've signed recently." I counted them off on my fingers. "SAS, Time Warner, Hyatt…" I trailed off.

Kishor already knew all this, and hearing it again wasn't likely to change his mind.

"I'm sorry, Don, but we're just not interested. We have a very clear goal in mind with the I-Cubed acquisition, and it doesn't involve digital marketing. It would be a waste of money and time for both of us. We have no intention to focus on this area. You should hang on to that element of your company and keep growing it."

That wasn't what I wanted to hear, but I appreciated his honesty. As much as I liked and respected Kishor, I still had concerns about our cultures meshing. I'd made sure that KPIT knew exactly how important the people at the company were to me. We'd negotiated retention bonuses and other elements to protect our folks after the acquisition. In my heart though, I was glad KPIT changed the deal because it meant we could keep a part of I-Cubed in the family as a spinout firm that we would call iCiDigital. With this new plan in place, we regrouped and moved on with the revised arrangement.

When it finally came time to meet with the leadership team in India, Doug, Lewis, and I got ready to fly to Asia. We studied the deal backward and forward, confident that most of our hard work was over. All that remained was this last trip to have meetings with key stakeholders in India. I would also be able to have a one-on-one meeting with Ravi, KPIT's board chair.

On the day of the flight, we rolled our bags through the line until we reached the Continental counter. A curly-haired clerk who seemed barely out of high school smiled as I approached his computer.

"Hi, there!" he said cheerfully. "What is your final destination today?"

"India," I said, handing over my travel documents and placing my bag beside the counter. It was going to be a long trip—Raleigh to Newark, Newark to Mumbai, and Mumbai to Pune.

The clerk looked at my ticket and passport. "Great. I just need to see your visa."

I shook my head. "I don't use Visa, but I have my American Express card."

"No, Mr. Thompson. I mean, you need a visa to travel to India," he said, the smile still on his face.

"What are you talking about? Is this a joke?" I was starting to feel like I'd missed something in this conversation. "I just need to check in for my flight."

The clerk then pulled out some paperwork and showed me that India required specific travel visas. I turned to Doug, who had organized the trip.

"Do we have our travel visas?"

Doug had overheard the conversation and was already on his phone with his assistant. After a brief pause, he looked up at me, his face deep red from chin to hairline. "We do not."

I turned back to the counter. "So there's no way I'm going to India today?"

The clerk shook his head, his smile finally beginning to fade. "No, sir, I'm afraid not. Probably not for a while. You have to apply for the visa, and that can take up to two months."

I inhaled and pressed my lips together, determined not to get angry. The attendant was just an innocent bearer of bad news. Doug, Lewis, and I stepped out of line and moved toward a bench where we could set down our bags and regroup.

"I'll call the travel agent right now," Doug said, swiping furiously across his phone.

I waved my hand dismissively. "Don't bother. You heard the guy. It can take months to get travel visas. I just need to call Ravi and let him know what happened."

Doug cleared his throat "You seem to be taking this pretty well. Are you mad?" He looked like a kid waiting to hear how long he had been grounded.

"Of course I am! I'm upset! I was supposed to go to India to get my millions of dollars today!"

I paused to let these words sink in. "But here's the thing. We can't do anything about it right now. I'll tell you what. If I'm at Cracker Barrel eating pancakes within twenty minutes, it's all good."

Doug and Lewis paused, clearly wondering whether I might be having a mental breakdown.

I tapped my watch and coughed. "Nineteen minutes."

Doug raced outside and flagged down a cab. Sixteen minutes later, I was sitting in a restaurant booth about to dig into a big stack of buttermilk pancakes.

"So we're good?" Doug asked tentatively, his fork hovering over his omelet.

I nodded as I poured the maple syrup. "Yeah. I mean, do I love that I was geared up to go to India, and now I have to go through all of this again in a few months? No. But we'll put it back together."

I'm a big believer in looking at things with a level head. Internally, I might be furious, but life has taught me enough to know that you don't solve problems with that kind of mindset. People often get bent out of shape in the moment, especially when there are bruised egos in the mix. But I knew my team would take care of the situation and come together to fix the mistake, so the best thing to do was to take it in stride, plan our next step, and enjoy my hard-earned pancakes.

About six weeks later, our expedited visas finally came through. I was relieved that the situation had been resolved without too much difficulty. KPIT understood the oversight, and we straightened out the holes in our planning process that had led to it. Of course, I was excited about moving the deal closer to completion. The trip though? That's a different story. I am sure there are a million amazing things to see and do in India, but this was not a sightseeing trip. Plus, fifteen hours on a plane is just no fun.

I worried about picking up a stomach bug while there. It's miserable to get sick on any trip, but on this one, I literally could not afford it. Feeling lousy would put me at a disadvantage during the final negotiations. I had to be at the top of my game to get the best deal for me and my team. I knew Kishor and Ravi were likely going to take us to the nicest places because they were gracious hosts who took hospitality seriously. But as Grant had taught me, it's always good business to be prepared for the downside too. To me, unfamiliar food was a potential downside. Trying to anticipate every angle, I packed bottled water and nearly two weeks of nonperishable food. That way, nothing could keep me from performing at my best.

Fortunately, I didn't need to resort to my stash of peanut butter crackers too often. We stayed in a nice Marriott hotel, and since Jackie—back to work after her father passed away, and not responsible for the travel flub—had already shared my food preferences with the KPIT team, there was something I could enjoy at every meal. KPIT treated us like royalty, going above and beyond to make us feel comfortable and welcome. Part of that was a cultural emphasis on hospitality, but in this case, that wasn't exactly the *whole* story. They were showing us all the great things about being a part of the KPIT team.

Of course, my team was doing something similar. We wanted to keep the deal moving forward and get the very best price we could, so we needed to make a good impression. At the end of the trip, when I finally met with Ravi Pandit face to face, that meant taking a big step and making a small personal sacrifice: I wore a blazer.

Throughout my ten years as a CEO and twenty years in the tech industry, I'd never worn a suit to a business meeting. I just didn't see the need for it. Most of the people I worked with were engineers, more impressed by Java skills than tailored suits. I wore khakis and polo shirts. The fanciest I got was adding a quarter-zip sweater.

The meeting with Ravi took on a whole new meaning. I was negotiating for all the people who had ever worked at I-Cubed and for their families. This deal was a way of thanking them for all they'd done in the past by helping to secure their futures. That knowledge motivated me as I stood outside the hotel waiting for our car in the ninety-degree heat, sweat already making my shirt stick to my back.

In that heat, I couldn't ignore the doubts that kept surfacing. I was willing to do just about anything for my company and my team. If wearing my only sports coat would get them a better deal, then I wouldn't think twice. But what about *after* the deal went through? The KPIT employees wore suits every day—would I be expected to do that once we joined their team? The thought seemed to make my collar feel even tighter, my jacket even heavier. This wasn't a fashion question, but it was about style. Suits and the whole mentality that went along with them—formal, rigid, traditional, hierarchical—just weren't my business style, and they weren't I-Cubed's either. If I were asked to change my leadership style after this acquisition, I wasn't sure that I could—or would want to.

If I were in a meeting with another American business leader, I would have gone in expecting to dive right into goals and projections. In India, however, I learned that even top executives want to spend some time getting to know you before you start talking about business. This aspect of negotiations is not just a formality. They genuinely care to know more about who you are. I appreciated that perspective since it was my sincere interest in others that had led me to many of the most important lessons I had learned.

Ravi and I spent the first ten minutes chatting. That's a long time for two executives in the middle of a deal, but it gave me a chance to get to learn who Ravi was outside of his work. Everything I learned that day added to my impression that he was a brilliant man who cared deeply about other people. Social responsibility was a key part of the KPIT culture and of Ravi personally. We connected over our mutual love of learning and our commitment to consistent self-improvement.

I left the meeting without any doubt that I trusted and respected Ravi. I felt comfortable with his candor and commitment to his team. The only thing I still wasn't comfortable with was how our cultures would fit together. We were being acquired as a part of their plan. While that was just the nature of an acquisition, it seemed to me that the plan was already set in stone. Ravi assured me that I-Cubed would have a say in its future direction. If, however, we were one piece in KPIT's giant puzzle, that meant only they knew what the full picture would look like.

On the plane back to the U.S., I pushed those doubts aside for the hundredth time. The board had already voted for the acquisition, and my company needed me to follow through. I liked KPIT, its leaders, and the negotiations had been going well from my perspective. I was just going to have to trust that they'd keep their promises.

Done

In April 2014, we closed the deal, selling the engineering and product lifecycle management parts of I-Cubed. My signature on those papers was a very big deal. I had fulfilled my grandfather's prediction that I would become the family's first millionaire.

21

A NEW PATH

My new job at KPIT was a pretty sweet setup. I got the senior vice president role, a generous salary, and a spot as one of the top fifty executives at a $500 million company. Plus, while I still had plenty of responsibility, I'd no longer be the guy it all came down to. I could relax on the weekends without worrying about what was happening back at the office.

Many people would have said I had the perfect job. I wanted to agree but my heart wasn't in it. Even before I'd officially begun, I heard a little voice of doubt whispering in my ear at night. Sure, I wouldn't bear as heavy of a burden, but that also meant that I wouldn't be running the show. The whole game had basically changed overnight. My team and I were just one small part of it.

I-Cubed had been absorbed by KPIT. The products and people were still there, but I-Cubed as I'd known it no longer existed. The day-to-day work remained the same, but we didn't have final decision-making power over anything. Everything from project management to resource assignment went through a much longer chain of command. *And no matter how cool this new job is,* that skeptical voice said, *nothing compares to running your own company.*

KPIT was truly a global company. Once I started running the North American product life cycle process, my team had to get used to relying on offshore resources and skills. The I-Cubed employees weren't thrilled with that arrangement. They didn't like the delivery quality we were getting from our Indian team, but instead of doing anything about it, they mostly just complained. The reality was that the change in culture and communication was harder and had greater consequences than we imagined.

However, a few people made a real effort to embrace the offshore model. Robbie, for instance, had been a junior manager. After the sale, he spent a lot of time working with counterparts in India. He wasn't an executive, but in keeping with our open-door culture at I-Cubed, he set a meeting with me. He had some new ideas about how to do things more efficiently, and I wasn't going to stand in the way of anyone who wanted to be a part of solving problems, rather than just identifying them.

"Come on in, Robbie." I motioned for him to take a seat at one of the chairs near my desk. "What's up?"

"Well, I heard what you said about people complaining about working with the Indian team. I thought I could help come up with a solution."

"I'm listening."

"See, I've worked with overseas counterparts on a few of our international projects in the past couple years, so I have some experience with how to improve communication and expectations across teams. I was thinking I could pull together a few people from our team and a few people from the Indian team to have some strategic vision meetings. We could bring you options and solutions to the problems rather than just continue the whining around the water cooler."

He paused, trying to assess my reaction.

"I love it," I said, sitting forward in my chair. "And what are you going to bring to those meetings? What's your take on the situation?"

"Well, I have a few ideas."

Robbie ran through his analysis of the problems and some strategies for how to address them. I nodded, threw in a couple ideas I'd been kicking around and jotted down notes on aspects of the problem I hadn't been able to see from my manager's vantage point. We only talked for about fifteen minutes, but we came closer to a solution than I had in any meeting since the conflicts had arisen.

"All right, it looks like this is a good stopping place," I said when the conversation had slowed. "I'm excited about where we are, and I'm glad you came in to see me today. If we can get some joint wins between the respective teams, it will help a lot. I can't tell you what a relief it is to think of a solution and get to work on it. I'm not used to all this red tape."

He laughed. "Yeah, it can be maddening. But—" He shrugged, "I guess that's what things are going to be like from now on, right? That's just how big companies are."

"Yeah, big companies," I said slowly. "I guess you're right."

It wasn't until Robbie gave a little cough that I realized my mind had wandered off. I shook my head.

"Well, thanks again for speaking up. You let me know when you get those meetings together, and we'll reconvene to talk next steps."

He agreed and walked out of my office. Almost right afterward, I had my weekly meeting with the in-office team leaders, managers, directors, and VPs. I wanted to do some extra prep for it, but after Robbie left, I just sat staring out my window at the trees in the parking lot, chin resting on my hand.

That's just how big companies are.

He was right, of course. I'd been perfectly aware that the gears ground more slowly in a huge organization like KPIT. There was no way a company that size could operate like we did back when the team had only seven people, or even like I-Cubed did in more recent years with 125 employees. There were more channels to go through, more checks and balances, and more people who needed to come to consensus. I'd known that going into the job.

But there was a difference between knowing that information and feeling it. The conversation had pushed me to take a closer look at my reaction. The truth was, I'd been more excited and animated in that discussion with Robbie than I could remember having been in months. My leadership strategy had always been to empower employees to make changes, try new strategies, and get creative about moving past roadblocks—all the things I'd just seen Robbie doing. But along with my excitement, there was also the reality check that his plan would need approval from another half-dozen people. In that scenario, there was a real possibility that it would die somewhere along the chain of command.

I didn't hate my job by any means. In fact, there were parts of it I truly enjoyed. Yet, my overall feeling was not joy but frustration, the feeling of wading through wet sand just to get the smallest task accomplished. The effort it took to do less work in more time began to wear me down.

North America and Beyond

The months flew by in a blur of new faces, products, and skills. Before I had time to acclimate, my contract with KPIT was about to expire. The flexibility my position now offered allowed me to increase my involvement in outside projects, things I really enjoyed, like advising small businesses, sitting on boards for education initiatives, and spending more time with new mentees. As my one-year mark approached, I still wasn't certain what I wanted my next move to be. There were elements of working for a large global company that I didn't like, but then again, it was a good job—stable, lucrative, and prestigious. Yes, I had irons in a few other fires, but I didn't know what my work would look like if I veered off what seemed like a clear, safe, steady course.

When Kishor offered me the opportunity to expand my role at KPIT, to go from managing just the North American PLM market to the European market as well, I seriously considered it. The position would have offered more influence, freedom, and money. Even for someone like me with a strong self-image, it felt good to be recognized for my achievements.

If I had announced when we signed the deal that I would stay on at I-Cubed only for the required year when we signed the deal, nobody would have blinked. That was standard operating procedure in mergers and acquisitions. But frankly, I hadn't thought that far. Now that there was a bigger and better opportunity, I had to start making big decisions about my future. I'd never been one to turn down an offer like the one I'd just been given, but something kept me from jumping on it right away.

Red Beans and Advice

One night in the fall of 2015, when my kids were with their mother and work was over for the day, I called my mom to see if I could take her out to dinner.

"Oh, that's such a bother. Just come over here. I'm making red beans and rice."

As much as I loved to treat my mom, I would never say no to her specialty. After the wonderful meal, I leaned back in my chair.

"Delicious, as always. Nobody makes beans and rice like you do."

She wagged her finger at me teasingly. "Don't tell your granny that. She'd never let you hear the end of it."

"Well, she can still be the Bogalusa Beans and Rice Queen," I said, grinning. "I'm sure she won't mind if you take the crown for the Research Triangle."

"You want some dessert?" she asked.

"No, thanks. I'm pretty full, and I should probably be getting home to start packing."

"Packing?" Mom said, frowning. "Are you traveling again? Weren't you just gone?"

I nodded. "Yeah, two weeks ago. But I have to go back to New Jersey. There's a big meeting, and they need someone from the PLM division. And then I just found out that I have to go to Detroit next month. *Detroit*. In the *winter*."

I shook my head, then stood to clear the table, but I stopped saw my mother's face. She was still sitting, staring at me with her eyes narrowed. I could see the little wrinkle between her eyes that appeared when she was thinking.

"What?" I asked, puzzled. "Everything okay?"

"Of course, of course," she said. "It's just…well, I'm just surprised, that's all."

"Surprised at what?"

"After all you've been through, all you've achieved," she shrugged. "I never thought you'd be doing a job like this. That you don't love. That isn't you. I mean, you hate to travel."

"I don't *hate* to travel," I corrected her, smiling. "I just hate unnecessary travel. Like, why should I go all the way to Hawaii when I'm just as happy in the Bahamas?"

"That's not the point. I want to know if this work is really what you *want* to be doing. Is this where you want to be in your life? If it is, that's great," she continued. "It's a great job and a huge accomplishment. But if it's not... well, then I want you to think about it."

"Okay, okay. I hear you. It's just—" I sighed. "I worked all this time to get to what I thought was the destination, but it's not...it's just another turning point. Now I'm not exactly sure what's supposed to be next. What would I do if I weren't doing this?"

My mother fixed me with her no-nonsense glare. "Donald Thompson, don't give me that line—that you don't know what to do next. It's foolishness."

"Hey, come on now," I objected, slightly stung. "It's a serious question."

"Not if you use that brain of yours—and I know you have a good one. First of all, you have plenty of things you could do instead of working at KPIT. You have plenty of opportunities." She paused and gave a little shrug. "None of us knows exactly what's supposed to come next. We have to plan the best we can and then take advantage of the opportunities as they come along."

We sat silently for a moment.

"Don." she said with a softer voice. "I didn't mean to upset you or sound like I'm not proud of you. I *am* proud of you. You know that, right?"

I smiled. "Of course. Never had any doubt."

Her worried expression eased. She reached over to pat my arm.

"You'll figure this out and find the right path," she said gently. "You know how I know?"

I gave her hand a squeeze. "How?"

"Because you've been doing that your whole life."

Mom knew what I also knew about myself. I enjoy putting the pieces together and molding the clay to build great companies. It is in my DNA as a leader. Challenges inspired me.

Daughter, Teacher

As I'd predicted, I stayed up late that night, packing for my trip. The actual process didn't take long, but it went slowly because my attention kept wandering back to what my mother had said. Until recently, my doubts about KPIT and what was next for me had stayed just below the surface. Lately though, it seemed like every time I turned around, I was being pushed to confront the issue directly. Mom was just the latest person to bring up these questions.

The second conversation didn't focus on my career directly, and it wasn't with someone I usually asked for advice. It was with my daughter Ciera, my middle child—someone I typically gave guidance to, not the other way around.

Ciera was looking at colleges and had her heart set on Appalachian State University, a mid-size school in the mountains of Western North Carolina with a predominantly White student body. I honestly couldn't imagine my daughter in that environment. I wasn't sure why she was so determined to go to a school that didn't seem to suit her.

One night while the kids and I ate dinner, Ciera began talking about Appalachian State yet again. I listened to all her reasons for loving it, but as soon as she paused, I jumped right in.

"Why do you want to go there? No one there looks like us."

Ciera sat down her fork and turned toward me, her expression serious and intense. Across the table, Moriah and David stopped eating, their eyes going back and forth between me and their sister.

"Dad, you've spent my whole life teaching me to face my fears and push through them. If I don't do this because of fears of what I look like or what they look like, well, then I learned nothing you tried to teach me."

Ciera kept her eyes on me. I sat stunned into silence. My daughter had just summed up everything I believed was important and used it to point out that I was wrong, that she was living by her own values. Without meaning to, Ciera had also given me yet another reminder that I needed to figure out how to live up to those ideals myself.

There was only one way to respond. I smiled at Ciera. "Well, okay. When do we go visit campus?"

Freedom of Choice

As I prepared for my latest business trip, I found myself reflecting heavily on the discussions with my mom and Ciera. Although I was torn about what to do, I was still fully aware of my privilege and good fortune. Earlier in my career, this decision would have been more complicated. Thankfully, I no longer had to worry about things like credit card debt, making a down payment on a house, or affording college tuition. Whatever I did, I would still be able to provide for my family. In that respect, I had what I'd always wanted from financial success: I had choices.

So, the question only came down to what I really wanted. Did I want to stay with a huge multinational company where I had more resources than I'd ever had before and the chance to be part of projects spanning many technological spheres? Or did I want to strike out on my own with advising and consultancy? Maybe help scrappy startups fight it out in those early sink-or-swim years? Or get in on the ground floor of big visions?

Was I chasing security or adventure?

By the time my suitcase was packed, I knew which way I leaned. I was grateful for KPIT. The company had come along at just the right time for I-Cubed and shown a lot of confidence in my capabilities as a leader. If my business career hadn't gone the way it had—joining I-Cubed when it was smaller than a baseball team's starting lineup and coming up as Grant's right hand—I might have been perfectly happy staying with them.

Or maybe not. A part of me suspected that working for a large company—an organization where change was slow and no matter how much they valued me, I'd always be one of many—simply didn't fit with me as a leader. I'd been raised to push boundaries, ask questions, dream bigger, and I'd learned early on that the best way to do that wasn't to follow the path of least resistance. I didn't care about doing what made sense to someone else. What mattered was that it made sense to me. The more I thought about it, the more obvious it was that the best choice for me was moving on from this job and building a new phase of my career that was tailor-made and custom-fit.

Finding My Inner David

The next day, I was on a plan to New Jersey. The flight attendant said it was time to shut our laptops, so I pulled out my Kindle instead. As I waited for it to power up, I swatted away thoughts about my next move. *I'm not deciding that yet*, I reminded myself. *I'm taking some time to think it over.*

Then, I flicked through my library, trying to find something good to read. As much as I was trying not to think about work, trying to be patient and let the answer to come to me, it seems someone else had another idea. On the dim screen, one book stood out: Malcolm Gladwell's *David and Goliath: Underdogs, Misfits, and the Art of Battling Giants.*

I couldn't help it. I laughed out loud. The universe can be pushy sometimes. This seemed like the final sign I needed and was seeking. My doubts and questions disappeared. I'd finally made my choice. Even though I usually say don't believe in signs, I do think a strong coincidence can be a good reminder, and this one felt crystal clear.

It was time I returned to giant slaying. I wanted to use my experience and my resources to inspire others to be great job creators, not just lifelong job seekers. That is my calling. It was then, and it is now.

22

BEYOND THE CHECKBOX

Breaking up is just as difficult for entrepreneurs as it is for young lovers. Selling a company, leaving an opportunity, or saying goodbye to a team and business you helped create is hard. Really hard. But after the conversations with my parents and that on-the-nose title of Gladwell's book, I knew I was ready to move on.

That conversation I'd had with Kishor in the airport hotel a year earlier still haunted me. "You think too small," he said, and his words felt true. As proactive as I had been in leading I-Cubed's culture, growth, and development, I had kept my dreams a bit too short of what I thought I could actually achieve.

All of a sudden, I was back in Coach Pagano's office, being accused of false stepping and afraid to admit what he saw clearly. Instead of exploding forward to see what I could achieve, I was making decisions with reserve, uncertainty, and maybe a little fear. "If you dreamed bigger," Kishor had added, "we probably wouldn't be able to buy your company now."

My direct manager at KPIT was Sachin Tikekar, who was president, a founding board member, and just as brilliant about business and technology as Kishor. "Thanks for talking to me about the possibility of expanding into Europe," I said to Sachin on a video call the following week. "I know I could do great things with that role, but instead, I'm going to resign."

Sachin was surprised. I had only been contracted for a year at KPIT, but they had seen me work and were extending an incredible opportunity. Still, he understood. "Would you reconsider?" he asked.

There was no need. I missed the athletic agility of a small business and the camaraderie that comes with small, tight-knit teams. Most of all, I missed the opportunity to innovate and chase new goals without needing input and permission.

Yet, I also felt grateful for my time at KPIT. People say they're "grateful for the opportunity" more often than they mean it. Usually, it's just a polite way of saying "get lost." But when I expressed my gratitude to Sachin, I meant every word. "It's time for me to do something different—choose my next adventure," I told him.

He smiled. "I know exactly what you mean."

No Rest for the Weary

I had no firm plan after leaving KPIT, but one thing was certain: I wasn't just sitting around waiting. I'd done well enough with my income and investments that I didn't have to work again in the true sense of the word. Nonetheless, a life of beaches and golf courses wasn't for me. I wanted to keep busy, have my finger on the pulse of another company, and help it grow.

When I was young, hungry, and desperate to get out of that god-awful Mr. Cash subprime mortgage company, I had only one requirement from a job: give me an opportunity to earn a six-figure income. As long as that opportunity didn't involve ripping people off, I didn't care what form it came in. Now, I was in a different place. Money was no longer my driving force. I could decide who I chose to work with, while also doing work that mattered to me.

I said goodbye to my team—some hugs, some lumps in throats, and many promises to keep in touch—and the next day, I started calling people in my network. I'd been mentoring a few startups and transitioning into board memberships. I'd also been an angel investor in a few companies that looked promising and strong. Many of these investments went fantastically well.

With the right tweaks, the businesses were able to turn a corner and see huge upticks in revenue. But, some of my other investments were…well, to put it mildly, *not good.*

Back on the Football Field

Ever since my college days, I dreamed of owning a football team. I pictured myself sitting in a luxury box while my team was winning the Super Bowl. But, let's just say I didn't exactly have enough cash to purchase a multi-billion dollar NFL franchise.

So, I did the next best thing. As my relationship with KPIT ended, I'd bought one of the Elite Football League of India's new expansion teams. I first read about the league in 2013 in the *Wall Street Journal.* What piqued my interest—besides the idea of an American football league in India—was the list of early investors, including former NFL player and coach Mike Ditka, Super Bowl champion quarterback Kurt Warner, and A-list Hollywood actor Mark Wahlberg. Although it seemed strange on paper, the effort appeared serious.

When I learned the league was expanding, I contacted league officials expressing my interest. At first, they shut me down. "This is a closed league, and we have enough owners," was the message I kept hearing. But my dogged ambition drove me on. After several calls, some meetings, and an enormous amount of work and effort, I became the franchise owner of the Navi Mumbai Sabers in 2015.

Then the real work began.

Building a team is tough. I put together an administration, hired good managers and coaches, and we began assembling a team. I even flew some players into Greensboro, North Carolina, so they could train with some of America's elite football professionals. I was optimistic that I would recoup my investment within two years.

One day, I also had the idea to bring arena football to the mountainous High Country of Western North Carolina. I scribbled some ideas on a napkin, met with league officials, trudged through negotiations, and in July 2016, we announced the creation of the High Country Grizzlies arena football organization, which would play its inaugural season in early spring 2017.

Despite big dreams, high hopes, and lots of effort, both of my teams were hemorrhaging cash. I learned one hard lesson about team ownership in India—unless you own the facilities where you play, you have to rent, so I got a contract for the stadium. That is, until someone else came along and offered the landlord more money, so he took it. I won't go into the particulars of landlord-tenant laws in India, but they're certainly a little less strict than in the States.

Another thing I learned about India? Monsoon season is truly outrageous. You have to get your timing just right because, when the monsoons hit, everything shuts down. We got the timing wrong, and the city was deluged. The whole venture was riddled with opportunities to fail.

The Navi Mumbai Sabers' last social media message was posted on December 25, 2016, wishing everyone a Merry Christmas. The league is still in operation to this day—if you call two games a year "in operation."

At least I still had the Grizzlies, who kicked off their 2017 season with high hopes and big energy. Despite many promotions, outreach to create opportunities for interns, and a ton of community involvement, the team lost a lot of games and did not draw enough fans in its first season.

I could see where this was headed. It's difficult to launch a new thing if you can't be there all the time driving it. I had fantastic people working for me, but still, the people working *for* you will almost never be as committed as you are. Toward the end of the season, I decided to cut my losses and sell the team, wishing luck to the new owners.

Owning both an Indian football team *and* an arena football team taught me lessons in how to lose money quickly. I could have been a YouTube star filming myself driving down the street throwing big wads of $100 bills out my window or setting them on fire. I still would have wasted less money than I did by owning non-NFL football teams. Frankly, I should have known better. It didn't work for the first XFL, or the India Football league, or the USFL, but yeah, I thought I could do it better than they did. I could make it work!

Chalk that up as pretty darn stupid.

Failure is part of life and business, and these two failures certainly hurt. But the key to moving past a failure is that, while your wounds mend, you look for the lessons. Yes, I lost money, but I learned a lot too. The smartest decision I made at that time was not to bank on any one thing but to spread myself across ownership, boards, investment, and multiple opportunities.

I also mentored a number of younger CEOs and had a seat on their boards. It's an honor and a privilege to have a part in another businessperson's growth and development. They were doing amazing things in their companies and experiencing phenomenal growth. Soon, I would become more involved in one of these companies than I could have ever foreseen.

Forging West

Greg Boone was one of the people who had worked with me at I-Cubed. Over the years, he grew into a leadership role and was selected to lead the new company with the part of I-Cubed's technology that KPIT did not acquire. They called the company iCiDigital. I served on that board until it was sold.

While I was still chairman there, I ran across a small digital marketing agency called Walk West. They did a fantastic branding job for another business I was involved with, and Greg had approached me about the idea of acquiring them for iCiDigital. He had already started initial conversations with Brian Onorio, the company's founder and CEO.

"Don," Greg said to me after a board meeting, "I think you should talk to him. He's really smart and ambitious."

About a week later, Greg, Brian, and I met for coffee at Starbucks. We kicked the acquisition idea around with some small talk before I decided to dive in deep. "What do you want to do and be?" I asked.

Brian didn't waste any time. "I want to produce world-class creative work that truly matters."

He had my attention and was super smart. Brian was the sort of rare computer science engineer who also really liked people. But he had some obstacles to overcome, including struggling to do his most creative work while building the business at the same time, all on his own. Entrepreneurs can get into that space when they're afraid to risk hiring the one or two more people they need to grow their vision. By waiting, they end up limiting their own success, trying to do everything themselves. For him to do work that mattered, I knew he had to generate enough business so that he wouldn't always be stuck chasing the next deal.

In the end, although we moved into the idea of acquisition, we didn't reach an agreement. Brian and I valued Walk West's worth differently.

Still, I saw something special in Brian—something unique. He was not just technically and creatively strong. He also had good business instincts. I've met many people who excelled in one area, but finding a mix like Brian's is rare. I know only a handful of people who have that sort of blend, so I knew that Brian was somebody worth betting on.

In later discussions, Brian and I were able to work out some concrete details. I became the chairman of the board at Walk West. Over the next few years, in addition to all the other work I was doing, I mentored Brian on getting out of the entrepreneurial trap and growing his company. With Brian's smarts and ambition, I couldn't wait to see what he would accomplish.

Here We Go Again

In 2017, Brian approached me with a new product idea—a digital platform that took the old-fashioned, emailed sales proposal into the cloud, where teams could create templates, collaborate, and submit to clients complete with lots of end-user metrics. It was a fabulous idea, but there was an issue.

"Brian, I can instantly see a market for this idea," I said, "But I'm not sure how it fits within the Walk West brand."

"I know. And I love what we've done together. You've been an immense help at Walk West."

At that time, Walk West was beginning to see exponential growth—the processes I helped Brian put into place were starting to gain traction. It had grown from a small company where Brian was the only full-time employee to a small but sturdy team handling significantly larger accounts.

"I've been running this company for ten years," Brian explained. "I feel like maybe it's time for me to move on to something else."

It was clear that he was passionate about his idea. I also knew that Brian had the drive to make it work. But, as chairman of the board and a major shareholder, that left me with a choice to make. I could let Brian go run his new business and bring in a new CEO. Or I could just take it over and become the new CEO myself.

Despite my past successes, I was not exactly excited about the latter option. Think of it this way: being a father is great, but once you're a grandfather, you don't want to start over again with a new baby in your house 24/7.

Over the ensuing weeks, we continued looking at various options. In the end, we made two decisions together. First, Brian would retain a seat on the Walk West board while he started a new company, Proposa. As an entrepreneur, I understood Brian's restlessness. Of course, I loved his new project and made sure I invested there.

The other decision? In January 2018, I officially stepped in as Walk West's new CEO.

As the new sheriff, I immediately saw some things that weren't being run the way I liked. One key to developing a strong work culture is to hire strong people, but the other—maybe more important—piece is finding people who are well-aligned your organization's core values of how to do work. In other words, they can't just be good individual contributors. They have to be great teammates too. Early on, as I dove deeper into the operations and culture at Walk West, I recognized a disconnect between my intense work style and the overly relaxed culture that existed.

I knew Brian always put in the hours, worked weekends, and got gritty and resourceful when he had to. These are the reasons I had chosen to work with him and continue to support him. What I didn't realize, though, was that few others at Walk West shared his work ethic. Like a new football coach, I realized what had to be done and brought in members of my team to achieve our mission.

Taking over a leadership team is never easy, especially when you have to make a culture shift. Some will adapt and others will cheerfully join in because the new culture is a better alignment for them. Others will fight you to the end, but they won't last long. I know other digital cultures offered lots of leeway and flexibility. Walk West was no longer that type of company. If you want to work 36 hours a week and extended lunch hours, that's fine. Not here.

I got some pushback and happily gave people time to adjust, but if there was a clear misalignment, then I knew they should be working where they could find more joy. I was no longer going to be held hostage by "indispensable" employees like Chris at I-Cubed.

When I stepped in, Walk West was already expanding. However, given the opportunity to lead their day-to-day processes, workflows, and people, we figured out how to make it grow faster. In 2015, Walk West had been a three-person teaam: just Brian and two part-timers with revenues of $300,000. Now, we turned Walk West into a multi-million dollar agency.

As I settled into my new role, I did have some self-doubt. I wondered to myself, *Can I do this again?* And I know I'm not alone in those feelings. Many entrepreneurs and leaders who have left or sold a successful company can't help questioning, "Was I just lucky? Was it an accident? Maybe it was just my team that made it so successful." I had to push those thoughts out and focus on the work ahead, which I was truly not looking forward to. I had assumed that the tough grind of CEO-ship was behind me, but also, I had made a commitment, and I don't back down from my promises.

With the groundwork Brian had laid and my new push to refine Walk West's processes and strengthen its work culture, larger companies took notice. In late 2018, Walk West was named one of the fastest-growing privately-owned companies on *Inc.* magazine's famous "Inc. 5000." We ranked at number 647 with 779% growth.

Over the next year, we continued aggressively pursuing larger digital marketing accounts, landing clients such as Cisco, Lenovo, and Merz Aesthetics. In 2019, we landed on the "Inc. 5000" a second time and in 2020, a third. Our team had worked to take Brian's baby from a basically one-person operation to an enterprise with revenues of $5.2 million. Those "was I just lucky?" questions in my head were silenced. I'd proven to myself that I could do it again—and with a marketing agency, in a whole new arena. My brand of growth worked. Assemble a solid team, keep improving the processes, and then, work your butt off. Along the way, we perfected our brand image and service offerings as we continued to push the edge of what we thought we were capable of doing.

Walk West emerged as a turnkey marketing solution offering everything from strategy concepts to full campaign production and management across a multitude of advertising channels. While the agency may not be one of the 5,000 fastest-growing companies forever, it will continue to grow and mature. On June 1, 2021, I turned over the chief executive role to Karen Albritton, remaining chair of the board. My next adventure was about to begin.

Finding Diversity

Through it all—KPIT's acquisition of I-Cubed, consulting and board work, football team ownerships, all of it—Jackie Ferguson continued working with me. Our relationship only grew closer over time, as we both realized how perfectly matched we were in and outside of work. We thought the same way and felt the same things. Put simply, we belonged together. In June 2019, we made it official. Jackie became my wife and her wonderful daughter, Diana, joined my family too. As my relationship with Diana developed, we found common points of interest and learned that we were kindred spirits. Sometimes, we'd even team up against Jackie's conservative and protective viewpoints, becoming allies as we developed our relationship, and drawing the three of us closer together.

Some married couples find it difficult to work together, but Jackie and I continue to have well-aligned values, visions, and goals, so we work together mostly without issue on projects old and new. As it happens, one day soon after our wedding, I invited her into my office on a whim. I had a spark of an idea. "Let's build a course about diversity and inclusion," I said.

She immediately got that look in her eye that said: *Here goes Don again with another big idea.*

I didn't let it distract me. "Here's what I'm thinking. What we're hearing in the market is that organizations want more diverse marketing so they can reach more diverse people, but they just don't know how to do it. My idea is to help business leaders embrace diversity and inclusion. We can teach them how to do it well. Because we know that diversity is not only good for people but also makes a big impact on an organization's revenue and profitability. I think this is the time, right now, while the general public is starting to pay more and more attention to these issues."

She relaxed and leaned in. "That's actually a great idea."

Walk West was already more diverse than most marketing firms. It had an incredibly strong team with a high number of women and people of color, especially in leadership, but we knew it was the exception not the rule.

Jackie seemed to launch like a rocket ship, immediately excited about the potential and possibilities. Over our years together, I've seen her accomplish a huge number of extraordinary things with the same fire I saw that day. It wasn't surprising. This diversity course idea spoke directly to her. Growing up in a multiracial, multigenerational, white-collar, blue-collar, multiregional household, her life had been full of conversations with unfiltered perspectives from people with different life experiences. Diverse backgrounds, identities, and perspectives? That was her home. We decided to dig in, assemble a team, and create a more fleshed-out concept for how this course might become a part of the business.

As usual, Jackie delivered. In a few weeks, she had created a plan that included four leaders from Walk West getting the Certified Diversity Executive (CDE) designation awarded by the Institute for Diversity Certification: Jackie, me, Kurt Merriweather, and Sharon Delaney-McCloud. While still getting certified, Jackie put in more than a thousand hours of research creating comprehensive and engaging material. She worked with then-intern Kaela Sosa to build the course, while Kurt and I figured out how we would sell it.

This new venture was more than just a one-off diversity and inclusion initiative within Walk West. We envisioned a company that would serve as an educational platform for people and for businesses, helping to solve a growing problem for organizations in all industries. Put briefly, the world is growing more diverse. Businesses that don't know how to tap diverse markets and embrace diverse employees are only going to fall behind.

The CDE certification itself required three days of in-class learning, a written test, and a personal project. The five-module online course we wrote—*Diversity: Beyond the Checkbox*—served as our project. It was well-received by the Institute, so that made us even more excited about what we were creating.

The CDE test itself was no joke. It was close to three hours long in a proctored facility where they took your possessions to thwart cheating. I hadn't felt so pressured since I sat through the SATs! Jackie passed the test on her first try, but it took me two attempts. This course was not easy. But, all four of us completed the requirements and received our CDE designation.

We were proud of that accomplishment but more impressed by all the things we'd learned about diversity and inclusion in the process. As much as I thought I already knew about the topic, it's true that teaching any topic is one the very best ways to learn. In building our course, I was forced to realize some of my own blind spots and biases. I had never considered topics like neurodiversity, where a person's cognitive differences are recognized and respected like any other element of being human. And I'd never thought about hidden disabilities, such as autoimmune disorders or chronic pain. It was an enlightening experience.

Around that time, I found another advocate and influencer who helped to shape my thinking—my first-born, Moriah. Even from an early age, whether on a walk, a car ride, or at dinner, Moriah would question me—and frequently challenge me—about my beliefs and behavior. I remember her watching for how I engaged respectfully and intentionally with servers at restaurants, even while checking an email, reading a menu, and responding to a text message all at once. She was good at insisting that I treat people with respect. I remember her asking, more than a few times, "Dad, can you look at what you said as if you were hearing it from a female perspective?"

Like so many people, I didn't really think about some of these issues until I had proximity to them—proximity that revealed how the world was treating people I respect and love. Moriah helped me view things through the lens of a young woman trying to make her way in the world. Seeing through her eyes, I knew I wanted to help create a better playing field for her and so many others.

A few months later, my team had created an online educational platform for our course, and the product was ready for beta testing. We reached out to clients, partners, and others from a variety of backgrounds. In the end, we had more than fifty people enrolled in the beta test. When they completed the course, we asked them to submit a quick survey for honest feedback.

Jackie couldn't wait to share the results "It's a success! 4.6 stars out of 5!" she said, grinning.

I smiled with her and rejoiced in our success. She had done it and brought me along for the ride. I couldn't be more impressed.

Giant-Slayer

In the short time since we launched *Diversity: Beyond the Checkbox*, The Diversity Movement has already grown to a multi-million dollar products and services company that has improved workplace culture for thousands and thousands of people. Using a variation of the model I used at I-Cubed, our team starts by learning as much as possible about our clients, gathering data and listening, and then prescribes a customized solution that helps business leaders, middle managers, and frontline employees reap the business benefits of diversity, equity, and inclusion. It's more than a project now. The Diversity Movement is personal to me.

Having Black children with intersectional diversity, I want their talents and work ethic to be the only criteria for their success. This company can move the needle in making that desire a reality for them *and* have an exponential impact on society across a larger scale.

That's why The Diversity Movement has my full attention these days. My job as CEO is to make everything work better through incremental improvements and big picture thinking, and there are a lot of working parts. At our core, we're a tech company, but we're also consultants, data analysts, expert content creators, and educators. We're in the growth stage, and that excites me.

If we can build a relationship with one CEO who has thirty thousand employees, and then we help that CEO think better and more broadly about diversity, equity, and inclusion, we can create a 1-to-30,000 relationship. That means, through only one point of contact, I'm helping to influence change in 30,000 people, their families, and their communities. That is significant.

I'm also focused on executive coaching: training C-suite leadership in diversity, equity, and inclusion (DEI) so that we can continue to have a more widespread influence. Every day, I'm helping to transform my fellow leaders so they can then transform their organizations and everyone those organizations touch.

More than anything else, that's what motivates me now—the drive to create a better world through positive, sustainable culture change. By teaching my C-suite colleagues about the return-on-investment from good DEI strategy, I'm helping to create stronger work environments where everyone feels welcome, respected, and encouraged to contribute. I'm helping unlock workplace excellence on a global scale, from the comfort of my office. That's pretty cool.

Back on that plane a few years ago, when I opened my Kindle and saw Malcolm Gladwell's book, I knew that my future path would lead away from KPIT, but I couldn't have predicted it would lead me here. I'm a David who needs to find Goliaths to slay. Prejudice, bias, inequity, exclusion? Yeah, I think I can handle those.

I've done my own share of giant-slaying already. Now, I am using what I've learned—and what I've earned—to help other underdogs win their battles. And there are so many underdogs. I'm just warming up my sling.

CONCLUSION

s I enter the second half of my life (yes, I plan to live to be at least one hundred), I find myself reflecting more frequently on my mistakes, successes, lessons learned, and the blessings inherent in each of them. I want to remain active in business but maybe not quite so active as those eighty-hour workweeks at I-Cubed and Amway. When Jackie and I married in 2019, she became my teammate in our new era together. As I transitioned from my previous roles and into my work at The Diversity Movement, my business decisions grew more in alignment with my personal pursuits.

I used to think I had a professional life and a personal life. Yet the older I get, the more I realize there's really only one life, and I want to live it well. That realization informs who I spend my time with and what I spend it on, and it makes me even more proud of—and committed to—the work that Jackie and I are doing at The Diversity Movement.

In short, we're helping craft a new future of work. Our team is changing the way companies do business so more people can be invited to the table and can have a chance to earn their own success, even if they've spent their whole lives being sidelined and underestimated.

I believe deeply in corporate social responsibility and the triple bottom line of people, planet, and profit. Businesses must be fully aware of—and fully accountable for—their impact. At this moment, we each have a tremendous responsibility to help change the world. Whether you're a young professional, an entrepreneur, an emerging leader, a well-established business executive, or something else entirely, this is your time to commit to change.

Growing up in the 1970s, immediately following the civil rights atrocities, protests, and triumphs of the 1960s, I experienced lingering racial resentments, heard about the injustices my parents and grandparents had endured, and watched firsthand as my father was passed over for that coach promotion at ECU—a decision that, by all evidence, was based only on the color of his skin. So much has changed, yet so much has remained the same.

What we've seen recently is a stark reminder that you cannot out-earn racism, bigotry, or bias. No matter what I have accomplished, where I live, or what car I drive—to some people—I'll always be "just another Black man." To them, my life is less valuable than a White person's. It's painful for me to recognize this ugly truth, but it's also the reality we must acknowledge as we plan for and create a better future.

Today, we have no choice but to acknowledge injustice and inequity because the evidence is everywhere. Of course, bigotry and bias have always existed, but with the murder of George Floyd, something seemed to snap. Because of the COVID-19 pandemic, most people were home and witnessed that crime. Social media, 24-hour news cycles, and smartphones with video cameras in our pockets allowed us to have a collective experience of those long nine minutes and also forced a collective reckoning.

In the past five years, racial equity movements have spread at full force in cities across America and the world. The names of Ahmaud Arbery, Breonna Taylor, George Floyd, Jacob Blake, Daniel Prude, and so many others are still imprinted on people's minds. It's critical that we seize the moment and maintain momentum toward justice and equity. The human attention span is fleeting, and it's only a matter of time before we're focused on the next big thing.

That means we only have a short window—maybe a year or two—to cement some of this new way of thinking into our collective DNA and create a better set of examples for our young people to follow. That's part of my responsibility as a leader, and I encourage every leader in a similar position to stand up, speak out, and change the narrative.

Jackie and I talk with each other about these things almost every day, but what really interests us is the opportunity to talk about these big and difficult issues with people in the larger world from a position of credibility. The Diversity Movement gives us that platform. It's a place where we can "put a dent in the universe," to borrow a phrase from Steve Jobs.

The Diversity Movement helps unlock workplace excellence by using diversity, equity, and inclusion as tools for its work. We're not interested in just checking the boxes. We want to help build work environments—and teach people the skills they need—to spark, nurture, and sustain real change. We want to see people who have been marginalized, underrepresented, and underestimated in the workplace given equal opportunity to earn positions, appointments, or promotions. We want to help provide loans and guidance for people of color, women, and professionals of all backgrounds and from all communities.

This responsibility can feel daunting at times, but it's also opening up new opportunities because, frankly, DEI creates better business environments, and better businesses make more money. When you have a more successful organization, you also have more opportunities to win in the marketplace. Believe me, I'm not asking everyone to hold hands and sing "Kumbaya" while the company's profits plummet. I'm saying that the numbers support organization-wide DEI efforts.

More inclusive companies are more profitable, productive, and innovative. They make better decisions. They recruit better talent. And they reach a bigger market segment. So, by committing to a more inclusive workplace, you win on two counts: both socially and financially. Soon, you may not have a choice between the two anyway. The younger generations expect business leaders to work for both social good *and* financial prosperity.

The world is at a crossroads. We've got some pretty big decisions to make and some pretty big obstacles in our way. But, what I've learned throughout my life—and what I hope you've learned in reading this book—is that obstacles are only opportunities to prove what you can do. Every day, you have a chance to shape the future and make it better. You have a chance to make the journey a little smoother and more fair for people around you and people you won't ever meet.

In that way, my work at The Diversity Movement feels like an extension of what my parents did for me and Amie. They paved a smoother road so we could have a better chance to earn our own success. I was fortunate to be raised with the never-quit, hardworking, optimistic mindset my parents modeled. Now, I'm excited to pass that model forward.

Maybe you're being underestimated yourself. Don't let the world tell you what you can do. There were plenty of people who underestimated me and what I could become, but the key to my success is that I didn't let somebody else's expectations of me define how big my dreams could be. I believed in the American dream, even if sometimes America didn't return the feeling. The good news is that the world is evolving. Now is our chance to build a more inclusive future and a culture that believes in every one of us so we can reach our highest potential. Let's keep going.

ACKNOWLEDGMENTS

My story contains both laughter and tears, as well as trials and triumphs. Through it all, my favorite word has been thankful.

I have been blessed with parents who instilled in me a relentless desire to pursue my goals and the understanding that winning requires an enduring commitment to get better every day. My parents' example of perseverance and resilience is one of the greatest gifts they could have bestowed. My sister Amie is—and always will be—a source of pride. I am grateful for her friendship.

Big Daddy and Granny showed me what it means to have a fierce loyalty to protecting family and building a foundation through sacrifice for the next generation.

My children are my reason! Moriah, Ciera, and David saw me work through exhaustion with the hope that, as a result, their lives would be stronger. They missed me as much as I missed them at times, but they would always forgive me for falling asleep during a movie or being a little late to a game, and I am thankful for that. My love for them drives me. Diana came to me a little later in my journey and the loving relationship we have cultivated has been a special gift to my life and a joy.

Jackie, my wife and partner, is without question the rock that gives me the strength to keep pushing. Her love and loyalty has shown me that I do deserve personal happiness. Professionally, Jackie's work ethic, talent, and integrity has created a lasting impact in all that I do.

Grant Williard is my mentor and friend. He's the one that opened the door to the limitless possibilities of business. Yet, it is his partnership and marriage to Laura that has been (and remains) a union I deeply admire.

Thank you to the employees of I-Cubed who believed in me when I was a rookie CEO with lots to learn, areas for growth, and situations to navigate. I deeply appreciate your confidence and trust.

My success has been a collective effort. I know that my accomplishments are not mine alone. To all my past teammates on the sports field and over the years in the boardroom, I say "thank you" for staying with me while I worked to become a better leader. At The Diversity Movement, I'm grateful to the team and particularly our co-founders: Jackie, Kurt Merriweather, Kristie Davis, Sharon Delaney McCloud, and Kaela Sosa. A very special thank you to Roxanne Bellamy and Bob Batchelor for helping make *Underestimated* better, as well as the team at Morgan James Publishing.

Finally, thank you to the bullies in my life. Everyone needs to learn to rise up and overcome challenges. The bullies gave me an opportunity to learn and develop a true warrior spirit.

ABOUT THE AUTHOR

Donald Thompson is CEO and co-founder of The Diversity Movement. Known globally for its groundbreaking diversity, equity, and inclusion (DEI) programming that drives real-world business results, the company was named to *Inc.* Magazine's 2021 Best in Business List in DE&I Advocacy. Recognized as a *Forbes* Next 1000 honoree, Thompson was also named to the *Business North Carolina* Power List of the 100 leaders making a significant impact on organizations, industries, and communities. *Fast Company* named the "MicroVideos by The Diversity Movement" platform a 2022 "World Changing Idea." The right-sized digital learning library is also part of DEI Navigator, a subscription service designed for small- and mid-sized organizations to benefit from the company's extensive content, client services, and expertise.

An advocate for workplace excellence, Thompson has innovated in applying business objectives to DEI work, pushing the boundaries of what it means for an organization to transform culturally, while attaining strong returns for employees and shareholders. As an angel investor, he focuses on building companies that have transformative value.

Thompson's career centers on growing and leading companies. His expertise is goal achievement, influencing company culture, and driving exponential growth as an entrepreneur, public speaker, author, podcaster, Certified Diversity Executive (CDE), and executive coach. Recognized as a leader who brings a broad executive perspective across multiple industries, Thompson serves as a board member for Easterseals UCP, Vidant Medical Center, Raleigh Chamber, TowneBank Raleigh, and several other organizations in the fields of technology, marketing, sports, and entertainment.

Thompson writes a weekly leadership column for *WRAL TechWire* and has written for many other publications, including Entrepeneur.com and CNBC. An engaging keynote speaker, he entertains and engages audiences by demonstrating how DEI initiatives can change the world by transforming the way we work together. As a leadership and executive coach, Thompson helps executives utilize new tools and thinking so they can rapidly develop better management skills and leadership abilities as they work in the ever-evolving business landscape.

Thompson lives in Raleigh, North Carolina, with his wife, Jackie, and has four adult children.

A free ebook edition is available with the purchase of this book.

To claim your free ebook edition:

1. Visit MorganJamesBOGO.com
2. Sign your name CLEARLY in the space
3. Complete the form and submit a photo of the entire copyright page
4. You or your friend can download the ebook to your preferred device

A **FREE** ebook edition is available for you or a friend with the purchase of this print book.

CLEARLY SIGN YOUR NAME ABOVE

Instructions to claim your free ebook edition:
1. Visit MorganJamesBOGO.com
2. Sign your name CLEARLY in the space above
3. Complete the form and submit a photo of this entire page
4. You or your friend can download the ebook to your preferred device

Print & Digital Together Forever.

Snap a photo   Free ebook   Read anywhere